The economics of large-value payments and settlement: Theory and policy issues for central banks

The economics of large-value payments and settlement: Theory and policy issues for central banks

Edited by
Mark Manning, Erlend Nier, and Jochen Schanz
Bank of England

OXFORD
UNIVERSITY PRESS

HG
1811
.E26
2009

OXFORD
UNIVERSITY PRESS

Great Clarendon Street, Oxford OX2 6DP

Oxford University Press is a department of the University of Oxford.
It furthers the University's objective of excellence in research, scholarship,
and education by publishing worldwide in

Oxford New York

Auckland Cape Town Dar es Salaam Hong Kong Karachi
Kuala Lumpur Madrid Melbourne Mexico City Nairobi
New Delhi Shanghai Taipei Toronto

With offices in

Argentina Austria Brazil Chile Czech Republic France Greece
Guatemala Hungary Italy Japan Poland Portugal Singapore
South Korea Switzerland Thailand Turkey Ukraine Vietnam

Oxford is a registered trade mark of Oxford University Press
in the UK and in certain other countries

Published in the United States
by Oxford University Press Inc., New York

British Library Cataloguing in Publication Data

Data available

Library of Congress Cataloging in Publication Data

Data available

Typeset by SPI Publisher Services, Pondicherry, India
Printed in Great Britain
on acid-free paper by
the MPG Books Group, Bodmin and King's Lynn

ISBN 978–0–19–957111–6

1 3 5 7 9 10 8 6 4 2

Foreword

The modern objectives of central banks – monetary and financial stability – developed from their early roles in the field of payment systems. To ensure that its liabilities continue to be perceived of higher quality than those of any other issuer, the central bank – as the institution at the apex of the payment system – has to exercise close control over the terms on which they are made available to the banking system. This is the origin of the monetary stability objective: preservation of the role of the ultimate settlement asset as a store of value and unit of account. It also gives the central bank a strong interest in the stability of the financial system. A reliable and resilient infrastructure for distributing the ultimate settlement asset is a key condition of that stability – and of implementing monetary policy effectively.

Today, central banks around the world continue to provide the ultimate settlement asset in the form of cash and electronic balances in central-bank money. They exert influence through ownership, operation and oversight of key components of the financial infrastructure. But their position at the heart of the monetary economy is subject to the same forces for change that are transforming the rest of the economy. In particular, developments in technology, the financial innovation they allow, and the globalization of finance are reshaping the payments landscape. In response to higher trading activity – nationally and across borders – and the development of new, more complex financial products, payment and settlement systems have to evolve. While the payment infrastructure has stood up well so far, the deepening crisis in financial markets in recent months is also likely to bring new challenges and requirements.

Policymakers, in turn, have to ensure that settlement risk remains contained. The most fundamental change in recent times has been the introduction of intraday finality in payment and securities settlement systems. For example, most countries with a large financial sector have moved to real-time gross settlement in payment systems, and delivery-versus-payment in securities settlement systems. The introduction of Continuous Linked Settlement (CLS), which reduces credit exposures in the settlement

v

of foreign-exchange transactions, is another recent example of an innovation to mitigate credit-risk exposures arising from the settlement process. The economics of such policies, and their broader implications, are extensively discussed in this volume.

But rapid developments in the wholesale payments sphere will continue to pose fresh challenges for regulators and central banks. One development is the increased degree of interdependencies between systems. Some payment and settlement systems are linked directly (for example, because the net liquidity flows of one system are settled in another); but even in the absence of direct connections, interdependencies are created because systems have common participants, or because they rely on common service providers. Greater international co-operation between overseers, and joint stress tests between system participants may be called for to reduce the risk of contagion, while allowing participants to benefit from these links. Other issues are raised by the increased provision of payment and settlement services by multinational banks. In response, overseers of payment systems may need to strengthen their dialogue with banking supervisors. More generally, central banks and supervisors will need to decide which parts of the changing infrastructure landscape need to be overseen: to what degree; against which standards; and by whom.

Policy should be based on robust analysis of the economic forces that drive developments and determine the risk profile of payment systems. And over the past decade or so, the academic and central-banking communities have greatly advanced the study of the economics of payments. To date, however, there has been little attempt to draw together the insights gained from this growing body of research in a form that is accessible to a reader with a background in economics but no specific training in monetary theory or payments. This volume seeks to offer just such a synthesis. It seeks to explain the methods used and the conclusions of the work and to link them to the policy issues faced by central banks. I hope that it will encourage more academics to address payments questions. It should also provide policymakers with a useful review of the work done so far and a guide to current and future policy challenges.

Sir John Gieve, Deputy Governor, Financial Stability
Bank of England, 2008

Acknowledgements

The editors and authors are very grateful to Ian Bond, Forrest Capie, Charles Goodhart, Charles Kahn, Chris Mann, Stephen Millard, Jim Moser, Stephen Quinn, Robert Ritz, William Roberds, Peter Sinclair, Ellis Tallman, John Veale, Anne Wetherilt, Toby Wilkinson and three anonymous referees for their comments and contributions.

The editors would also like to thank the Research and Statistics Group at the Federal Reserve Bank of New York for permitting the reproduction of Figure 10.3.

Contents

Contents

List of Figures

List of Tables

List of Boxes

Contributing authors

Kemal Ercevik joined the Bank of England in 2004 after graduating from University College London with a degree in Economics. He worked as an analyst on payment system policy issues for three years before being sponsored by the Bank to take an MSc Financial Economics degree at the University of Oxford. He currently works in the Capital Markets team within the Financial Stability Directorate of the Bank.

Marco Galbiati obtained his PhD in Economics at the European University Institute, after a spell as private wealth manager in an Italian Bank. He joined the Bank of England in 2006. His research is on game-theoretic and agent-based models of payments and clearing systems.

Claire Halsall joined the Financial Stability Directorate of the Bank of England in 2006 after completing an MPhil in Economics at the University of Oxford. Since joining the Bank Claire has worked on a wide range of policy issues in payment systems and central counterparty clearing houses.

John Jackson joined the Bank of England in 2000, beginning his career in a reserves management team in the Markets Directorate. He spent five years doing policy and research work on payments, clearing, and settlement in the Financial Stability Directorate, co-authoring several research papers on a range of topics. For the last year he has been working in the Bank's Banking Services Directorate, heading up a team that provides analytical support to the operational teams which run the sterling RTGS system and provide back office settlement for Open Markets Operations. John holds Masters degrees in Physics and Economics, from Durham University and Warwick University, respectively.

Mark Manning joined the Financial Stability Directorate of the Bank of England in 2002, after several years working as a fund manager in the City of London. Since joining the Bank, Mark has specialized in policy and research in payments, clearing, and settlement, co-authoring several research papers and articles in this area and participating in various international policy and working groups. Mark is currently on secondment from the Bank of England at the Reserve Bank of Australia, where he heads the Payments System Stability section of the Payments Policy Department. Mark holds Masters degrees in Economics and Finance, from University College London and the London Business School, respectively.

Ouarda Merrouche joined the Financial Stability Directorate of the Bank of England in 2007 after a spell in academia. She holds a PhD in Economics from the European University Institute. Before joining the Bank she worked as a short-term consultant for the IMF and the World Bank. Her research interests include banks' liquidity management during operational outages in payment systems, the macroeconomic consequences of innovations in payment systems in transition economies, the consequences of payment system outages on money markets, and the efficiency of money markets.

Erlend Nier holds a PhD in Economics from the London School of Economics. He joined the Bank of England in 2001 and held a position as Research Manager in the Bank's Financial Stability Directorate. During his time at the Bank, Dr Nier has led research and policy work on a range of financial stability issues, including capital and liquidity standards for banking firms, payment system design, and linkages between financial stability and monetary operations. His current position is Senior Financial Sector Expert with the IMF's Monetary and Capital Markets Department, on secondment from the Bank of England.

Armed with a Modern History degree from Worcester College, Oxford, **Ben Norman** joined the Bank of England in 1994. He started there as a business analyst on the team developing the UK RTGS and EU TARGET payment systems. Following spells in the Bank's IT, Monetary Analysis, Statistics and Banking Departments, plus a year taking an MSc Economics degree at the LSE, he has been managing a range of payments research and policy issues since 2005.

Jochen Schanz holds a PhD in Economics from the European University Institute. He worked as an economist for an investment bank before joining the Bank of England as an economist in 2005. During his time at the Bank, he has worked on market infrastructure questions, focusing on the link between system design, banks' short-term liquidity management, and systemic risk. His interests include the regulation of financial markets and the governance of firms providing infrastructure services.

William Speller joined the Financial Stability Directorate of the Bank of England in 2006, holding an MSc in Economics from Stockholm School of Economics and having worked as a credit analyst for a commercial bank. He specializes in liquidity and capital regulation and macro-prudential policy.

Peter Zimmerman worked as a credit analyst for a hedge fund before joining the Bank of England in 2007. He holds a Masters in Economics from Trinity College Dublin. His interests include payment policy issues and network theory.

Even though all contributing authors are or have been affiliated with the Bank of England, this volume reflects the views of authors and should not be taken as representative of the views or policy agenda of the Bank of England. Where the authors weigh the benefits and costs of public-policy intervention in payments, their conclusions may not coincide with those of the Bank of England.

Introduction

'We'd always thought that if you wanted to cripple the US economy, you'd take out the payment systems. Banks would be forced to fall back on inefficient physical transfers of money. Businesses would resort to barter and IOUs; the level of economic activity across the country could drop like a rock.'

Alan Greenspan, Chairman of the Board of Governors of the US Federal Reserve System, 1987–2006.

Today's complex web of market infrastructures – payment, clearing and settlement systems – is a response to frictions that arise when goods and financial securities are traded.

In general equilibrium models, developed famously by Arrow and Debreu (1954), such frictions are assumed away. Every agent can trade costlessly with everyone else, while the 'Walrasian auctioneer' ensures an allocation that matches individual needs. Each agent immediately finds a trading partner, there is no need for money, and no role for either central banks or payment systems to support the flow of money through the economy. Moreover, in the Arrow–Debreu world, agents can commit to contracts, ensuring that all obligations will be honoured. There is, therefore, no need for sophisticated mechanisms to enforce commitment or manage the risks associated with non-performance.

Sadly, in the real world, trading frictions *do* exist. There is then a role for money, a role for central banks, and a role for a payment and settlement infrastructure that both supports the flow of money and provides mechanisms for management of the risks associated with limited enforcement of contracts.

1

With a view to clarifying policies to address risks in payment systems, central banks have over the past few years devoted considerable resources to the study of the economics of payments. In parallel, this field has begun to establish itself as a new subject for scholarly research, drawing in academic students and researchers. To date, however, there has been little attempt to draw together the key insights gained from this growing body of research.

This volume seeks to offer just such a synthesis. It charts the frontier of our knowledge to date and puts it in the context of a comprehensive overview of the policy issues faced by central banks in this sphere. In particular, it explores: central banks' roles in payment systems; the risks on which central banks focus in their oversight activities; and the challenges central banks face as the payments and settlement landscape evolves.

The economics of payments is a multidisciplinary field, taking in branches of economics such as monetary theory, search theory, game theory and industrial organization. It also draws on techniques from network theory and makes extensive use of simulation studies to model complex interactions between payment-system members. For each of the topics covered, this volume highlights some of the most influential works in the literature. The volume also draws heavily on empirical insights, in particular offering an historical context to central banks' involvement in payment systems.

We hope that this book will appeal to a wide audience, including fellow policymakers, practitioners – either users or providers of infrastructural services – and non-specialist academic economists and students. Not only do we hope it will offer a good reference text, but also that it will stimulate active debate and encourage new research in this important field.

1 Money, banking and payments: historical evolution and the role of the central bank

What is a payment? One starting point is to consider the etymology of the verb 'to pay': it is derived from the verb 'to pacify'. In this context, the idea of pacifying goes back to an age before modern systems of payments had been developed: the concept is closely connected, for instance, to the medieval practice of *wergild*, whereby a guilty party paid a fine to its victims in order to prevent blood feuds. In today's usage, a payment still describes a transfer of value between agents.[1] By extension, any *organized* arrangement for transferring value between parties can be defined as a payment *system*. Thus, the Bank for International Settlements (CPSS, 2003c) defines a payment system as 'a set of instruments, banking procedures and, typically, interbank funds transfer systems that ensure the circulation of money.'

Such systems developed in the context of the broader evolution of money and banks and, eventually, central banks. In **Part I** of this volume, we explore this evolution, describing how central banks came to assume a role at the heart of the payments infrastructure, and illustrating why it is natural for this role to be combined with a responsibility for monetary and financial stability. We show how the role of central banks is intimately linked to the evolution of 'large value' or 'wholesale' payment systems that facilitate the flow of liquidity between banks.[2]

The early banks emerged from the business of moneychangers and goldsmiths. These early banks developed the first arrangements for making payments in-bank; that is, they enabled merchants to make payments to one another without having to hand over specie (e.g. gold and silver coins), on the basis either of deposits held with the same bank or of depositor receipts (effectively bank-notes). Over time, so as to accommodate transfers between customers of different banks, the banks started accepting claims on each other.

Once banks started building up claims on each other, they needed, at some point, to be able to extinguish or 'settle' these claims. Such 'final settlement' had to occur via the transfer of an asset that the creditor bank was prepared to accept: the ultimate settlement asset. At first, banks started settling interbank claims using specie. Later, they switched to settlement in assets convertible into specie: for example, by the 1770s, London bankers had switched from settling in specie to settling in Bank of England notes, deemed a superior form of settlement asset. By the mid-nineteenth century, banks had innovated further, and were able to settle claims across the Bank of England's books.

---

[1] And in this connection it is worth noting that a payment today is, like the *wergild* of Anglo-Saxon times, a transfer of value from one agent to another, i.e. a one-way transaction.
[2] Given our focus on wholesale systems and financial stability, we do not review the economics of retail payment systems, such as credit cards, where the literature on network effects and two-sided markets has been successfully applied to analyze competition. A survey of this literature can be found in Rochet and Tiraure (2004).

Elsewhere too, such as in the US or Canada during the nineteenth and early twentieth centuries, a single, central institution emerged at which banks could settle their claims. But this institution was not necessarily a bank – as the clearinghouse model of settlement demonstrated – nor did it necessarily issue the ultimate settlement asset. The connection between central clearing and settlement and central banking was therefore neither straightforward nor uniform in its evolution – at least not until the twentieth century, when several governments set-up central banks that, in providing the ultimate settlement asset, took over (or, in cases where it did not already exist, established) the central settlement function. During the course of the twentieth century, these central banks then also assumed the two key central-banking functions of ensuring monetary and financial stability.

With its liabilities used as the ultimate settlement asset, a central bank has an incentive to maintain their value by setting the terms on which they are made available to the banking system. There is therefore a clear synergy between a central bank's roles in providing the settlement asset and promoting monetary stability. Furthermore, to ensure that balances held in bank deposits – by far the largest component of the money supply in a modern monetary economy – can continue to function as a medium of exchange, the central bank will take a natural interest in the payment systems employed in the transfer of bank deposits. Indeed, a payment system that enables the transfer of commercial bank money and that utilizes central-bank money as its settlement asset is crucial for the implementation and transmission of monetary-policy decisions taken by central banks.

Similarly, there is a link between the provision of the ultimate settlement asset and a central bank's financial stability objective. The provider of the ultimate settlement asset can, in times of crisis, increase the supply of its liabilities to ensure that payments continue to be settled. Under certain circumstances, it might also effect emergency lending to prevent the failure of a solvent but illiquid institution.[3] However, in order to avoid moral hazard, there are benefits to reducing threats to the financial system *ex ante* if this can avoid the need to intervene *ex post*. Indeed, such threats may arise from weaknesses in the design or operation of the payment systems themselves.

---

[3] This capability is often described as a central bank's 'lender of last resort' function.

Today, central banks around the world still typically provide the ultimate settlement asset, at least for large-value and wholesale market payments, but often for major retail systems also. They sometimes also operate, or even own, key components of the payments and settlement infrastructure.

But over time the financial infrastructural landscape has become more complex, expanding well beyond the traditional domain of central banks. New payment systems and other clearing and settlement infrastructures have emerged, processing particular categories of payments and supporting post-trade processing in particular financial markets.

And monetary economies have become increasingly dependent upon the existence of this machinery, with values and volumes passing through core infrastructures rising rapidly over time. Central banks have, therefore, taken an active interest, typically via the assumption of an oversight role, in ensuring that the infrastructure more broadly is operationally effective, efficient and resilient, and that undue risks are not imposed upon system members and the financial system more generally.

That is, they have sought to ensure that the design and operation of the infrastructure itself does not pose a risk to financial, or systemic, stability. Systemic risk, in this context, may be defined as 'the risk that the failure of one participant in a transfer system, or in financial markets generally, to meet its required obligations will cause other participants or financial institutions to be unable to meet their obligations (including settlement obligations in a transfer system) when due.'[4]

2 Sources of systemic risk in payments and settlement

But what exactly could go wrong? This is considered in **Part II** of this volume. In payment systems, the key source of systemic risk is settlement risk: that is, the risk that settlement will 'not take place as expected' (CPSS, 2003c). Settlement risk has its roots in four broad categories of risk: credit risk; liquidity risk; operational risk; and business risk. These may be defined, as follows:

- *Credit risk*: the risk that a participant in the system defaults on its obligations within the payment system, imposing direct unanticipated losses on other members;

---

[4] CPSS (2003c).

5

- *Liquidity risk*: the risk that a participant/participants hold(s) insufficient liquidity in the settlement asset, disrupting the flow of liquidity in the system and leading to delay in or failure of its and other participants' settlements;

- *Operational risk*: the risk of losses arising from technical failure or other forced interruption to the operations of a payment system (or its core components), or those of its participants;

- *Business risk*: the risk of losses arising from either suspension (or termination) of a payment system's (or its core components') provision of services due to financial pressures.

Notice that some of these risks affect participants and others the system itself. Credit and liquidity risks, for instance, are a characteristic of the interconnections and strategic interactions between the banks involved and would exist whether or not they were members of a payment system. Where there is a system, however, it can be the channel through which these contagious effects are manifest. Whether the system transmits these effects depends on its design. Operational and business risk, on the other hand, can occur both at the level of the participant and at the level of the system.

2.1 Sources and mitigation of credit risk in payment systems

We first home in on credit risk, exploring how this risk might manifest itself and identifying the specific threats it poses to financial stability.

Credit risk in payment and settlement systems can be influenced significantly by payment system design and, in particular, the frequency of settlement. Historically, interbank payments were typically settled on a net basis. Under this mode of settlement, payment requests received by the banks are collected together over a period of time and the net amounts that the banks owe/are owed are calculated. At the end of the period, the banks settle these net amounts by paying the settlement asset into the system (if they owe) and receiving the settlement asset from the system (if they are owed).

But such systems can transmit individual bank failures more widely. This is because, if payments are credited to customer accounts before final settlement occurs, credit exposures between banks can build up and a failure of one participant in the system can lead to the failure of others.

In an early simulation study,[5] there was found to be significant scope for systemic spillover in the US CHIPS system, which, at that time, settled on a deferred net basis. Subsequent studies, building on this methodology and applying it to other systems, have identified less scope for spillover.

Nevertheless, over the past two decades, in part driven by public authorities, there has been a marked shift towards real-time gross settlement (RTGS) of (at least) wholesale, interbank payments. Under RTGS, each payment instruction submitted to the system is settled individually with finality in real time intraday, eliminating the interbank credit risk that arises from a delay in settlement. Similar considerations also prompted the adoption of delivery-versus-payment (DvP) in securities settlement and, more recently, payment-versus-payment (PvP) in the settlement of foreign-exchange transactions. The benefit of these risk-mitigating measures has been evidenced during the market turbulence of late 2007 and 2008, with settlement able to proceed smoothly across markets, notwithstanding the prevalence of counterparty credit concerns.

2.2 Sources and mitigation of liquidity risk in payment systems

RTGS systems do, however, carry risks of their own. In particular, such systems are 'liquidity hungry' relative to net systems. That is, participant banks require more liquidity to settle their payments in a timely manner. With RTGS now widely adopted, the focus of attention has therefore turned to liquidity risk.

Since holding liquidity may be costly, banks participating directly in an RTGS system have an incentive to delay non-time-critical payments in the expectation that incoming receipts will provide the liquidity for their outgoing payments. But if all banks are doing this, there is a risk of 'gridlock' in the system: the risk that all participants are relying on incoming liquidity, but no-one is in a position (or willing) to make the first payment. This strategic interaction has been the subject of considerable academic and policy interest in recent years.

In particular, it is important that appropriate system-design features are incorporated to manage the liquidity burden on member banks that arises in RTGS systems and to prevent either disruption to the flow of liquidity within the system or the diversion of flows to less robust vehicles/systems. To reduce the likelihood of liquidity shortages, central banks may decide to provide intraday liquidity on generous terms, for instance by charging a

[5] Humphrey (1986).

low (or zero) interest rate, and by accepting a broad range of securities as collateral. Indeed, with internationally active banks increasingly participating in multiple payment systems, there have been strong industry demands for increased central-bank acceptance of collateral denominated in foreign currency.

The design of the system might also be adapted to reduce the liquidity burden of RTGS, while not compromising on credit risk. In this regard, so-called *hybrid* systems have emerged in recent years, with in-built functionality to queue certain outgoing payments until offsetting incoming payments have arrived.

2.3 *Operational and business risk in payment systems*

While the literature has tended to focus primarily on credit and liquidity risk, it is clear that other sources of settlement risk – namely, operational and business risks – might also be important, particularly with concentrated provision of infrastructure, where 'single-point-of-failure' issues loom large.

The operational capacity of the central infrastructure and/or member settlement banks to process payments in the normal way could be compromised by a number of factors, both internal – e.g. technical failures sourced within the system itself or the way in which it is operated – and external – e.g. problems with a source external to the system such as general power failures, terrorist action or natural disasters.

Appropriate technical-level system design, accompanied by sufficiently robust operational procedures, should serve to minimize the likelihood of a failure with a source internal to the system itself. Effective contingency arrangements and workarounds – back-up facilities; contingency sites, etc. – might then reduce the impact of those incidents that do, nevertheless, occasionally occur.

But it is not only the ability of the central system to process payments that is crucial here: the effectiveness of liquidity recycling within the system also relies on uninterrupted operations at the level of the settlement banks. In the extreme, the inability of a settlement bank to send payments raises the possibility of a 'liquidity sink' developing in an RTGS system, as available liquidity becomes concentrated in the settlement account of the bank concerned. Intraday, this could cause liquidity shortages elsewhere in the system, which might in turn lead to significant delays to the settlement of payments between the unaffected settlement banks.

The likelihood that a member-level disruption will undermine the effectiveness of liquidity recycling in the system as a whole depends crucially on the structure of the payments network and the behavioural responses of other banks in the system.

Business risk, on the other hand, is the risk that the payment system provider becomes insolvent. A variety of tools may be applied to address this risk in payment systems. Of these, perhaps the most obvious is the application of capital requirements to payment systems. Other remedies might include ensuring the bankruptcy-remoteness of key assets applied by the infrastructure provider or *ex-ante* measures to ensure that system participants stand ready to contribute financially should business risk crystallize.

3 Governance and regulation of payment and settlement systems

Central banks often now assume a role in the oversight of payment and settlement systems, applying internationally agreed standards to the systems falling within their scope. Their intervention is typically justified by the argument that market participants do not fully consider the consequences of their actions on the rest of the payment system, and, by extension, on the rest of the economy: that is, by arguing that their actions give rise to systemic risk externalities. Many central banks continue to exert influence via ownership of their country's large-value system, or the operation of key components of the infrastructure. In **Part III**, then, we examine the various roles taken by central banks, exploring also the theoretical underpinnings of alternative regulatory and governance structures.

3.1 *Alternative models for governance and regulation*

Payment systems are characterized by increasing returns to scale and strong network externalities. These imply a tendency towards concentrated provision of payment and settlement services, which may not only be a source of systemic risk, but may also have implications for competition, access, pricing and innovation.

9

One potential mitigant here is mutual ownership, which is common in infrastructure provision. This can go some way towards aligning the incentives of the central provider with those of system participants, ensuring also that the system internalizes a high proportion of the costs associated with the crystallization of risks. However, there may be co-ordination failures among the mutual owners, as well as potential spillovers, beyond the immediate group of members, to the wider economy. There may, then, be a case either for external stakeholder representation in governance or for public intervention.

Issues around competition, access and innovation may be addressed by the competition authorities, if the mandate of the central bank does not extend to ensuring the efficiency of the provision of payment services. But in practice, at least for systemically important systems, there will tend to be close co-operation between the authorities, with the mitigation of systemic risk in payment systems almost always falling to the central bank in its financial-stability role.

3.2 Central-bank roles in payment systems

A number of roles might be adopted by central banks to influence risks to financial stability posed by payment and settlement systems. Three principal vehicles are identified in the literature:[6]

- *Public ownership*: an ownership stake in the entity governing the payment system;
- *Operation of the infrastructure*: active engagement in the design, implementation and operation of all, or a subset, of the software, hardware, communication networks, data centres and contingency sites underpinning the system;
- *Oversight of the system*: day-to-day monitoring of system performance to ensure compliance with a set of minimum standards and design principles.

Ownership and oversight, if supported by adequate (perhaps legal) powers of enforcement, can be substitutes. Indeed, a pure oversight model can overcome potential issues around governance failure and user disengagement, which are often associated with public ownership.

---

[6] Millard and Saporta (2007)

In practice, a variety of models of intervention are applied around the world, reflecting different legacy positions, different political economy environments, and different banking and financial structures. Models of oversight have, however, converged, with an increasing number of central banks assessing their systems against the standards laid out in the *Core Principles for Systemically Important Payment Systems* established by the Committee for Payment and Settlement Systems (CPSS) at the Bank for International Settlements (CPSS, 2001a). In partnership with the International Organisation of Securities Commissions (IOSCO), the CPSS has also established *Recommendations for Securities Settlement Systems* (CPSS, 2001b) and *Recommendations for Central Counterparties* (CPSS, 2004).

4 Future policy challenges for central banks

This convergence in standards for oversight in part reflects the evolution of the infrastructure landscape and, in particular, increasing international interdependencies. In **Part IV**, the final part of this volume, we survey this landscape to identify some of the important emerging themes early in the twenty-first century and examine the regulatory and policy challenges these may pose for central banks.

The payments and settlement landscape is changing in response to the emergence of cheaper technologies, financial innovation, globalization and regulatory change. Developments here pose a number of challenges for central banks and regulators, including setting the appropriate scope for oversight. An important policy question is how to respond to the increasing provision of infrastructure services by commercial banks, particularly where market participants seek multicurrency services. Lessons learned from the financial system stresses of 2007 and 2008 are likely to condition any regulatory and policy responses in this area.

4.1 *Banks operating as infrastructure providers*

Participation in a payment or settlement system may be direct or indirect. Direct participants hold accounts with the settlement agent. Indirect participants, on the other hand, settle across accounts held with direct participants (referred to as settlement banks). Payment systems in which some banks participate indirectly are referred to as 'tiered' systems.

Tiered structures can be liquidity efficient: settlement banks can internalize some of their customers' payments and can also recycle liquidity efficiently by using liquid funds received for one customer bank to settle payments for another. However, tiered structures may at the same time introduce new sources of risk. For instance, indirect participation introduces credit exposures between settlement banks and their customer banks. In addition, a customer bank depends on its settlement bank's ability to raise sufficient liquidity to effect payments on its behalf in real time. Business and operational risk may also be amplified, as the customer's ability to effect payments not only depends on its own operational availability and solvency, but also on that of its settlement bank.

Important questions therefore arise as to how firms providing infrastructure-like services should be regulated. A firm providing settlement-banking services – particularly one that internalizes a significant portion of payments – is, in essence, operating a payment system. Similarly, a custodian bank internalizing securities transactions is, to all intents and purposes, operating a securities settlement system. So, in respect of such segments of their business, should firms offering these services be subject to similar regulatory standards and oversight as traditional payment or settlement systems? More generally, how can the increased systemic importance of these firms be reflected in supervisory standards for banking firms?

4.2 Globalization, innovation and the changing infrastructure landscape

One driver of an increasing role for firms offering infrastructure-like services is increased demand for multicurrency settlement services, which might be more readily met by commercial bank providers. To this end, globalization may entail a greater role for firms operating as infrastructure providers. Indeed, the globalization of banking is shaping the evolution of the infrastructural landscape in many ways. This volume, therefore, spends some time considering the various policy issues that arise in this sphere.

The global integration of capital markets has spawned a small number of large internationally active financial groups, operating in many different markets and currencies. Facing a complex web of intraday and end-of-day cross-currency liquidity needs, an increasing number of these financial groups have responded by centralizing their liquidity-management function. That is, a central Group Treasury takes responsibility for management of subsidiaries' liquidity needs, and co-ordinates the movement of liquidity, and collateral, across parts of the group.

Centralized liquidity management requires arrangements that facilitate the cross-border transfer of securities and recycling of cross-currency liquidity surpluses. There have, therefore, been active calls to central banks to accept a wider range of foreign-currency collateral and to work with private providers to enhance infrastructural arrangements for mobilizing such collateral.

More generally, internationally active banks seek infrastructure providers with international reach. Hence, clearing and settlement systems are establishing cross-border links, and cross-border mergers are becoming more common. Such developments give rise to complex interdependencies between systems and, as infrastructures come ever closer together, these interdependencies might be expected to become stronger.

Financial innovation is another significant source of change in the infrastructure landscape. For instance, OTC derivatives markets have traditionally been cleared and settled bilaterally, typically with significant manual intervention. But as these markets have grown, and back-office capacity has been stretched, new automated infrastructure services have emerged. And, aided by technology, such services are unbundling traditional clearing and settlement functions, introducing competition at narrower niche points in the post-trade value chain. The financial market strains of late 2007 and 2008 have strengthened calls for further automation and centralization of the post-trade infrastructure in this space.

Finally, public intervention – either *ad hoc*, or more sustained regulation or oversight – has historically had implications for the evolution of the financial infrastructure. At the time of writing, the Code of Conduct in the EU has sought to promote competition in clearing and settlement by calling for interoperability and open access between clearing and settlement providers.

And other public-sector initiatives have the potential to alter the shape of the landscape markedly. For instance, the launch of the Continuous Linked Settlement (CLS) system for foreign exchange in 2002 has had implications for the broader infrastructure landscape, both in terms of its creation of new interdependencies and its influence on agents' behaviour.

4.3 *Where are we headed and why does it matter?*

It remains to be seen how the infrastructure landscape will evolve. Whatever the end-game, the changes triggered by globalization, financial innovation and public intervention pose a number of serious questions for central banks and other public authorities:

- What are the implications for system resilience?
- What is the appropriate scope for central bank oversight? And would the conduct or organization of oversight need to change in any way?
- What might be the implications for central banks' operational roles? And might there be implications for the future of central-bank money settlement?

Part I

Money, banking and payments: historical evolution and the role of the central bank

This first part of the book is all about why central banks are – and how they came to be – intimately engaged with payment systems and the wider market infrastructure.

In Chapter 1, we take a step back and explore the historical evolution of money and payments. This chapter draws out how payments came to be subject to organized arrangements and how central banks came to assume a position at the heart of the payments landscape, typically providing the ultimate means of settlement between contracting parties.

We continue, in Chapter 2, with an overview of the link between payment systems and central banks' typical core objectives of monetary and financial stability. We describe how a role in the provision of the ultimate settlement asset creates incentives for the central bank to ensure monetary and financial stability. More specifically, we demonstrate that a well-functioning payment system is critical to ensuring that money can continue to fulfil its textbook functions of store of value; unit of account; and medium of exchange in all states of the world.

We also briefly describe the more recent evolution of the market infrastructure, walking the reader through the variety of specialist infrastructures supporting activity in financial markets at the start of the twenty-first century. This provides the backdrop to a more detailed discussion of risk-management challenges associated with the payments, clearing and settlement infrastructure in Part II of this book.

1

The foundations of money and payments

In this chapter we step back to examine the historical evolution of central bank roles in payment systems, beginning with the early emergence of money and banking. From these foundations, we plot the subsequent development of banks, and then of payment and settlement systems. We then describe the development of central banks in the context of their settlement function, laying the foundation for the discussion in Chapter 2 of central banks' monetary and financial stability roles and their position in today's increasingly complex infrastructural landscape. A further objective of this chapter is to set the historical context for the directions in which payments may develop in future – some aspects of which are covered in Part IV of this volume.

1.1 The origins of money and payments

We defined payments in the introduction in terms of the transfer of value from one agent to another, and a payment system in terms of the set of rules and procedures governing the organized arrangements for transferring such value.

But before we move on to the origins of such arrangements, let us first take a step back and examine the 'transfer of value' that a payment seeks to achieve. At one level, value can be transferred by one agent giving to another anything that the receiving agent is willing to accept (by definition, as 'valuable'). Such acceptance is intimately connected with an expectation that whatever is transferred will be – and remain – valuable to its recipient. Where two agents exchange goods/services directly, such transfers are achieved by barter. As explained below, there are considerable frictions in barter transfers. By far the most common approach nowadays is to transfer value by monetary means.

So what is a transfer of *monetary* value? Money has traditionally been defined by its functions – as a unit of account, a medium of exchange, and a store of value.[7] Specifically in terms of its function as a medium of exchange, money is also defined as that which agents are willing to use in trade, to allow one agent to obtain a desired good, while the other agent can expect in turn to use such money as a means to obtain their (different) desired good (and so on). This definition includes commodity monies – for example based on precious metals (such as gold or silver), cowrie shells, and even salt – that have emerged throughout history and in various economies in order to catalyze trade.

Another way of defining money has sought to step beyond the traditional functional approach, and has characterized money (more narrowly) as any generally accepted debt instrument with a recognized unit of account whose issuer is both identifiable and willing to accept it back in payment at whatever point in time the issued instrument may mature (Tymoigne, 2006). Significantly, in comparison to the definition by functions, this definition of money emphasizes the importance of an identifiable issuer, and the acceptability to them of their money to extinguish debts that they are owed. But this definition does not sit easily with the notion of commodity monies: perhaps gold or silver could be issued, with the stamp of the issuing agent for instance stamped on at least one side of the coin; but other commodity monies such as cowrie shells or salt do not lend themselves to being 'issued' as such.

Nevertheless, this more recent definition fits more naturally with the so-called Cartelist theory of the origins of money, that is rooted in the idea that money gains its value not from the physical object that may represent it, but from the power and credibility (whether economic, political, religious, or other) of the issuing authority. This approach arguably complements the Mengerian theory of the origins of money, which attributes to the market the development of a (physical) medium of exchange, and argues that the value of money is derived from the way it eases the friction of a 'double coincidence of wants' that so hampers barter trade (Jevons, 1875; Menger, 1892).

---

[7] This trio of definitions has also been conflated into a single functional definition of money as a 'means of deferred payment': in other words, taking a commonly agreed upon unit of account, which then circulates as a medium of exchange, and that retains its value over time is equivalent to this single definition.

In short, Menger's approach builds upon the idea expressed earlier by Jevons that for trade to take place in a barter economy, a consumer needs to find someone who not only has the desired good, but who also wants that consumer's good in return. In practice, it occurs rarely that two agents each want the other's good, still less that they should have the correct quantities of each good available to be able to agree the terms of their trade, and then still less that these coincidences should materialize at the exact time that both sides of the bargain should actually desire these goods.

A number of respected intellectual authorities, going back at least as far as Aristotle, have placed emphasis on money's origins as a facilitator in exchange. Many of the more recent historical, anthropological and political economy experts have leaned more towards the Cartelist theory to explain the advent of fiat money (Goodhart, 1998b). Yet the actual origins of money come at a point in history when, by definition, an agreed numerical system had already been developed, i.e. by 3100BC (Tymoigne, 2006), but (crucially) before historically reliable, extant written evidence is available, as noted by Selgin and White (2002). For this reason, it is difficult to show as demonstrably false either one of the Mengerian and Cartelist theories. In any case, they may each have merit in explaining the origins of money.

For example, only a few centuries after the first coins were circulating in Asia Minor in the seventh century BC (Grierson, 1977), the Carthaginians may lay claim to (one of) the earliest fiat monies. It appears that they used leather money; the contents of the money were sealed and, as long as the seal was not broken, the money had value. This adds an early case study to the Cartelist evidence base.[8] On the other hand, long after the introduction of fiat money, an enforced 'social experiment' of a World War II prisoner-of-war camp in the early 1940s demonstrated how cigarettes could begin to circulate spontaneously as a commodity money, in order to enable exchanges among the prisoners. This lends more recent weight to the Mengerian approach (Radford, 1945).

Nor has pure economic theory given guidance as to which of the Cartelist or Mengerian approaches is more likely in practice to have been observed in history. For instance, in a series of seminal monetary theory papers, Kiyotaki and Wright (1989, 1991, 1993) start from the premise of agents searching for mutually agreeable trade with each other. They find

---

[8] We are indebted to Professor Forrest Capie for this reference, apparently sourced from a draft of a manuscript by Robert Mundell.

that, in overcoming the double coincidence of wants that barter entails, welfare is improved under a pure monetary (as opposed to non-monetary or mixed-monetary/barter) equilibrium – whether the money in question is commodity-based or fiat. But money simply appears – exogenously – in their model.

So, in the absence of a clear theoretical lead, we need to rely on an interpretation of the available historical (including archaeological) and anthropological evidence. The first (extant) physical media that arguably passed for money came on the scene in ancient Mesopotamia, in the shape of clay tokens. These were used to record deposits of and transactions involving agricultural produce like barley or wool, agricultural implements, or metals such as silver. From at least the seventeenth century BC onwards, some of these clay tokens were explicitly bearer instruments – stating, for instance, that its bearer should receive a specific amount of barley at harvest time, or that the bearer should be given a quantity of silver at the completion of his journey (Davies, 2002; Ferguson, 2008). It was subsequently, during the first millennium BC, that the first coins were manufactured – in Asia Minor. But there are also pointers to earlier barter exchange facilitated via a unit of account: for instance, in Homer's *Iliad*, where suits of armour were exchanged, and commodity gold exchanged for a slave, with oxen as the unit of account (Grierson, 1977; Tymoigne, 2006). This is an instructive episode in the development of money: even if it was not fully fledged 'money', having a standard unit of account represents an efficiency gain, since it serves to reduce the number of relative prices that agents would need to keep track of: in an economy of n goods, from $(n(n-1)/2)$ to $(n-1)$, provided n is greater than 2 (Millard, 2006).

There is further early evidence – also pre-dating the production of the first coins – to suggest even that just a unit of account could allow 'credit' to be recorded, which could then begin to function as money. Specifically, the religious authorities in Pharaonic Egypt in the second millennium BC may initially have used several units of account (referenced to uniform quantities of beer, bread and, subsequently, metals) to record flows of various goods between their different religious departments; yet it appears that they subsequently used such units of account to record dues they imposed on others. When some of the debtors could more than fulfil their dues, they obtained a net credit in terms of the unit of account, for which techniques to transfer developed (while others, who were short in meeting their obligations, could be granted loans, again expressed in the accepted unit of account) (Bleiberg, 2001; Tymoigne, 2006).

The theory that credit using a unit of account predated physical money as a medium of exchange makes sense above all if predicated on the earliest trade initially being undertaken locally. Among local communities, where all agents were known to each other, a tally of individuals' obligations could credibly be maintained. Nevertheless, as soon as trading relations became more complex, for example across long distances, where legal certainty could not be guaranteed, and between parties unknown to one another, the unit of account generally needed to take on some physical manifestation. Furthermore, it needed to be in limited supply and hard to counterfeit, yet (relatively) easy to transport. This reflected the inability of agents either to commit to repaying a debt at a future date, or to demonstrate their creditworthiness, for example by publishing their trading histories as evidence (Kocherlakota, 1998).

Whether the unit of account was an abstract or physical manifestation, under the Cartelist approach it predominantly derives its value from its issuer agreeing to accept it back in payment. One might, then, regard the physical manifestations of money as a form of collateral (Tymoigne, 2006). To the extent that some value is attributed to precious metals (such as for decorative reasons), then minting coin was a means of backing the unit of account with a substance that the issuer valued. But the face value of the coin would normally always be higher than the market price of the metal that made up the coin (Keynes, 1914; Wray, 2004). Otherwise (notwithstanding sometimes severe legal restrictions to the contrary) the incentive would be for holders of the coin to melt it and sell the metal as a commodity.

It has been argued that the value of the underlying collateral varied in proportion to the power/influence its issuer could wield. Thus, when Kublai Khan became the first issuer of paper money (on a fiat standard), in the Mongol Empire of the thirteenth century, this reflected his immense authority. His subjects accepted the paper money issued, because the Khan had the power to put them to death if they did not. Conversely, when in the 1290s the politically weak *Ilkhan* (ruler) Geikhatu tried to import the concept of paper money to Persia (even copying the earlier blue-print by using Chinese script, while adapting it to local conditions by adding a Muslim expression of faith), commerce in the region ground to a halt. This was despite severe penalties if anyone should use means other than this paper money to effect their business deals (Morgan, 1987).

Less extreme methods (than death) of forcing acceptance of a fiat currency were also available – such as a government determining that a particular issuance of a unit of account was 'legal tender' (meaning that creditors had to accept it from their debtors). In general, (military or religious) authorities prior to the formation of nation states, or (latterly) sovereign state governments, created debtors within the economy by levying taxes (or other obligations such as fines, including the Anglo-Saxon *wergild* cited in the Introduction above), and declared a willingness to accept monetary instruments they had issued in payment of these created debts. On this basis, money derives its value ultimately from its acceptability as a means of payment back to the issuer (notably, in the case of governments, in the form of taxes) (Innes, 1913).

The establishment of a particular form of money is subject to so-called 'network effects'. That is, the larger the number of agents willing to accept a given form of money, the greater the benefit to holding that money for use in transactions. It is then harder for new-entrant alternatives to gain currency (literally) (Selgin and White, 2002). So, once it has become established, a particular money, distinguished by its unit of account, is also able to perform its role as a medium of exchange among agents in the economy.

It generally takes the wholesale overthrow of a government for the money it has issued to lose its value altogether (though 'clipping' or other forms of debasement of coins in the middle ages, or overissuance of fiat money in more modern times, devalues money by means of inflation). But while money has acted as a means of payment for several millennia now, the documentary evidence suggests that, for a long time, any such payments among agents in the economy did not develop beyond simple bilateral relationships: one agent would produce a good, and a consumer would pay for it in cash. It required the emergence of banks to create the conditions for the economics of payments to develop in a more sophisticated way.

1.2 The emergence of banks, including the early central banks[9]

Modern banks developed from a number of different starting points. Tenth-century Arabic sources point to well-developed banking activities within Muslim territories: not only were the bankers of the medieval Middle East engaged in money exchange and the granting of loans, but they also regularly employed various payment methods. Cheques had been inherited from the Byzantines, and other payment instruments, such as the

---

[9] This subsection draws heavily on Norman, *et al.* (2007).

suftadja (a type of delegation of credit), were routinely used to allow both retail and government/wholesale payments to be effected between different cities in the region. But while western merchants and bankers would have observed these practices when trading in and with the Muslim territories, there is no direct evidence to suggest that the Middle-Eastern payment instruments were adopted like-for-like in Europe (Ashtor, 1973).

Rather, in western Christendom, in places where a wide variety of coins of different origin was in circulation, such as in thirteenth-century Venice, moneychangers expanded their specialist role of valuing specie,[10] to offer payment and other banking services based on the deposits held with them (Kohn, 1999; Mueller, 1997). Over the subsequent centuries, some of the more successful of these 'proto-banks' established themselves, even financing the English hundred-year war effort.

Indeed, the Peruzzi and the Bardi (both banking families in fourteenth-century Florence, who had built up a network of branches across Europe, allowing long-distance payments to be effected in-bank) were bankrupted when English King Edward III defaulted on his debt in 1348. They were succeeded by others, such as the Medici (in the fifteenth century), with a similarly extensive branch/correspondent network in key financial centres of Renaissance Europe. By the late-fifteenth/early-sixteenth centuries, the Fuggers of Augsburg (and other Southern German bankers such as the Hochstetters and Seilers) were the ones routinely providing loans to various European – notably Spanish – rulers (Kindleberger, 1993). Elsewhere, such as in mid-seventeenth century London, the origins of banking could be found among goldsmiths, who developed a similar banking business based on their specialist service of providing safekeeping facilities.

Whether western banks originated as moneychangers or as goldsmiths, merchants could deposit their (gold) coins with them in return for a receipt. Transactions could then be effected either across the moneychangers'/goldsmiths' books, or by transfer of the receipts they had issued, among other things helping to address a shortage of high-denomination coinage of reliable quality that characterized the monetary economy throughout much of early modern Europe (Sargent and Velde, 2002).

The distinction between payments across the books of an intermediary or by transfer of that intermediary's receipts (e.g. a bank-note) could come to shape the evolution of banking systems to this day. In some systems,

---

[10] Specie is the technical term used for coin money.

such as those of continental Europe, account-based payment methods with transfers across accounts of banks tended to predominate.

Elsewhere, such as in England (at least until the nineteenth century) or the US, issued notes were prevalent. (This is not to say that account-based transfers did not occur in predominantly note-issuing countries; or vice versa.) To the present day, there can still be a legacy of different payment methods, which, in part, reflect the chance of history – shaped notably by the political pressures and incentives that determine its course. Following Bismarck's unification of Germany, would German payments in the late-nineteenth/early-twentieth centuries necessarily have been effected predominantly across the accounts of the Reichsbank, had not the new pan-German central bank subsumed the well-established (257-year old) giro business of the Bank of Hamburg? Similarly, would notes have been as ubiquitous in the US, had the English system – dominated by (Bank of England) notes not provided a convenient precedent?

Different payment approaches also reflected the different costs through time of addressing the vulnerabilities that were peculiar to each. With an account-based system, there is a need to authenticate the account holder and keep records of the account holder's creditworthiness. Such a system is vulnerable to identity theft, and costly in record keeping. By contrast, with a store-of-value system (such as one based on issued bank-notes), there is a need to verify the integrity of the store of value that is circulating. Over time, particularly with the technological advances of the twentieth century, the costs of account-based systems have fallen relative to the costs of store-of-value systems[11] (Kahn and Roberds, 2009).

So, by the start of the fourteenth century, Venetian records appear to show that account holders at the same bank could effect payments to each other by book-entry transfer. But there is no conclusive evidence that these banks routinely accepted claims on each other; indeed, the reverse is implied both by the fact that a number of merchants held accounts at several Venetian banks in order to facilitate the collection of payments that were due to them, and by the proportion of (sometimes significant) cash deposits and withdrawals in some of the extant accounting records (Mueller, 1997). There was no strong impetus for the development of formal interbank clearing arrangements, although, like the merchants

---

[11] The reason why account-based systems were observed in early continental European systems is presumably because they were based at a branch and hence local in scope – in which case, the costs of identifying account holders and maintaining records were not prohibitive.

they provided services to, some of the banks themselves appear to have held correspondent accounts with each other, thereby providing the possibility for some means of netting off interbank claims. Arrangements along these lines may have been similar to those at medieval trade fairs (e.g. Champagne), where payments were mostly effected in-bank, with an initial set of credits/debits assigned to the accounts of sellers/purchasers, which were then (for the most part) extinguished by subsequent purchases/sales in the opposite direction. At the end of the fair, remaining (net) balances could be settled in specie (Kohn, 1999).

In the mid-fourteenth century, in the wake of a number of local bank failures, there were calls in Venice for a public bank to be set-up, with the capacity to enable payments to be made without the credit risk that is inherent in commercial bank money. Its development was more than two centuries in gestation, and came to fruition only when the public *Banco di Rialto* was set-up in 1587. But elsewhere in the Mediterranean trading area, municipal (so-called 'Taula') banks were set-up as early as the start of the fifteenth century – including in Barcelona (in 1401), Genoa (1407) and Valencia (1408). The Taula enabled banks to hold deposits as reserves and to use these to clear interbank payments. The business case for these early, what one might term 'proto' central banks was not always clear cut to contemporaries: in an early instance of a form of business risk, the Barcelona authorities banned the Taula from offering an interbank settlement function within a little more than a generation (1437). Even when the *Banco di Rialto* was imitated in other significant European trading cities – such as Amsterdam (1609), Hamburg (1619) and Nurnberg (1621) – their payments activity was limited to local payments within the one bank.

The ability to exchange claims on a bank reduced transaction costs relative to exchanging specie. As a general rule, commercial banks had further direct private incentives to start accepting claims on each other: by doing so, claims on any one bank were more widely acceptable, and all banks would be able to increase the issuance of their non-interest-bearing liabilities (which, in turn, funded interest-earning assets). This was a profitable business (Selgin and White, 1987). At the same time, the ability of any one bank to overissue was restricted by receiving banks returning claims promptly to the issuing banks for redemption. If a bank overissued its notes, then the other banks could overwhelm it with redemptions of its notes: the issuing bank then risked not being able to pay out on these, and its resulting illiquidity (even if it was not technically insolvent) would threaten its existence as a going concern. This is an example of liquidity risk.

25

Indeed, prompt redemption was an important way in which banks reduced one of the key costs of offering the service of accepting, on behalf of their customers, each other's claims: that of credit risk, i.e. if one of those other banks should become insolvent before that claim was redeemed. At the same time, redemption of claims was, itself, costly as well. Redemption costs arose in:

- clearing, i.e. calculating the amounts due to and from other banks, and confirming the availability of enough of the settlement asset at those banks in a debit position;
- holding a stock of the settlement asset, to meet the obligations due (i.e. an opportunity cost); and
- settlement itself, e.g., from the cost of transporting the settlement asset.

Over time, these costs were progressively reduced as various innovations were introduced. By the 1660s, the London goldsmiths were carrying out a banking business in issuing notes against specie deposits, and creating money by issuing further notes to borrowers. The claims that banks accepted on each other were then redeemed on a bilateral basis every few days, with the (net) difference settled in specie. The frequency of settlement was determined by the creditworthiness of the issuer: the more reputable a banker, the longer other bankers were willing to hold his notes (Quinn, 1997). The implicit cost of credit risk was being traded off against the more explicit costs of holding and transporting the settlement asset.

As economic activity grew, following agricultural and industrial advances in the eighteenth and nineteenth centuries, ever more payments needed to be made, over greater distances, and so volumes and values of interbank obligations increased. In response, the banks' clearing and settlement arrangements became more formalized. For instance, a general note exchange had emerged in Edinburgh by 1771, and was soon settling on a twice-weekly basis. From 1775 onwards, the Bankers' Clearing House in London was settling on a daily basis. Once these clearinghouses had been set up, it was a short step from settling obligations bilaterally, to doing so multilaterally (although it was only from 1841 onwards that the Bankers' Clearing House in London settled on a multilateral basis). The innovation of multilateral settlement further reduced the quantity of the settlement asset needed by participants to meet their net obligations.

A further cost-saving development, above all in note-based systems, was for the clearinghouse blue-print to be adopted outside the capital cities, emulating the pattern of local, *ad hoc* (bilateral) clearing observed earlier in London in the mid-seventeenth century. For example, during a four-decade period straddling the turn of the eighteenth/nineteenth centuries, banks set-up exchanges in most provincial Scottish towns where more than one bank was operating. Local clearings had also emerged in England by the mid-nineteenth century. Later, in Canada, ten regional clearing-houses were similarly established between 1887 and 1902, with daily settlement at each of four main centres. Although such regional arrangements fragmented the pools of liquidity that the banks needed to settle their obligations (at least until regional net obligations were forwarded on to the centre), they saved significantly on settlement-asset transportation costs.

These transportation costs were particularly acute when the settlement asset was specie or (gold) bullion. Not only was this cumbersome and costly to transport and exchange, but the process of transportation was vulnerable to a variety of operational risks – notably theft. To address the transport costs, banks innovated by using assets that were convertible into specie (and that all banks were willing to accept). By the 1770s, for instance, London's bankers had switched from settling in specie to settling in Bank of England notes. Notes issued by the Bank of England – as opposed to those issued by other London banks – were chosen for this function, presumably because of certain advantages uniquely enjoyed by the Bank, notably being the banker to the government, and the only legally permitted joint-stock bank.[12] The Bank of England acquired other such privileges later on, most notably in respect of restrictions on other banks issuing notes. As early as 1797 (and some would argue earlier) its liabilities were sufficiently credible that Pitt's permission for the Bank to suspend their convertibility for two decades (as the Napoleonic wars tested Britain's financial robustness) passed off with little fuss. This was due in no small part to the other banks' voluntary use of Bank of England notes as a convenient means of effecting settlement (Selgin and White, 2002).

In Scotland, exchequer bills appear to have become the preferred settlement asset, certainly by the time a formal agreement was drawn up in 1846, when previously both specie and drafts on London were used to effect final settlement. In Canada the alternative to gold as the ultimate

---

[12] Throughout the eighteenth (and into the nineteenth) centuries legal restrictions on other banks meant that they could not be set-up with more than 6 partners, thereby restricting the capital available for these banks to grow their business. By contrast, the Bank of England was uniquely exempted from this restriction, allowing it to develop a significantly larger circulation of its notes.

settlement asset was the Government-issued 'Dominion Note' (which was itself only partly backed by gold – a further cost-reducing innovation).

Whether it was specie/gold or some paper that was (partially/wholly) convertible, a vulnerability to theft remained, however, as long as the settlement asset needed to be physically transported, either bilaterally between banks or to a (central) clearing house. There is some limited evidence that note-based systems responded to this threat. For instance, at one point the Bank of England issued seven-day bills, which were like bank-notes, but not payable on sight; hence, they were less vulnerable to theft. By settling interbank obligations over accounts at a bank, this vulnerability could be eliminated entirely. In addition, it allowed further efficiencies to be exploited.

In the United States, the Second Bank of the United States used its accounts to play an active role in providing inter-regional payment services for the two decades (1816–1836) that its charter was granted. And during the 1820s, Boston banks appointed a single agent for clearing and settling notes in Boston – the Suffolk Bank – which cleared the notes of several New England banks on a multilateral net basis and settled their positions in deposits that they held with it. The Suffolk Bank clearing and settlement arrangements were superseded when, in the 1850s, the mutually owned Bank for Mutual Redemption replaced it and continued to perform a similar clearing and settlement function. Meanwhile, on the other side of the Atlantic, deposits at the Bank of England (as opposed to Bank of England notes) were used to effect settlement of the Bankers' Clearing House obligations from 1854 onwards.

While the US Bank for Mutual Redemption did not exist for long before the upheaval of the US Civil War in the 1860s, the Bank of England and others, such as the newly established Reichsbank in Bismarck's newly unified Germany, were becoming their countries' 'central banks'. This is not to suggest that it was inevitable that one institution should come to sit at the centre of a country's payment system. In Canada, for instance, a mutual Bankers' Association was set-up (in statute) at the start of the twentieth century, formalizing the organization of the regional clearing arrangements that had developed during the previous decade. Nevertheless, as technology constraints lessened (and specifically in the case of the Canadian system, as telegraphic communication between different regions became feasible), so there were strong economies of scale pushing for centralization. By 1927, settlement of Canadian banks' obligations (still in Government-issued Dominion Notes) was centralized at the Royal Trust Corporation.

Even where one institution did come to sit at the centre of a country's payment system, it was not necessarily the case that it would become the central bank. Continuing the Canadian case study, the Royal Trust Corporation was wholly unrelated to the Bank of Canada that took over its settlement role when it was set-up in 1935. Similarly, in post-Civil War US, a system of mutual clearinghouses was set-up, which even issued joint liabilities of its members to settle in during periods of financial instability. The Federal Reserve, established in 1913, represented a new departure in US monetary history.

Whether they were historically involved in payment and settlement functions and (then) evolved into what was regarded as a central bank, or whether they were set up by governments who determined their roles in statute, modern central banks still typically play a key role in their countries' payment systems. As argued in the next chapter, a central bank's role as provider of the settlement asset leads naturally to its typical core objectives: the pursuit of monetary and financial stability.

2

Payments and monetary and financial stability[13]

To this day, central-bank liabilities are typically used to settle claims between payment-system participants, and central banks often strengthen their influence via a role in the ownership, operation or oversight of key components of the financial infrastructure.

This chapter explores in more detail why central banks typically assume these roles. Section 2.1 begins with an explanation of the distinction between settlement in commercial and central-bank money, and describes how the 'payments pyramid' evolved. Sections 2.2 and 2.3 explore why a role in payments is core to the functions typically associated with central banking today: the maintenance of price stability and financial stability. Indeed, we argue that both aims can be captured in a 'broad' definition of the pursuit of monetary stability: the central bank should ensure that money can perform its functions of unit of account, store of value and medium of exchange in all states of the world. Smoothly functioning payment systems clearly contribute to this objective.

In this regard, Section 2.4 explains why payment and settlement systems are important for the real economy and how they contribute to economic growth, with Section 2.5 providing an overview of the structure of the modern infrastructural landscape and the role of the central bank – and central-bank money – within it.

---

[13] This chapter draws heavily from Manning and Russo (2008).

2.1 Central-bank money as the ultimate settlement asset

As we saw in Chapter 1, economic agents have, over time, sought ever more efficient ways to conduct their payments business. To avoid having to directly exchange precious metals or currency in settlement of their obligations, agents sought arrangements by which they could instruct their banks to settle claims on their behalf, either by transferring deposits across their own books (if paying another customer of the same bank), or transferring deposits via interbank arrangements (if seeking to transfer funds to a customer of another bank).

Claims thereby arose between the banks, which had somehow to be settled. Hence, banks had to select a settlement asset that was acceptable to all and establish a mechanism and a set of rules – a payment system – by which such settlements were to take place. We discussed the range of solutions that were developed over time in Chapter 1. Today, central banks provide the ultimate, or final, settlement asset. Below the central bank, there is typically a hierarchy with a top tier of banks – so-called settlement banks – settling directly across the books of the central bank

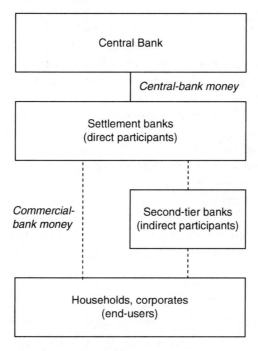

Figure 2.1: Hierarchy of settlement relationships

and offering settlement in their own liabilities – or 'commercial-bank' money[14] – both to banks in the tier below and to end-users of payment services. This hierarchy is often referred to as the 'payments pyramid' (Figure 2.1).

Hence, central bank and commercial bank money settlement co-exist.[15] In particular, households and firms typically settle in commercial bank money at their own bank, relying on convertibility of their deposits into central-bank money (typically cash). Importantly, if a commercial bank runs out of reserves – or collateral that can be posted with the central bank to obtain reserves – it loses its ability to purchase bank-notes from the central bank. Its promise to convert its customers' deposits into central-bank money on demand then becomes worthless; this may prompt a bank run as depositors rush to convert their deposits into cash.

2.2 Payments and monetary stability

To safeguard the demand for its liabilities in settling interbank claims (and maintaining a stock of bank-notes), the central bank will seek to control the terms on which they are offered to the banking system: the quantity provided and the price. Thus, monetary stability is necessary for the acceptance of central-bank money. Tucker (2004), for instance, states that '... demand for [Bank of England] money [relies] on two preconditions: the integrity of our balance sheet and, in a fiat money system, a decent monetary policy. Without them, agents might drift to using final-settlement assets which could provide an alternative unit of account for the economy.' The integrity of the central bank's balance sheet may still play a role even when the central bank's balance sheet is backed by the government. The argument is that a financially healthy central bank may enjoy a greater degree of independence from the government. Independence, in turn, may support a central bank in its pursuit of monetary stability.[16]

In practice, the monetary-policy objective is usually cast in terms of price stability. For instance, the Bank of England seeks to maintain 'stable prices and confidence in the currency', discharging this responsibility

---

[14] Also referred to as 'inside' money.

[15] This theme is explored in CPSS (2003a).

[16] Kydland and Prescott (1977) and Barro and Gordon (1983) make this point in a formal setting. The strength of the empirical evidence is discussed in Alesina and Summers (1993) and Stella (2008). More recent and comprehensive evidence is provided by Stella and Klueh (2008).

with reference to an explicit inflation target. Similarly, the European Central Bank has an explicit objective to 'maintain the Euro's purchasing power and thus price stability in the Euro area.' And the US Federal Reserve conducts 'the nation's monetary policy by influencing the monetary and credit conditions in the economy in pursuit of maximum employment, stable prices, and moderate long-term interest rates.' Central banks pursue this objective via the implementation of monetary-policy decisions, to which there are two broad elements.

First, banks generally satisfy their demand for reserves by borrowing from the central bank in regular open-market operations, conducted by the central bank.[17] Banks eligible to participate in such operations increase their holdings of reserves by borrowing against eligible collateral assets – such as government bonds – either via a repurchase, or 'repo', agreement or a collateralized lending operation. Short-term operations are typically carried out on terms close to the central bank's policy rate. Longer term operations are normally at a rate which reflects market expectations of the future path of the policy rate.

Second, the central bank typically stands ready to accommodate – via standing lending and deposit facilities on published terms – shorter-run fluctuations in the banking system's demand for end-of-day balances in central-bank money.

Figure 2.2 presents a stylized version of the central bank's balance sheet, reflecting these elements. We explore the interaction between the precise methods to implement monetary policy and banks' short-term liquidity management in Chapter 4.

Repo operations are typically settled in the securities settlement system. Banks participating in open-market operations then lend out some of the liquidity obtained from the central bank to other banks; such loans generally

Central-bank balance sheet

Assets	Liabilities
Fx reserves	Bank-note issue
Lending to banks	Reserve account balances
Outright securities holdings	Capital

Figure 2.2: Stylized central-bank balance sheet

[17] Banks' demand for reserves arises from their need to purchase the central bank's bank-notes, among other things.

also settle in the securities settlement system (if collateralized), or in the large-value payment system (if uncollateralized). Hence, the integrity of *both* the large-value payment system and the securities settlement system are crucial for the central bank's ability to conduct its monetary operations.

But as regards monetary operations, a central bank's interest can reach beyond systems that settle in central-bank money. In a typical industrialized economy today, most money is held in the form of commercial-bank deposits (or inside money). The extent of economic agents' reliance on transfers of commercial-bank money to settle claims arising between them, and the accuracy of settlement banks' forecasts of their customers' flows, ultimately underpins the banking system's day-to-day demand for reserves (outside money). Hence, the central bank needs to take an interest in the functioning of the payment systems that determine this ultimate demand.

2.3 Payments and financial stability

We argued in the introduction to this chapter that a central bank's financial stability objective nests within a broadly interpreted monetary stability objective. Financial instability, manifested, say, in contagious losses among banks or disruptions to payment systems and other components of the financial infrastructure, would directly undermine the ability of money to perform its functions. In times of stress, the provider of the ultimate settlement asset would have the capacity to increase the supply of its liabilities to ensure that payments continued to be settled. In certain circumstances, it might also expand its balance sheet so as to prevent the failure of a solvent but illiquid institution: that is, it might take on the role of lender of last resort.

Yet, historically, the lender-of-last-resort role was not always assumed naturally by the established settlement agent. For instance, the Bank of England became the provider of the ultimate settlement asset late in the eighteenth century, while still a private bank with private shareholders, providing banking services to private companies as well as to the government. Throughout the nineteenth century, the Bank of England was repeatedly called upon to support other banks, notably when financial crises threatened the stability of London's financial system. The resulting conflicts of interest prevented it from performing fully the public functions that one associates with a modern central bank. This tension can be observed in some other countries where one private institution had evolved to perform settlement.

Here, it is interesting to contrast the differing outcomes in New York and Chicago during the Bankers' Panic of 1907, which can in large measure be explained by the responses of the local clearinghouses. In New York, membership of the clearinghouse was largely restricted to national and state banks. Trusts, seen locally as serious competitors to the banks, were by-and-large excluded from the clearinghouse. In Chicago, on the other hand, Trusts were direct members of the clearinghouse, alongside national banks. Moen and Tallman (2000) report that the clearinghouses in both cities stood ready to offer emergency lending assistance during the crisis, but tended to favour direct members. In New York, conflicts of interest arising from the competitive threat posed by the Trusts added a further dimension to the clearinghouse's lending decision.

Eventually, such conflicts could be overcome only by making the central bank a public-sector institution. The Bank of England, for instance, was nationalized in 1946. Elsewhere, in countries where no obvious candidate for central bank had emerged (whether through responsibility for settlement or otherwise), there was a general trend during the twentieth century for governments to set-up public central banks from scratch. The emergence of the Federal Reserve in 1913 was in part a response to the Bankers' Panic of 1907.

So, there were economies of scope in bringing together the role of settlement agent with that of the central bank: in short, it made sense for banks to settle payment obligations in normal times at the same institution from which they would hope to gain liquidity in extreme circumstances.

In seeking to minimize the frequency with which it is called upon to conduct emergency lending, and in the spirit of controlling its balance sheet and maintaining price stability, the central bank will wish to reduce systemic threats to the financial system. But some of these threats may derive from the design and operation of payment and settlement systems themselves, particularly when the dependence on such systems is high.

Around the world, then, central banks have taken a keen interest in ensuring that the payments and settlement infrastructure is operationally effective, resilient and robust. And they have taken a leading role in mitigating systemic risks that might arise within the settlement process (see Part II for a detailed discussion of the potential sources of such risks). Crystallization of systemic risks in the infrastructure could compromise activity in modern financial markets, thereby disrupting the smooth transmission of funds from savers to investors and compromising the functioning of the modern monetary economy. This is particularly so during periods of market turbulence, such as that in late 2007 and 2008. The continued confidence in the financial market infrastructure was crucial in allowing trading in key securities markets to continue during that period.

2.4 The value of payment systems to the real economy

In an economy without payment systems, economic agents would have to hold, or at least be able to access readily, sufficient cash to fund all (potential) market transactions in which they might wish to participate during a given period.[18] They would have to hold much more cash than in the presence of well-functioning interbank payment systems. But cash is an unproductive asset. Rather than holding more cash, the agent could decide to trade less, which could reduce welfare.

The idea that the need to hold the required settlement asset could prevent agents in an economy from settling their obligations, and hence could inhibit trade, has a long history in economic thought. An often-cited example of this phenomenon is the large seasonal variation in short-term interest rates seen in the US prior to the establishment of the Federal Reserve, which Friedman and Schwartz (1963) attribute to a shortage of currency during the harvest season when trading flows were high. However, it was only in 1996, with the publication of two influential papers by Scott Freeman (1996a, 1996b), that the implications of this tendency were formally modelled.

Freeman (1996b) uses a two-period overlapping generations framework to analyze an economy in which agents trade using debt (inside money), which is then settled in a later period via a payment of outside money. This is a useful representation of the co-existence of commercial bank and central bank money. By assumption, debtors and creditors cannot settle their claims directly; hence, they require recourse to a market in which debt can be resold to third parties against outside money. Freeman shows that if there is insufficient outside money, the claims trade at a discount, inhibiting the underlying real economic transactions.

Freeman demonstrates that the intervention of a monetary authority, which can temporarily create additional outside money and lend it out so as to allow debt markets to clear at par, can be welfare enhancing. It can be shown that such a policy need not have a permanent effect on the price level as the additional outside money created can be retired once the loans have

---

[18] See Svensson (1985) and Lucas and Stokey (1987) for examples of how the literature on general equilibrium models of monetary exchange makes this 'cash-in-advance' constraint explicit.

been repaid. As we shall see in Chapter 4, this argument also applies to policies typically adopted by central banks as regards the provision of intraday liquidity in payment systems: intraday credit is provided relatively cheaply to facilitate settlement during the day, whereas overnight and longer term loans are offered at a sufficiently high rate to ensure price stability.

In a model similar in spirit to that of Freeman, Williamson (2003) shows that the efficiency of trade depends on the existence of an outside asset – central-bank money – or centralized arrangements for settling claims between agents: a payment system. Williamson first shows that, with spatial separation and an absence of centralized payment arrangements, households' 'cash-in-advance' constraint binds: relative to the optimal allocation, households hold insufficient cash and so will consume too little. Upon introduction of a centralized clearinghouse – operated by the central bank and settling net on a daily basis across the central bank's books[19] – households are able to exchange private debt with the clearinghouse. As a result of the combined use of private debt (inside money) and outside money (reserves), welfare rises.

But even though payment systems can improve welfare, it is not guaranteed that they emerge when agents have the choice between cash and a form of inside money. He *et al.* (2005) investigate the conditions that have to be met. They set out a theoretical model of the transition from an early monetary economy to one with financial institutions and payment systems. They find that a payment system is more likely to be introduced the cheaper it is to use, the greater the risk of 'theft' in a cash-only world, and the higher the gains from trade. Lester (2006) and Millard and Willison (2006) have built on this model, incorporating settlement and operational risks in the use of payment systems, and investigating welfare implications.

Once established, agents depend heavily on such systems to support their transactions, but typically go about their business without a second thought as to whether their transfers will be settled as expected. The prolonged absence of, or a loss of confidence in, the systems on which agents rely for the transfer of bank deposits could therefore have a severe impact, resulting in a retreat from inside money and a costly return to cash – *in extremis*, a return to barter – with potentially stark implications for the level of activity in the real economy. As Alan Greenspan, former Chairman of the Board of Governors of the US Federal Reserve System

---

[19] In the model this is equivalent to the free provision of daylight overdrafts from the clearinghouse (central bank).

notes in his memoirs: 'We'd always thought that if you wanted to cripple the US economy, you'd take out the payment systems. Banks would be forced to fall back on inefficient physical transfers of money. Businesses would resort to barter and IOUs; the level of economic activity across the country could drop like a rock.' (Greenspan (2007), page 2).

A vivid example of the loss of inside money as a medium of exchange is the Great Depression (Box 2.1). Between 1929 and 1933, the value of payments processed by the major US dollar settlement systems fell by more than 60% as confidence in the banking system disappeared. While this episode was not strictly a disruption to the infrastructure employed in settling interbank claims, it offers some clues as to how the real economy might respond to a prolonged disruption of this kind.

Box 2.1: THE LOSS OF INSIDE MONEY AS A MEDIUM OF EXCHANGE
IN THE GREAT DEPRESSION

One notable feature of the Great Depression of the 1930s in the US, which was precipitated by the Wall Street Crash of 29 October 1929, is the failure of banks – 608 in the last two months of 1930, and over 9000 in total up to 1933. When a bank failed, authorities would usually impose restrictions on cash withdrawals, meaning that customers might not receive their money for a long time, if at all.

Gerali and Passacantando (2007) argue that the lack of confidence in banks led to decreased appetite for bank money and an increased demand for alternative payment instruments. The value of cheques handled by the US Federal Reserve declined by 57% between 1929 and 1933, compared with a 49% contraction in nominal income over the same period. The total value of payments cleared fell even further – 66%. Deposits fell sharply as people withdrew their money and kept it outside the banking system.

Many local communities in the US introduced scrip money – effectively they printed their own money – or employed barter systems. Irving Fisher (1933) estimated at the time of his writing that about one million people in the US depended on barter, in whole or in part. At one stage, one of the US states, Oregon, planned a $75m stamp scrip issue. Stamped scrip involved purchasing a stamp of small value (such as 3 cents for a $1 transaction) and attaching it to the note for each transaction made. Once a sufficient number of stamps had been attached to the note, it could be exchanged for cash. Even the manufacturers of the Monopoly board game used their presses to print substitute money for their town. However, in 1933 Roosevelt prohibited the use of 'emergency currencies' and attempted to restore public confidence in banks, bringing an end to the use of scrip.

Gerali and Passacantando disagree with economists who argue that the lack of an expansionary monetary policy from the Fed was to blame for the depth of the crisis – they see the decline in the transactions value of the money supply as an important factor.

In the event, the contraction in settlement activity was more than proportional to the overall reduction in economic activity during the Depression. Gerali and Passacantando (2007) show that, in localized communities, forms of barter emerged, as well as new locally accepted alternative forms of money. These workarounds substituted only imperfectly for inside money, however, as they were generally available only for trade in defined communities where informational frictions were sufficiently low.

The Irish banking strike of 1970 offers a more recent case study of major disruption to the modern machinery for effecting payments (Box 2.2). Murphy (1978) and Central Bank of Ireland (1971) provide a comprehensive overview of the strike, which lasted more than six months. During this time, households – in particular – were unable to transfer bank deposits. In the event, the real economic impact was much more muted than might have

---

Box 2.2: WHEN A PAYMENT INSTRUMENT DISAPPEARS: THE IRISH BANKING STRIKE OF 1970

The Republic of Ireland suffered three banking strikes in 1966, 1970 and 1976. The longest of these occurred in 1970, when the Associated Banks were closed for over six months.[20] During this time, customers found it almost impossible to withdraw cash from their bank accounts and were forced to find alternative means of payment.

The four Associated Banks (Bank of Ireland, Allied Irish Bank, National Irish Bank and Ulster Bank) had current and deposit accounts comprising 85% of the Irish money supply, as measured by M2, in 1970. Although these were closed during the strike, merchant and foreign banks remained open, offering services to corporations in particular.

Furthermore, customers near to the border could avail themselves of services in Northern Ireland, and some people even managed to access banking services in Great Britain. Since the Irish pound at that time was fixed to sterling at a one-to-one ratio, UK bank notes were freely accepted in the Republic at face value and there was no currency risk. Indeed, during the tourist season in the summer, British tourists brought over much-needed cash in the form of sterling, thus helping to alleviate the crisis. The total amount of sterling in circulation increased from £5mn in April to £40mn by the end of the strike. However, these injections of sterling were limited to certain areas and it would take more time for that cash to filter through to places that did not have the advantage of foreign banks, tourists or proximity to the UK (if it reached them at all).

The timing of the strike could not be described as a shock. Indeed, in anticipation of the strike, banking services were gradually scaled back over the preceding two months, allowing customers to engage in banking business and build up stocks of cash. Furthermore, Irish households had already been through a three-month banking strike in 1966, which surely helped to reduce any panic.

(continued)

---

[20] The strike lasted from 1 May to 17 November 1970.

Box 2.2: (Continued)

In all three strikes, Irish households found an effective workaround measure. When they wished to make a payment, they wrote cheques to each other, so that the bearer could cash them after the crisis had ended. Effectively people printed their own money, and acted as a guarantor of the payment.

How could the seller be sure that the person writing the cheque would not default? Ireland at that time was a much more rural and tight-knit society than it is now, and typically people would only do business in their local area. Therefore they might know the person and trust them, or failing that they could enquire in a local shop or pub as to the creditworthiness of the payer. In the cities this might be less feasible, but then in larger cities, it was more likely that alternative banks or sterling would be available.

Conclusion

Prima facie, this incident – an almost total lack of inside money to effect transactions for more than six months – should have had a big impact on the wider economy. Why was this not the case?

- The (albeit limited) access to alternatives – non-Associated banks and sterling – especially for businesses and city-dwellers.
- The strike was anticipated and something similar had been experienced before.
- Close-knit communities lowered informational frictions.
- There were no concerns about the solvency of banks.
- It was known that the strike would end at some undetermined point in the future,[21] so people felt assured that the cheques would be honoured eventually.

It is perhaps remarkable that households were willing to assume credit exposures to each other for a prolonged period. It is likely that in a larger economy with interactions between strangers, there would have been a far more adverse impact.

---

been expected – economic activity continued to expand, though somewhat more slowly. But agents' behaviour *did* change, as did risk exposures between them.

In particular, it is interesting to observe the workarounds adopted by those most affected by the strike. With banks fully expected to reopen in due course, cheques drawn on pre-closure bank accounts continued to circulate. Agents were thus accepting credit risk on each other for a prolonged, and indeed, unknown, period: between the date of issuance of the cheque and ultimate settlement once the banks reopened.

---

[21] Admittedly, the end-point was unknown. The *Irish Times* of 16 May reported that roughly half of the banks' employees had moved to London to take up work. Apparently planes were being chartered to bring bank workers to London. The public would thus have known how far the workers and banks were from agreement, and that the strike would be prolonged.

It seems that this workaround system was able to function *purely* by virtue of low informational frictions: the spatial proximity of those issuing and accepting cheques ensured that there was sufficient information on the creditworthiness of the issuer. One might posit that, in a world with a larger number of transacting agents, unknown to one another and perhaps highly dispersed, the real economic effects would have been far more severe.

Indeed, Kahn and Roberds (2009) argue that the record keeping embedded within interbank payment arrangements can increase opportunities for efficient trade. In a world with imperfect information and limited enforcement, inside money transfers reveal potentially valuable information about the identity of the transacting parties and provide evidence that a trade has taken place. In a similar vein, Koeppl *et al.* (2006) and Temzelides and Williamson (2001) draw out the importance of periodic settlement in the presence of informational frictions.

Finally, Merrouche and Nier (2009) attempt to establish the benefit of a well-functioning payment system to the real economy by exploring empirically how the transition economies of Eastern Europe responded to payment system reform during the 1990s and early twenty-first century. The authors find support for the notion that payment-system reform resulted in agents' increased use of inside money rather than cash as a payment medium, which in turn boosted the ability of the banking system to create credit. The authors also explore a second channel: that is, advanced payment arrangements offer greater scope for liquidity sharing in the interbank market, which might allow banks to reduce precautionary holdings of central-bank reserves. The evidence for this channel is somewhat weaker, with significant support emerging only where excess reserves were particularly high before payment-systems reform.

2.5 The broadening and deepening of financial market infrastructure and implications for central banks' financial stability objectives

From the origins described in Chapter 1, the arrangements that support the settlement of payment and securities transactions – in the following referred to as '(financial) infrastructure' – have become broader and deeper. And in their financial stability role, central banks take an interest in the smooth functioning of the financial infrastructure as a whole. But given its central importance, central banks typically take a particularly strong interest in the identification and mitigation of risks that might disrupt settlement in the large-value payment system (LVPS), in which ultimate settlement occurs across the central bank's books. In Chapter 8, we show that such interest might be discharged via operational involvement, oversight of system rules and procedures, or outright ownership of the system. Here, we briefly describe the main elements of these broader infrastructural arrangements and show how the large-value payment system has come to sit at the core of a complex web of financial infrastructure.

During the nineteenth century, trading in financial instruments – the exchange of equities, bonds, derivatives, etc. – led to the development of regulated exchanges. Centralized post-trade infrastructures – central counterparty clearinghouses (CCPs), central securities depositories (CSDs) and securities settlement systems (SSSs) – later emerged in support of such trading activity. Today, these infrastructures play a critical role in the financial system, their rules, processes, resilience and efficiency crucial to minimizing the frictions to trade in financial markets; and their disruption able to compromise financial stability materially. Box 2.3 briefly describes the roles assumed today by central counterparty clearinghouses, central securities depositories and securities settlement systems.

Box 2.3: CENTRALIZED INFRASTRUCTURES FOR CLEARING AND SETTLEMENT

Central counterparty clearinghouses (CCPs) initially emerged to support trade on derivatives (futures) exchanges. With long pre-settlement periods, agents are exposed to 'replacement cost risk', the risk that, before settlement, the counterparty defaults and the trade has to be replaced – potentially at a loss. With anonymous trading, agents would be reluctant to carry such counterparty risk and hence central counterparty clearing emerged as a vehicle by which each party transacts with a high-quality counterparty. Via a legal process known as novation, the clearinghouse interposes itself as the buyer to every seller, and the seller to every buyer. Central counterparties have since expanded their operations to other markets, notably equities, bonds and some OTC derivatives.

Central securities depositories (CSDs) are the bodies into which new securities are issued and 'held' (today, generally in dematerialized form). CSDs typically also operate the **securities settlement system (SSS)** in which trades are settled (the transfer of securities in exchange for the agreed settlement asset – typically central-bank money). CSDs perform functions such as corporate actions (calculation of dividends, etc.), custody (the safe-keeping of securities) and sometimes also stock-lending, repo and collateral management.

In the early 1970s, the **international central securities depositories** (ICSDs), Euroclear Bank and Cedel (now Clearstream Banking Luxembourg) were established to provide CSD services for the eurobond market. Via a network of links to multiple CSDs around the world, these entities today offer a variety of services to international financial markets, notably global custody, collateral management and tri-party repo (where the ICSD acts as an intermediary between two parties in a repo transaction).

Table 2.1 provides an overview of volumes and values processed in selected securities settlement systems. Both volumes and values in these systems are large, with securities worth the equivalent of each country's annual GDP turned over every one-to-two weeks.

Table 2.1: Daily values and volumes in selected securities settlement systems

SSS		Value (US billions) 2006	% of GDP 2006	Volume (thousands) 2006
Canada	CDS	212	17	401
France	Euroclear France	615	27	130
Germany	Clearstream Banking Frankfurt	206	7	234
Italy	Express II	325	18	113
Japan	BOJ	643	14	15
UK	CREST	717	30	246
US	Fedwire	1491	11	88
	DTC	708	5	1157

Source: CPSS (2008a).

In the domain of payments, dedicated systems have emerged, processing particular categories of payments and supporting particular markets: cheques and retail electronic systems for payments between individuals, and international systems, such as continuous linked settlement (CLS), which settles foreign exchange transactions. We will return to a more detailed discussion of the settlement of foreign-exchange transactions in Chapter 5. Box 2.4 describes three important types of retail payment systems.

Box 2.4: RETAIL PAYMENT SYSTEMS

Automated teller machine (ATM) sharing schemes allow cardholders to withdraw cash from the ATM of a bank with which they are not an account-holding customer. A significant motivation for banks and building societies to participate in schemes has been to limit the cost of installing independent ATM networks for a customer base spread across the country, but there are also often significant convenience benefits for cardholders. Obligations between member institutions in ATM-sharing schemes are typically settled on a deferred net basis (see Section 3.1).

Cheques and other paper payment instruments are among the oldest non-cash payment methods and remain popular in a number of countries today. Cheques are a flexible payment method, especially as the payer need only know the name of the recipient and not their account details. They are processed in different ways around the world, but today are frequently converted into electronic messages for efficiency. Depending on the system, the paper instrument itself or a scanned copy generally follows this message to the paying bank. Obligations between member institutions are typically settled on a deferred net basis.

(continued)

Box 2.4: (Continued)

Direct debits credits. Electronic retail payments such as direct debits and credits are characterized by their low values and high volumes. Electronic retail payment systems process these payment instructions and determine each member's net liability. By netting payments between institutions, these systems facilitate the bulk processing of large numbers of low-value payments and reduce the draw on members' liquidity. Today, most banking customers (individuals and businesses) in developed countries use some form of electronic payment, substituting away from cheques and other non-cash, paper payment instruments. The number of personal electronic retail payments is overtaking, or has overtaken, the number of personal cheque payments in many developed countries.

Table 2.2 documents values and volumes passing through selected retail payment systems. Volumes are substantial, but nevertheless (annual) values are relatively low, often only about as high as the country's (annual) GDP. The table also indicates a transition from paper-based systems (cheques) to electronic systems (such as direct debit/credit) in recent years.

Table 2.2: Annual values and volumes in selected retail-payment systems (direct debits and cheques)

	Annual value (% of GDP), 2001		Annual value (% of GDP), 2006		Annual volume (millions), 2006	
	Direct debits	Cheques	Direct debits	Cheques	Direct debits	Cheques
Canada	23.6	464.3	32.6	266.8	662.0	1325.4
France	47.0	147.7	54.7	123.2	2736.8	38270.0
Germany	188.4	42.7	157.8	25.9	7363.3	108.9
Italy	16.3	96.2	20.3	81.2	480.0	453.8
Japan	N/A	176.3	N/A	93.9	N/A	134.2
UK	55.8	196.0	64.9	129.5	2857.8	1778.0
US	98.8	391.9	102.3	316.3	8663.9	30557.4

Sources: CPSS (1997, 2007b, 2008a).

Volumes and values passing through the large-value payment systems have been rising over the course of the twentieth century but, as shown in Table 2.3, have remained broadly constant relative to GDP during the past decade. But values continue to be large: in the G7 countries below, *daily* values are of the order of 20% of the respective country's *annual* GDP.[22]

Large-value payment systems not only settle obligations arising in wholesale interbank markets, but also net obligations arising in other (e.g. retail) payment systems. Via links with clearing and settlement systems, they also underpin activity in the broader financial markets. Figure 2.3

[22] Bech *et al.* (2008) provide details.

Table 2.3: Daily values and volumes in selected large-value payment systems (LVPS)

	LVPS	Daily value (US $ bn) 2006	% of GDP			Daily volume (thousands)		
			1996	2001	2006	1996	2001	2006
Canada	LVTS	146	7	10	11	9	15	19
France (a)	TBF	670	6	23	30	18	15	18
Germany (a)	RTGS +	748	17	13	26	74	94	150
Italy (a)	BI-REL	187	7	9	10	21	40	43
Japan	BOJ-NET	862	31	15	20	15	20	22
UK	CHAPS £	424	15	19	18	57	87	131
US	CHIPS	1560	17	12	12	211	238	308
	Fedwire	2263	13	16	17	325	443	528
EU	TARGET	2674		17	25		211	329
	EURO1	239		3	2		117	189

Sources: CPSS (1997, 2007b, 2008a).
(a) These national large-value payment systems have now migrated to TARGET2.

illustrates the central position of large-value payment systems, highlighting their interdependence with a range of ancillary systems. For example, banks' net positions in retail payment systems are ultimately cleared via the national large-value payment system. And in those countries in which a competing large-value payment system exists – such as the US CHIPS

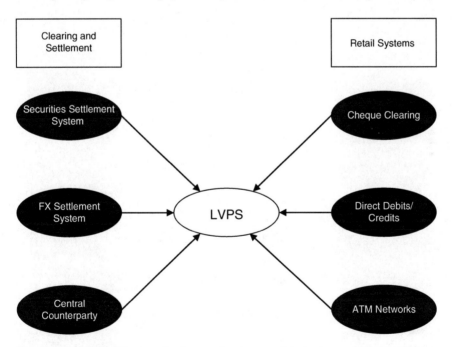

Figure 2.3: Dependence on the large-value payment system

system, which operates as a privately owned alternative to the US Fedwire system – ultimate settlement is again typically achieved via pay-ins to/from the main large-value system.

The large-value payment system is also typically linked to the securities settlement system (to effect the cash leg of a securities trade) and margin payments to central counterparties are also typically transferred via the large-value payment system (see Chapter 5).

Given the central position of large-value payment systems in the financial infrastructure, Part II of this book focuses primarily on the risks that can emerge in these systems (in Chapters 3 and 4). Risks specific to clearing and settlement in wholesale financial markets (including for foreign exchange) are discussed further in Chapter 5.[23] Interdependencies between systems, which now often extend internationally, are considered in more detail in Part IV.

---

[23] Further discussion of issues that are specific to retail payment systems, such as credit and debit card systems, are outside the scope of this book. CPSS (2003d) provides an overview of policy issues for central banks in retail payments.

Part II

Sources of systemic risk in payment and settlement systems

Part II of this volume explores sources of systemic risk in payment and settlement activity. Systemic risk may be thought of as 'the risk that the failure of one participant in a transfer system, or in financial markets generally, to meet its required obligations will cause other participants or financial institutions to be unable to meet their obligations (including settlement obligations in a transfer system) when due' (CPSS, 2003c). In payment systems, the source of systemic risk is settlement risk: that is, the risk that a payment fails to settle. Settlement risk has four broad underlying components: credit risk; liquidity risk; operational risk; and business risk. These may be defined, as follows:

- *Credit risk*: the risk that a participant in the system defaults on its obligations within the payment system, imposing direct unanticipated losses on other members;[24]

- *Liquidity risk*: the risk that a participant/participants hold(s) insufficient liquidity in the settlement asset, disrupting the flow of liquidity in the system and leading to delay in or failure of settlement;

---

[24] Importantly, when we refer to credit risk in the context of payment and settlement systems, our concern is with credit exposures that arise purely as a result of the design and operation of such a system: a function of any lag between the time at which a bank assumes an exposure to another bank on behalf of its customer, and the time at which such exposure is extinguished. We are not referring here to credit exposures that arise naturally between banks in the normal course of their economic activity, even though these are also generated and extinguished via transfers passing across payment and settlement systems.

- *Operational risk*: the risk of losses arising from technical failure or other forced interruption to the operations of a payment system (or its core components), or those of its participants;

- *Business risk*: the risk of losses arising from either suspension (or termination) of a payment system's (or its core components') provision of services due to financial pressures.

Figure 3.1 provides some examples of events that can trigger these risks.

Other decompositions of settlement risk can be found in the literature. For instance, principal risk and conditionality risk (the risk that the recipient of either delivery or payment acts as if its counterparty has fulfilled its obligations before it has actually done so, see our discussion in Section 3.1) both fall under our definition of credit risk. And credit risk in foreign-exchange transactions is sometimes referred to as foreign-exchange settlement risk, or 'Herstatt' risk (see Chapter 5). Settlement failures can also give rise to replacement cost risk: the risk that the failure of a party to fulfil its obligations forces its counterparty to replace the trade, possibly on less favourable terms (or, if no acceptable trading opportunity is available, not to trade at all).

More specific types of operational risk may also be identified. For instance, the Basel Committee on Payment and Settlement Systems (CPSS)[25] refers to

Risk		Risk Events	Examples
Credit risk		Settlement member insolvency	Heavy financial losses by settlement member
		Settlement agent insolvency	Heavy financial losses by settlement agent
Liquidity risk		Failure by settlement member to submit payments promptly	High cost of liquidity
Business Risk		Insolvency of infrastructure provider	Costly project overrun by infrastructure provider
		Withdrawal of service by system infrastructure on financial grounds	
Operational Risk	External to the system	Disasters	Terrorist attack, Natural disaster
		Utilities failure	Loss of power/water. Loss of access to office space.
		External threat to network	Hacking, denial of service attack, etc.
	Internal to the system	Supplier failures	Failure of organization to whom critical functions have been outsourced
		Systems/Network failures	Human error; software error; computer virus
		Systems/Network capacity breach	Limited processing capacity
		Employee misdeed	Fraud, forgery, theft, extortion, other intentional unauthorized activity by systems' staff.

Figure 3.1: A breakdown of risks by different trigger events

[25] In the *Core Principles for Systemically Important Payment Systems*, CPSS (2001a).

security risk in the context of the integrity of information technology systems. Similarly, *legal* risk[26] – the risk of loss arising from the unexpected application of a law or regulation or because a contract cannot be enforced – can contribute to settlement risk. For example, the legal risk surrounding the enforcement of netting arrangements was one of the drivers of the move from deferred net settlement to real-time gross settlement in the 1990s (Chapter 3); that is the move to transaction-by-transaction settlement of payment instructions as they are received.

Part II proceeds as follows. First, in Chapter 3, we explore how credit risk arises in large-value payment systems. We survey the literature that assesses the importance of this risk and describe the main ways in which it can be mitigated. In this context we describe the shift to real-time gross settlement (RTGS) in large-value payment systems. While the RTGS model addresses interbank credit risk arising in payment systems, it does place a higher liquidity burden on system participants. In Chapter 4, then, we investigate strategic incentives arising in RTGS systems to delay payments in order to save on liquidity and examine the consequent implications for liquidity risk. We explore mechanisms for the mitigation of liquidity risk, considering aspects of system design and central-bank policy. Chapter 5 discusses specific types of credit risk that arise in the clearing and settlement of foreign exchange, securities and derivatives transactions – as opposed to the settlement of clean payments – and the arrangements that have been developed to manage these risks. Finally, in Chapter 6, we explore sources of business and operational risks and potential risk mitigants. Here, we draw heavily on case studies to draw insights as to the potential consequences of operational failure and the implications of alternative responses by participants or the authorities.

---

[26] See, for example, Jenkinson and Manning (2007) for the importance of a clear legal and regulatory environment.

3

System design and sources of credit risk in large-value payment and settlement systems

The focus of this chapter is credit risk in payment and settlement systems. We begin with a discussion of how the design of a large-value system might affect the propensity for unintended credit-risk exposures to arise between participants.

Two basic settlement models are typically applied in interbank payment systems: deferred net settlement (DNS); and real-time gross settlement (RTGS). Netting allows users to economize on the liquidity required to complete settlement, but may give rise to the build-up of interbank credit exposures during the interval prior to settlement. In an RTGS design, on the other hand, payments are settled gross and in real time, leaving no scope for interbank exposures to accumulate within the system. Liquidity demands will, however, tend to be higher.

Having described how interbank credit exposures can arise in DNS systems, Section 3.1 goes on to discuss the likely magnitude of such risks. Section 3.2 discusses how these risks might be managed, with Section 3.3 introducing the concept of RTGS. We conclude by briefly discussing the trade-offs faced when opting for a certain mode of settlement in Section 3.4, and describe some of the drivers of the observed shift towards RTGS internationally.

3.1 Deferred net settlement in large-value payment systems

Under DNS, payment instructions are accumulated over time and then settled periodically on a net basis, typically once a day. Netting may be bilateral or multilateral – more often, the latter – with banks needing to generate liquidity only equal to their net obligations.

The magnitude of the net liquidity demand in a DNS system depends on the length of the time interval between payment submission and net settlement; and the nature of the network of obligations between the parties. In general, the longer the interval over which payment instructions accumulate before settlement, the greater the likelihood that offsetting instructions will be submitted to the system. And if the netting process is applied not only to pairs of agents (bilateral netting), but also to 'chains' of agents (multilateral netting), liquidity demands can be reduced significantly (see Box 3.1).

We first explain the source of credit risk in DNS systems (Section 3.1.1). We then provide an overview of studies attempting to quantify this risk (Section 3.1.2) and finally explain how this risk can be managed (Section 3.2).

Box 3.1: THE EFFECTS OF NETTING ON LIQUIDITY NEEDS

Suppose banks B1, B2 and B3 have the following payment obligations:
B1 pays 3 to B2; B2 pays 5 to B3; B3 pays 1 to B2 and 2 to B1.
The total liquidity the system needs to complete settlement is, therefore, as in Figure 3.2 (assuming, for expositional purposes, that all payments are settled simultaneously).

Settlement type	No netting (gross transfers)	Bilateral netting[a]	Multilateral netting[b]
Total liquidity needs	11	9	2

Figure 3.2: The effects of netting on liquidity needs

Notes:
(a) Under bilateral netting, a given bank's needs reflect its net positions *vis-à-vis* each other individual bank in the system. Positive positions do not generate a liquidity need (the bank is a net receiver); negative positions, on the other hand, do.
(b) Under multilateral netting, each bank's needs reflect its net positions *vis-à-vis* the rest of the system. Again, positive positions do not generate a liquidity need, while negative positions do.

More generally, consider n banks, and imagine that their n^2-n *bilateral* net positions $x^{i,j}$ are drawn from a normal distribution with zero mean. While the expected sum of all $x^{i,j}$ is zero, the sum of their absolute values, $x = \Sigma \Sigma \mid x^{i,j} \mid$, has a positive expected value. Consider instead the *multilateral* net position (call it y^i for bank i), and again sum up the absolute values to obtain $y = \Sigma \mid y^i \mid$. It can be shown that $E[x]/E[y]$ scales with the square root of $n-1$. So, if settling net positions is costly (due to liquidity costs, or other transaction costs), the larger the system, the greater the savings from adopting multilateral netting – although gains increase at a decreasing rate (as a square root). Jackson and Manning (2007b) illustrate this in the context of multilateral netting of exposures in a central counterparty clearinghouse.

3.1.1 Sources of credit risk in DNS systems

As Kahn and Roberds (2009) point out, netting requires the exercise of legally robust prior claims upon agents within the payment system. And notwithstanding the greater liquidity efficiency, the DNS mode of settlement can exacerbate interbank credit risk: if banks credit their customers' accounts during the day, before final settlement has occurred, they effectively extend credit to each other. Such risk will crystallize if a bank then defaults on its net obligation when due.

Box 3.2 explores further how credit risk arises, distinguishing between the time the (customer) payment is effected and the time it is settled via an (interbank) payment.

Box 3.2: THE DISTINCTION BETWEEN CUSTOMER PAYMENT AND INTERBANK SETTLEMENT

To develop a deeper understanding of how interbank credit risk emerges in DNS systems it is useful to recall the payments pyramid, introduced in Chapter 2 (Figure 2.1), and to distinguish between the customer payment (a transfer of value effected in commercial bank money) and interbank settlement (a transfer of value effected by use of the ultimate settlement asset). Consider a customer, C1, of Bank B1, who wishes to make a payment to a customer, C2, of Bank B2, using accounts held by C1 with B1 and by C2 with B2 (initial stylized balance sheets of B1 and B2 are shown in Figure 3.3). How is this done?

Bank B1

Cash / Specie	100	Loans from Banks	100
Loans to Banks	100	Customer Deposits	100
Customer Loans	100	Equity	100
Total Assets	*300*	*Total Liabilities*	*300*

Bank B2

Cash / Specie	100	Loans from Banks	100
Loans to Banks	100	Customers Deposits	100
Customer Loans	100	Equity	100
Total Assets	*300*	*Total Liabilities*	*300*

Figure 3.3: Stylized balance sheets of banks B1 and B2

(continued)

Box 3.2: (Continued)

Assume the customer payment from C1 to C2 is of value 50. The customer payment involves bank B1 reducing its deposit liability to C1 by 50, while at the same time making arrangements for Bank B2 to increase its deposit liability to C2 by 50. To effect the payment, the banks exchange messages. In bank B1's accounts, the reduction in the liability to C1 is matched by an increased liability to bank B2. And in bank B2's accounts, the increase in the liability to C2 is matched by an increased claim on bank B1. Figure 3.4 illustrates these changes. Notice that bank B2's balance sheet has expanded.

Bank B1

Cash / Specie	100	Loans from Banks	150
Loans to Banks	100	Customer Deposits	50
Customer Loans	100	Equity	100
Total Assets	*300*	*Total Liabilities*	*300*

Bank B2

Cash / Specie	100	Loans from Banks	100
Loans to Banks	150	Customer Deposits	150
Customer Loans	100	Equity	100
Total Assets	*350*	*Total Liabilities*	*350*

Figure 3.4: Stylized balance sheets of banks B1 and B2 after payment

This situation might – and, as noted in Chapter 1, in the past did – persist for some time. Indeed, if Bank B1's customers were paying more to Bank B2's customers than was the reverse, Bank B2 would increase its claim on Bank B1 over time, and its balance sheet would continue to expand. It is this increasing exposure of the receiving bank to the sending bank that is the source of credit risk in payment systems.

At some point, Bank B2 will want to exchange its (interbank) claim on Bank B1 for some other claim or asset. As we saw in Chapter 1, historically Bank B1 would send specie to Bank B2 (notes or bullion). At this point, Bank B1 would extinguish its liability to Bank B2 and reduce its specie assets accordingly; Bank B2 would write down its claim on Bank B1 and write up its specie assets. This is settlement: an (interbank) payment that involves the elimination of Bank B1's (interbank) liability to Bank B2 and Bank B2's exchange of an (interbank) claim on Bank B1 for a claim on another asset (in this case specie). At the end of this process – compare Figure 3.5 – Bank B1's liabilities have reduced by the amount of the original customer payment; while Bank B2's balance sheet remains larger due to the increased liability to its customer.

Bank B1

Cash / Specie	50	Loans from Banks	100
Loans to Banks	100	Customer Deposits	50
Customer Loans	100	Equity	100
Total Assets	*250*	*Total Liabilities*	*250*

Bank B2

Cash / Specie	150	Loans from Banks	100
Loans to Banks	100	Customer Deposits	150
Customer Loans	100	Equity	100
Total Assets	*350*	*Total Liabilities*	*350*

Figure 3.5: Stylized balance sheets of banks B1 and B2 after payment and settlement

Over time, settlement in specie was replaced by settlement in claims on another commercial bank. Bank B1 and Bank B2 would both have an account with Bank D, typically of a higher credit standing than either B1 or B2. Bank B1 would extinguish its liability to Bank B2 by instructing Bank D to write down its liability to Bank B1 and write up its liability to Bank B2. B2's claim on B1 would thus be exchanged for a claim on Bank D. But the credit standing of commercial banks being prone to abrupt changes, the commercial bank in whose books B1 and B2 held 'settlement' accounts was in time replaced by a central bank (see Chapter 1).

The manner in which credit risk will crystallize in the event of a participant failure, and the allocation of losses arising, will depend crucially on the behaviour of banks before, and at the time of, settlement. As noted, interbank credit risk arises in a net system only if the surviving banks have credited customer accounts before settlement has occurred. If they have not done so, claims will only arise between the end-customers of the surviving banks and those of the failed bank (or the failed bank itself, if it has debited its customers' accounts before settlement). Some authors, notably Selgin (2004), argue that banks are under no obligation to credit customer accounts in advance of settlement and, indeed, such advance payments may be unwound without legal penalty. According to this argument, interbank credit risk in DNS is merely an illusion.

Surviving banks may anyway choose to protect the multilateral net settlement by meeting the shortfall associated with a failed bank's pay-ins

– indeed, as will be discussed further below, system rules may provide for this via a loss-sharing arrangement. But the larger the number of defaulting banks, the less likely it is that the remaining banks will be able to meet their own settlement liabilities (Chakravorti, 2000).

Notwithstanding that payments are more likely to be offsetting the longer the interval before settlement, there remains a risk that some banks accumulate large multilateral net debit positions. Settlement risk in a DNS system will therefore typically be more pronounced the longer the interval before settlement. Furthermore, the risk may be greater with a more extensive network of connections, because the chain of failed payments could originate from any one of the participants. Thus, the very features that make a DNS system efficient may also make it fragile.

3.1.2 Simulation studies of contagious default in DNS systems

Several studies have attempted to determine the potential risk to financial stability that may arise in DNS systems by simulating a bank's failure to settle its payments. Many researchers have built on the simulation methodology adopted in a path-breaking study by Humphrey (1986), in which the author analyzes (historical) data from the Clearing House Interbank Payment Systems (CHIPS) in the US. Box 3.3 discusses the relative merits of using artificially generated and historical data.

Box 3.3: SHOULD SIMULATIONS USE ARTIFICIAL OR HISTORICAL DATA?

Simulation studies can base their predictions on either historical data, or generated data.

The advantage of using historical data – where they are available – is that they have been observed and are, by definition, realistic. The downside is that, in exploring the counterfactual using actual data, one implicitly assumes that banks would not alter their behaviour under an alternative scenario, for example when one bank in the system fails. Also, the fact that one can observe only one history implies that it is impossible to exactly 'repeat the experiment' in search for statistical regularities. Inferring that an event occurs with probability x from the fact that it occurred in a fraction x of observed days is a delicate step.

These shortcomings can be overcome when artificial data are used, generated according to an assumed data-generating process. For example, the researcher may specify that, on average, 100 payment instructions drawn from a particular distribution arrive at a given bank within an hour. Results generated using simulated data may be subject to the critique that they are too dependent on the assumptions made about the data-generating process. These assumptions, however, can at least be verified by comparing simulated with observed histories.

For a randomly selected day in January 1983, the author simulates the default of a participant with a large end-of-the-day net credit position, removing all payments sent and received by this participant.[27] Although this participant was in a net credit position in aggregate over all banks in the system, the removal of its transactions and calculation of a revised settlement leads to an increase in the net settlement obligations of a number of banks. Where an otherwise healthy bank has insufficient capital to fund the increase in its net settlement obligation, it too is deemed to 'fail', and its transactions are also removed from the system. The process is iterated until no new failures arise. Humphrey observes sizeable systemic effects: out of 134 banks, as many as 50 fail within six iterations. The results are robust to the choice of day. The author also finds a 'surprising [...] variability of [...] institutions affected' across experiments. This leaves the consequences of a failure hard to predict and so potentially hard to deal with.

McAndrews and Wasilyew (1995) follow a similar methodology, but use synthetic data to quantify the underlying drivers of systemic spillovers. The authors find that the risk of contagious default is increasing in the value of payments settled and the number of banks participating in the system. Furthermore, greater likelihood of interaction between banks can lead to increased spillovers, with a highly concentrated banking system likely to exhibit a greater propensity for contagion.

Several more recent studies draw different conclusions, questioning the relevance of systemic spillover in DNS systems. Angelini *et al.* (1996) build on Humphrey's methodology in a study of the Italian large-value system, but apply different thresholds beyond which a bank is deemed to fail. The authors' results diverge markedly from those in Humphrey (1986), with on average only about 4% of failures being large enough to trigger systemic problems. As the authors suggest, this could reflect differences in the participation structure between the Italian system and CHIPS. At the time of Humphrey's study, only a few banks were processing a large amount of transactions; hence, the failure of any one of these institutions could generate systemic effects.

---

[27] The impact of the initial failure would presumably have been even greater had the participant had a large overall net debit position. However, Humphrey seeks to capture the circumstance in which at least some system participants, perceiving a potential problem with a participant, partially adjust their exposure to that participant prior to settlement. Such adjustment would involve limiting the effective daylight credit extended to the questionable participant in the system by paying away less to their own customers on its behalf. This would have the effect of constraining the participant's capacity to build up a net debit position in the system.

Similarly, in a study of the Finnish interbank payment system, Kuussaari (1996) concludes that there is little risk of contagious default. One reason for this is that counterparty exposures typically do not exceed 10% of a bank's own funds (only occasionally rising as high as 50%). Another reason is that 'large counterparty risks do not form long interbank chains that could lead to a domino effect'. Bech *et al.* (2002) in a study of the Danish interbank netting system (PBS), and Northcott (2002) for the case of the Canadian Automated Clearing Settlement System (ACSS), also conclude that systemic risk is relatively low.

When judging the effects that the failure of a single bank may have on other banks, not only the size of the failed bank matters but also the network of interbank exposures (Bech and Soramäki, 2005b). For example, if bank A has the largest net debit position, but this is *vis-à-vis* a highly solvent bank B, B can absorb the loss, and no further failures occur. Bech and Soramäki show that while banks with larger net debit positions are generally more likely to trigger a contagious default, there are exceptions, and the relationship becomes weaker when banks in general are assumed to be less resilient to losses.

3.2 Managing credit risk in DNS systems

As highlighted in Section 3.1, DNS systems can offer a highly efficient means of settling payments by allowing payments to be accumulated and settled on a multilateral net basis. However, the accumulation of large numbers of unsettled payments can create sizeable credit exposures between users. This creates two risks. First, if a user is required to make a net pay-in at the end of a settlement period and fails to do so, multilateral net settlement for the system as a whole will be unable to proceed as planned, potentially creating large gross exposures between banks. Second, surviving users potentially face credit losses if they have credited customer accounts prior to final settlement.

A range of measures can be put in place to deal with the failure of a member (or members) to make pay-ins as required. A common benchmark is that these measures should, at a minimum, ensure that if the member with the largest net settlement obligation fails, settlement between the remaining banks will be reasonably undisturbed. Measures consistent with this benchmark include: a strong legal basis for netting; and mechanisms that allow for a limited unwind of multilateral netting. Where a firm legal basis for netting is achieved, the simplest way to reduce credit exposures is to increase the frequency of netting cycles. This, however, comes at the cost of higher liquidity needs. Hence, there is a trade-off between credit exposures and liquidity demands. The nature of this trade-off can be affected by a number of tools including: credit limits within the system; a including common collateral pool; and risk-based loss-sharing agreements among survivors.

The higher the value of payments settled, and the more 'important' the payments settled – for example, if their settlement is necessary for the completion of settlement in another system – the stronger will be the case for incorporation of such measures. But even the failure to settle small payments can damage the payer's reputation, particularly in stressed market environments. For instance, an operational problem disrupting settlement might be mistakenly interpreted as a sign that the payer is illiquid, perhaps even insolvent, and, at a minimum, increase the payer's funding costs.

3.2.1 *Legally robust netting*

The most fundamental measure to mitigate credit exposures in DNS systems is to have robust legal agreements in place that ensure the enforceability of bilateral or multilateral netting arrangements. The key risk to netting comes from insolvency law: in some jurisdictions, agreements to net obligations are not recognized as binding. If the finality of an (interbank) payment was not ensured – that is, if the payment was not irrevocable and unconditional – a liquidator might be able to enforce the unwinding of netting agreements. The gross exposures between users of a DNS system could be several orders of magnitude larger than their net positions, leaving some participants unable to meet their obligations. Hence, defaults might ensue, triggering 'domino effects' in the system. Where a DNS system operates across borders, or has users based in other countries, it is important that netting arrangements be designed to ensure that they will be legally valid in all relevant jurisdictions.

3.2.2 *Partial unwind of netting*

Within the framework of legally robust netting, DNS systems often have rules and technical algorithms in place to maximize the value of settlements even when a participant has failed.

One option is partial unwinding: netting is preserved between surviving members of the system, but some or all of the transactions submitted by failed members are removed from the netting calculation. Though preferable to a complete unwind of the net, such an approach could still leave some participants with sizeable unexpected exposures, potentially triggering knock-on defaults.

3.2.3 Access criteria

Limiting membership to entities with high financial standing clearly increases the resilience of the system, as it reduces the probability that the net will be unwound due to member default. For instance, direct membership might be restricted to entities subject to close prudential supervision. In other cases, membership may be limited to those entities with access to central-bank facilities; or perhaps those with a credit rating above a certain threshold. Ultimately, risk-management priorities may conflict with competition and efficiency objectives, which might argue in favour of open and non-discriminatory access. Furthermore, restricting membership will lead to a higher degree of 'tiering' in the system, which carries its own risks (see Chapter 10).

3.2.4 Net debit caps

Many DNS systems allow participants, and the system operator, to set upper limits to a bank's (bilateral) exposure to another bank, or to its (multilateral) exposure to all other banks. The system operator can use information on all banks' bilateral limits to judge a bank's risk, and further restrict an individual bank's net debit position. Where limits can be adjusted in real time, participants are able to react swiftly to news about the credit status of other participants. *Ex ante*, such a feature can preserve good incentives among participants to monitor each other and to proactively manage liquidity. The likelihood of a credit event may fall as a result. However, there is equally a risk that proactive variation of net debit caps could itself accelerate a credit event by starving a troubled bank of liquidity.

3.2.5 Loss sharing and collateralization

A perhaps more robust method of protecting a net system from the consequences of member default is to have a loss-sharing arrangement in place, whereby the defaulter's remaining funds and pre-posted contributions from survivors are used to meet any shortfall. This is typically achieved by requiring that members contribute to a common collateral pool, which would usually be held and administered by the settlement agent for the system. As discussed in detail in Bank of England (2005), two key considerations arise when designing a loss-sharing arrangement using a common collateral pool: first, to what extent should the cost of a default be met by survivors; and second, how should costs be allocated among survivors?

It would seem desirable to ensure that, as far as possible, the defaulting institution bears the cost of its failure to pay. This both reduces the incentives for institutions to default opportunistically in the face of very large payment outflows, and minimizes the potential for contagion should the need to cover the losses of a defaulter trigger knock-on failures in the system. Set against this, however, agents could face sizeable opportunity costs if required to pledge sufficient collateral in advance to cover a potential loss equal to their largest possible net debit position. Indeed, full collateralization in a DNS system would undermine the liquidity efficiency it sought to deliver. In practice, a balance needs to be struck between the costs of collateralization, and the potential losses imposed on others due to only partially collateralized default.

Various methods exist to share among survivors any shortfall that remains when a defaulter's collateral has been exhausted. If netting can be preserved, a simple approach is to share the multilateral net shortfall in proportion to the defaulter's actual bilateral net debit positions *vis-à-vis* survivors. This has the benefit of encouraging monitoring by agents, particularly where a collateral pool is used in tandem with bilateral limit functionality. The chief drawback is that it can lead to a very uneven and unpredictable distribution of losses among agents – simply because not all system participants will have a bilateral net credit position *vis-à-vis* the failed bank.

When losses are born by fewer users, the risk of contagion rises. Thus, more sophisticated approaches have been adopted. For example, contributions may reflect the level of exposures each agent *typically* brings to the system, independently of the size of exposures on the day the default occurred. Another possibility is to link contributions to any bilateral credit limits each member has extended to the failing bank or banks. Examples of both approaches are outlined in Box 3.4.

An important consideration in the design of loss-sharing arrangements that depend on collateral is the speed with which such collateral could be mobilized to meet a shortfall. It is essential that funds are available to allow prompt settlement in case of default, but there is a tension between achieving this objective and minimizing the opportunity costs of posting collateral. That is, the opportunity costs incurred by agents are likely to be higher if they are required to post low-yielding liquid assets.

Box 3.4: LOSS-SHARING ARRANGEMENTS FOR UK RETAIL SYSTEMS

BACS and the C&CC are retail payment systems that offer daily net settlement, and that together process all sterling direct debit and credit, cheque and standing order payments in the UK. A loss-sharing agreement, known as the *Liquidity Funding and Collateralisation Agreement*, was signed in April 2005.

The agreement consists of a loss-sharing agreement backed by a common collateral pool. Each settlement member of BACS and the C&CC contributes collateral according to the amount of risk that it brings to the two payment systems. This risk measure is based upon the size of each member's average net debit settlement positions across both BACS and the C&CC and the volatility of those positions. The value of the total collateral pool is based upon the 'largest single debit amount' (LSDA) for any member across both BACS and the C&CC over all three-day periods in the preceding year. A three-day period reflects the time horizon over which exposures in the two systems remain unsettled. Each member's share of the collateral pool is calculated using the equation below, where each member's share of risk is calculated as the average sum of net debit amounts for that member at any time, plus one standard deviation:

$$\frac{\text{Current LSDA} \times \text{Member's Share of Risk}}{\text{Sum of all Members' Shares of Risk}}$$

In Bank of England (2005), this method is shown to be effective in reducing the potential for systemic risk, when compared to distribution of losses on the basis of realized bilateral positions with the defaulter. This is because it ensures a more even distribution of losses by removing the possibility that a subset of agents is not required to contribute, and also because in the systems in question there is a strong correlation between the risk a bank brings to the system and the size of that bank. This avoids outcomes in which smaller banks face losses disproportionate to their size. The design of the common collateral pool supporting the loss-sharing agreement seeks to balance liquidity risk and the opportunity cost of collateralization. This is achieved by accepting a broad range of collateral types within the pool, including less liquid assets, but requiring that members commit to contributing liquid funds to enable settlement to take place in the event of a failure to pay.

3.3 Real-time gross settlement in large-value payment systems

Under RTGS, the settlement asset is transferred at the time the payment instruction is submitted to the system. Each payment is settled on a gross basis with finality intraday. As a result, no unintended credit exposures arise between banks. However, banks will typically need to hold more liquid assets than under DNS to ensure that payments can be settled without delay. Building on the example in Box 3.2, Box 3.5 illustrates how RTGS eliminates (interbank) credit risk in the settlement process.

Box 3.5: ELIMINATION OF INTERBANK CREDIT RISK IN RTGS SYSTEMS

This box builds on the example in Box 3.2. Recall that we considered a customer, C1, of Bank B1 who wishes to make a payment to a customer, C2, of Bank B2. C1 and C2 have accounts with their bank (shown in Figure 3.3). Payment – the process whereby banks alter their liabilities to their customers at their customers' request – created a liability in B2's accounts to C2, matched by a claim on bank B1.

Interbank credit risk can be avoided when, upon receipt of a payment instruction, Bank B2 does not increase its (deposit) liabilities to C2 unless it has already received a balancing asset (for example specie, or a claim on a central bank) from B1. Modern RTGS payment systems ensure such timely receipt of the balancing asset. Before each individual payment instruction is sent from Bank B1 to Bank B2, Bank B1 instructs the central bank to debit its account and credit B2's account. Once confirmation of the transfer is received, the payment instruction is sent and Bank B2 writes up its liability to C2. That is, *settlement precedes payment*. This ordering is encoded in the processing arrangements and cannot be changed by the participating banks.

In contrast, as we explained in Section 3.1 in DNS systems, *payment precedes settlement*. Banks send payment instructions during the day to each other, but they are not settled until the end of the settlement cycle (e.g. at the end of the day) when the central bank is instructed to debit and credit the banks' relevant accounts in its books. As a result, interbank exposures accumulate.

In theory at least, one could imagine a 'continuum' of systems, running from indefinitely postponed settlement (where banks accept each other's liabilities without bound), to a DNS system that settles in very short intervals and hence requires nearly as much liquidity as an RTGS system. As we will see in Chapter 4, elements of gross and net settlement can be combined in so-called 'hybrid' systems, which attempt to capture the advantages of both models.

It is important to understand, however, that even RTGS does not imply that a bank needs to hold sufficient liquidity in advance to meet all potential upcoming obligations. Rather, liquidity can be recycled within the period: banks can typically fund a significant proportion of outward payments using incoming flows.[28] The efficiency of liquidity recycling in this context will depend on the timing profile of banks' in- and outflows and the connectedness of the network of banks within the RTGS system. We discuss these

---

[28] As discussed in the next chapter, banks may be able to improve liquidity recycling in a RTGS system by co-ordinating the timing of their payment flows. McAndrews and Rajan (2000), Armantier *et al.* (2008), and Becher *et al.* (2008a) examine this question empirically in the context of the US large-value payment system, Fedwire, and the UK's CHAPS Sterling.

Box 3.6: THE IMPACT OF TIMING AND NETWORK STRUCTURE
ON LIQUIDITY NEEDS

Consider three banks B1, B2 and B3 making payments as in the left panel of Figure
3.6. If B1 pays to B2 first, and B2 then pays to B3, the total liquidity need for the system
is 10: B2 can use the liquidity received from B1's payment to settle its own obligations
to B3. If instead B2 pays first, 17 units of liquidity are required as no recycling occurs.
Hence, *the timing of payments* is important for liquidity requirements.

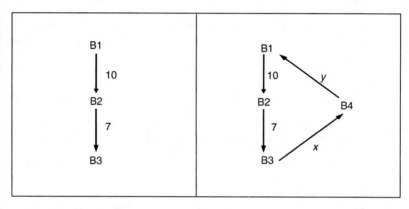

Figure 3.6: The impact of timing and network structure on liquidity needs

Suppose now the payments network is 'closed' by another bank B4 (right panel).
B4 allows some liquidity (x or y, whichever is smaller) to be 'recycled', because B1
receives back some of 'its own' liquidity, which it can then use to settle further
payments. Hence, the *shape* of the payments network is also important for the
magnitude of liquidity requirements.

---

determinants extensively in Chapter 4. Box 3.6 illustrates the effect the
network structure can have on the possibility to recycle liquidity.

3.4 The choice of settlement model: drivers of the widespread adoption of RTGS in large-value payment systems

The balance between liquidity efficiency and credit risk has been a key
determinant in the evolution of payment systems. Nowadays, as in the
past, retail systems typically settle on a net basis. In wholesale systems,

however, the use of RTGS has increased dramatically: in 1985, only three RTGS systems existed; this number had risen to 16 by 1995 and to 91 by 2005. The shift began in developed economies, but has since spread to developing and transitional economies (Bech *et al.*, 2008; and CPSS, 2005a).

Berger *et al.* (1996) introduce a framework for thinking about the cost–risk trade-off between RTGS and DNS, exploring how technological, financial and regulatory changes affect the optimal level of risk. Risk reduction is costly. On the other hand, externalities in payment systems can be sufficiently strong that privately owned providers may not invest sufficiently – from society's point of view – in risk reduction. This point can be simply illustrated by the diagram in Figure 3.7.

In Figure 3.7, curve FF represents a technological frontier, or the set of risk/cost combinations that could possibly be attained, given a particular set of technological, financial and regulatory constraints. Indifference curve II represents society's preferred risk/cost combinations. Given FF and II, the socially optimal risk/cost mix is represented by point A. However, suppose that the system is operated under private ownership. If a private owner places a lower value on risk reduction than does society, his preferences will be represented by a steeper curve, I'I'. In this case, he would choose the price/risk combination, B, in which the level of risk is higher than in A. Public intervention may then be required to adjust

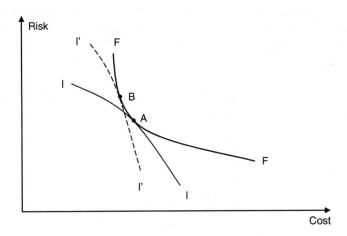

Figure 3.7: The cost–risk trade-off in the provision of payment services

Note: FF is the technological frontier. II and I'I' are the social and private indifference curves. A and B are the combinations of risk and cost chosen, respectively, by a public and a private system designer.

incentives/choices and shift outcomes towards the social optimum. Technological, financial or institutional innovations can alter the shape of frontier FF. The tangency points A and B would then also change, perhaps altering the case for public intervention.

Some studies (Schoenmaker, 1995; and Selgin, 2004) have argued forcefully that the adoption of RTGS must be welfare reducing: they deem that the higher liquidity costs incurred when settling gross outweigh the costs of credit risk that DNS can introduce.

Others disagree, offering further reasons why RTGS may be preferable, notwithstanding higher liquidity costs. For instance, the above studies assume that participant default is independent of the settlement model adopted. Kahn and Roberds (1998), on the other hand, consider it a choice variable. Their model shows that, if the bankruptcy regime allows a failing bank to increase the priority of the equityholders relative to interbank claimants, a bank operating in a DNS system may have an incentive to default strategically. Because this incentive is absent under RTGS, inefficient defaults occur less frequently in such systems.

Lester *et al.* (2007) model the endogenous emergence of a dominant settlement rule as an equilibrium choice. The principal trade-off in this model is that between default costs (which arise only under DNS), and real-time transfer costs (both technological and liquidity costs associated with processing on an RTGS basis). The authors show that RTGS will not be chosen in equilibrium if real-time transfer costs are too high. This characterizes the period pre-1990s, when the cost of computing power was a constraint to the establishment of real-time settlement rules. However, as real-time transfer costs fall, multiple equilibria are shown to emerge, with RTGS and DNS co-existing. And if transfer costs are sufficiently low, and default costs sufficiently high, RTGS may be socially optimal. (See Figure 3.8.) The decision to switch from one settlement rule to another cannot be captured in the model due to its lack of dynamics, and the authors leave

Transfer cost		
H	RTGS	Autarchy
L	DNS and RTGS	DNS
	L	H Default cost

Figure 3.8: Existence of DNS and RTGS equilibria in Lester *et al.* (2007)

for future research an analysis of the role for government intervention in overcoming potential co-ordination failures.

In the event, the switch to gross settlement was indeed largely driven by public intervention. One important factor here was the rapid rise in volumes and values of payments, which heightened concerns over credit risk in DNS systems.

4

Liquidity risk in large-value payment systems

With RTGS having become the dominant settlement model for large-value payment systems around the world, the focus of attention has naturally shifted away from credit risk, to liquidity risk.

A long-established finding in the monetary economics literature is that the presence of a 'cash-in-advance' constraint can inhibit trade (Svensson, 1985; Lucas and Stokey, 1987). However, it is only recently, with the widespread adoption of RTGS, that this fundamental insight has been applied to the analysis of payment-system design. A number of studies – including those by Freeman (1996a, 1996b), cited in Chapter 2, but also Green (1997), Lacker (1997) and Kahn and Roberds (2001a) – have adapted neoclassical monetary models to settings more closely resembling those seen in modern payment systems. This body of work has highlighted the finding that, in the absence of well-designed arrangements for liquidity provision, the need to hold sufficient liquidity balances to make payments in real time can impose significant costs on banks.

In the presence of a high cost of generating liquidity, banks may choose to delay settlement, awaiting the flow of incoming funds (see Section 4.1). In an RTGS system, such behaviour may lead to 'gridlock', or heighten the potential impact of operational risk late in the day. A central bank will, therefore, pay close attention to how both the design of the system and its own arrangements for liquidity provision might affect the efficiency of liquidity recycling through the day.

Liquidity is typically provided by the central bank through intraday credit facilities (Sections 4.2–4.4). However, the central bank will want to ensure that it provides liquidity in a way that does not compromise its monetary stability objectives. Furthermore, it will seek to manage any credit exposures that arise from the provision of liquidity, while at the same time taking care not to impose too high a cost on system participants.

This chapter considers such issues, while also discussing a number of ways in which, for a given cost of liquidity to users, the liquidity efficiency of the system can be enhanced, e.g. by prescribing deadlines by which a settlement bank has to transmit a certain value of its payments on a given day, or by adapting the design of the system to ensure that banks' incoming and outgoing flows are more closely co-ordinated (Sections 4.5 and 4.6). The chapter closes with some thoughts as to how payments with different characteristics may be optimally channelled via systems offering different trade-offs between credit risk and liquidity efficiency.

4.1 Liquidity and the incentive to delay payments

In this section, we consider how banks' behaviour in RTGS systems might depend on the cost of liquidity, going on to assess the potential implications for liquidity risk. We examine alternative approaches to analyzing and modelling banks' behaviour and, where available, consider empirical evidence on the timing and funding of payments. Section 4.1.1 presents the basic trade-off a bank faces between incurring higher costs of liquidity when it pays early, and incurring (monetary or reputational) costs when it delays the execution of a payment instruction. We then look in more detail at the game-theoretic modelling of this trade-off in Secion 4.1.2. More complex models can be investigated using simulation-based techniques (Section 4.1.3). Finally, we review some empirical evidence for this trade-off in Section 4.1.4.

4.1.1 *The trade-off between liquidity cost and payment delay*

Intraday liquidity to support payments activity is often made available by the settlement agent, typically the central bank, with the cost of liquidity dependent upon the extant collateralization or pricing regime. In a collateralized regime, the cost to the liquidity-short participant is the opportunity cost of holding eligible securities and posting them with the settlement agent (and hence forgoing alternative, potentially more productive, investments). In a priced regime, the liquidity-short participant faces a direct charge in respect of its unsecured overdraft with the settlement agent.

Several authors – including Angelini (1998), Kahn and Roberds (2001a), Bech and Garratt (2003), Bech (2008), Buckle and Campbell (2003) and

Willison (2005) – highlight the potential implications of costly liquidity demands on banks' behaviour within payment systems. They emphasize the risk that high liquidity costs will encourage banks to delay their payments, awaiting the receipt of incoming payments to fund their outflows. Such behaviour can disrupt the recycling of liquidity[29] in the system, ultimately imposing welfare costs on banks' customers. Furfine and Stehm (1998) note that, in the extreme, payment delays can lead to gridlock; i.e. the situation in which the failure of some transfer instructions to be executed (because the necessary funds or securities balances are unavailable) prevents the execution of a substantial number of other instructions.[30] Payment delays can also amplify the impact of an operational outage late in the day, to the extent that a large body of payments remain unsettled in a potentially capacity-constrained system.

But a bank may find that delay too is costly. Certain payments are time critical and hence a bank may face pecuniary or reputational costs if it delays. If each bank's payments behaviour is visible within the system, delay may also trigger adverse responses from other participants. For instance, others may withhold payment flows to the delaying bank.

The following section offers some intuition, but more research needs to be done to fully describe how these costs and benefits of delay depend on the design of the payment system and other aspects, such as the cost of intraday and overnight credit and the number of participating settlement banks. From the perspective of an authority responsible for financial stability, the important question is whether system or cross-market externalities could push the cost of delay materially beyond the private cost faced by each bank itself.

4.1.2 Game-theoretic approaches to modelling bank behaviour under RTGS

Several researchers have used game-theoretic techniques to model the trade-off between the cost of raising liquidity and the cost of delaying

---

[29] Notice that the concept of liquidity recycling has an analogue in the macroeconomic literature: the velocity of money, that is, the frequency with which a unit of money is spent (often measured as annual nominal GDP divided by the money stock). The chief difference is one of magnitude: while estimates of the velocity of money are around 10 in a year, estimates of the turnover ratio in RTGS systems (measured by the total value of payments over the liquidity needed to fund them) range from about 2 to well over 100 (depending on the system) in a *single day*. See, for example, Becher *et al* (2008a) for the United Kingdom's system, and Heller and Lengwiler (2000) for the Swiss system.
[30] CPSS (2003c).

payments. One of the early papers adopting this approach is Angelini (1998), in which banks maximize their expected profits with respect to choices over the value of payments to be withheld and interbank borrowing and lending.

Here, a bank's revenue from payments processing is decreasing in payment delays, with delayed transfers deemed to reduce customers' future demand for a bank's payments services. At the same time, however, banks face a cost of generating intraday liquidity from the central bank to satisfy their payments needs. The basic form of Angelini's problem builds on that used in the literature analyzing the demand for precautionary reserves under uncertainty.[31] The author applies this approach in a two-bank-two-period setting, showing that each bank will optimally delay its outgoing payments until the marginal expected decline in revenues arising from delay equals the marginal cost of generating liquidity.

But there are externalities to each bank's choice. One bank's decision to delay imposes costs on other banks in the system: facing a shortfall in their own incoming payments, they will need to increase their own liquidity holdings if they are to continue to offer timely settlement for their customers. Furthermore, payment delays may have an adverse effect on the quality of information flow in the system. In particular, because it is difficult for a bank to distinguish between naturally low payment inflows and low inflows resulting from payment delays, banks will tend to operate with higher reserves of liquidity relative to the co-operative equilibrium. This leaves them with fewer funds to invest in productive assets. The precise outcome will depend on parameter values: the sensitivity of revenue to payment delays, relative to the costs of holding precautionary reserves and generating liquidity intraday.

Bech and Garratt (2003) also adopt a two-bank–two-period framework. The authors examine bank behaviour in the payment system under alternative regimes for obtaining intraday liquidity from the settlement agent. They show that, with fully collateralized intraday credit, the game takes the form of a prisoners' dilemma. In this setting, relative costs of liquidity and delay determine the outcome, with banks facing an incentive to delay payments whenever liquidity costs exceed delay costs. This equilibrium is socially inefficient, since both banks would be better off paying early. Importantly, the authors assume that a bank's opportunity cost of posting

---

[31] Baltensperger (1974).

collateral with the central bank increases the longer the collateral is held with the central bank. In practice, this is true if banks can indeed make use of collateral that they only receive back from the central bank a few hours before markets close. Otherwise, banks have no incentive to delay payments in Bech and Garratt's framework.

Under a regime of priced (and uncollateralized) credit, on the other hand, the game takes the form of a stag-hunt.[32] Here, it is in the banks' interest to synchronize their payments, since neither will incur a cost if their payments offset within the time period over which overdraft fees are calculated. The co-ordination problem reduces to a decision as to whether to synchronize early or late in the day: 'hunting a stag', or avoiding both delay and borrowing costs, is only successful if both banks pay in the morning. 'Hunting a hare', or paying in the afternoon, avoids borrowing costs (but not costs of delay) independently of whether the other bank pays in the morning or the afternoon. Consequently, two pure-strategy equilibria exist: in one, both banks pay in the morning; in the other, both pay in the afternoon. The theoretical literature on stag-hunt games offers numerous suggestions for how players might co-ordinate on the efficient equilibrium. For example, some argue that players should be expected to co-ordinate on the risk-dominant equilibrium.

An interesting topic for research is whether, and how, banks co-ordinate in practice on the efficient equilibrium (see below). Synchronization of payments is indeed observed in Fedwire, where intraday credit is priced, but less so in CHAPS, where the Bank of England does not charge for intraday credit but requires banks to fully collateralize their overdrafts (see Section 4.1.4).

Mills and Nesmith (2008), in a model adapting Bech and Garratt (2003), consider an alternative rationale for delays. That is, banks may withhold payments while they await information on the ability of others in the system to send funds. With a positive probability that others will fail to make their payments by the end of the day, banks will be reluctant to pay early, for to do so entails some positive probability of being left with an overnight overdraft. It will be interesting to analyze whether this

---

[32] A stag-hunt game is a stylized description of a situation in which benefits from co-operation arise. Two individuals go out hunting. Each can individually choose to hunt a stag or a hare. Each player must choose an action without knowing the choice of the other. If an individual hunts a stag, he must have the co-operation of his partner in order to succeed. An individual can catch a hare by himself, but a hare is worth less than half a stag.

behaviour has been observed during the stressed environment of 2007/08, given concerns over the financial standing of some payment-system participants.

There remains, however, a question as to whether these arguments are not overly simplified. For instance, there is some stylized evidence that banks monitor others' behaviour, and reward prompt senders by paying promptly in return. Thus, careful monitoring of bilateral balances can encourage banks to co-ordinate on a 'pay early' equilibrium.

So far, few models investigate these incentives in detail. One promising avenue might be to regard liquidity as a public good, to which settlement banks contribute in turn. The related literature (see, for example, Marx and Matthews, 2000; and Lockwood and Thomas, 2002) finds that, under certain conditions, the efficient level of the public good will be provided. In particular, some 'delay' in the contributions is a *necessary* feature of the equilibrium and serves to encourage other agents to contribute as well. But the analogy is not perfect, in particular because liquidity is not strictly a public good as it can only be used – at least in the first instance – by the receiver of a payment.

Another mechanism that could encourage early payment in systems with few participants is explored by the literature on repeated games. Bech (2008) formalizes the intuition in an extension of Bech and Garrat (2003). The idea is that, at the end of the day, a bank can infer from the time profile of its incoming payments which banks paid early, and which paid late. Late payers could then be punished by withholding payments due on the following day(s). The mere threat of this penalty, the economic literature argues, could be sufficient to ensure that banks pay early.[33]

In practice, banks could monitor the behaviour of their counterparties through the application of bilateral net sender limits. This could be achieved either by the payment system's central scheduler, or by banks' in-house payment processing engines. Becher *et al.* (2008a) model the application of such limits, showing that they can improve incentives to make payments on a timely basis: if, by sending out a payment, a bank triggers the release of a queued payment from its counterparty, it can increase the probability of receiving a payment in return.

---

[33] Variations of the 'Folk Theorem' formalize this point in more abstract settings. See Gibbons (1992) for an introduction, or Mailath and Samuelson (2006) for an advanced treatment.

Bilateral limits may, however, be difficult to calibrate. Payment flows between banks are variable and, as Angelini (1998) observed, it is hard to distinguish between situations in which payments are being withheld and those in which no outward payment instructions have been received. Given the high intensity of monitoring involved, decentralized approaches seem likely to work best when the number of banks in the system is relatively small – or at least when payments activity is highly concentrated.[34]

4.1.3 *Simulations and agent-based modelling*

Researchers using game-theoretic techniques are often required to abstract significantly from reality to be able to solve their models and are often constrained by the sometimes strong assumptions required to deliver analytically tractable solutions. An alternative route is to allow for a more complex environment, for example with more banks and a more complicated structure of the game, but assume that banks use a simple decision rule to determine their actions.

Beyeler *et al.* (2007), for instance, develop a stylized model in which banks employ simple rules to determine whether to make or delay a payment. For example, in the basic version of their model, they assume that banks only delay the execution of a payment instruction if they do not have sufficient liquidity. In a more elaborated version, banks can add or borrow funds, but their decision to do so is governed by an exogenous function of their liquidity needs – not by an optimization process. Applying these rules in a simulation, the authors explore the dynamics of liquidity recycling in the system with alternative initial conditions for system level liquidity and different assumptions about the availability of a market for intraday interbank liquidity sharing.[35]

The study demonstrates that, at low levels of liquidity in the system, payment queues begin to build as banks await incoming liquidity. When a liquidity-constrained bank receives an incoming payment, it can release a queued payment, triggering a 'cascade' of settlements within the system as recipient banks successively work off their queues. As a result, with low levels of liquidity in the system, instruction times and settlement times are decoupled, but settlement times are correlated due to the cascades effect.

---

[34] See Section 10.1.2 for an overview of how concentrated payment systems are empirically.
[35] See Section 3.1.2 for simulation studies of DNS systems.

With ample liquidity in the system, on the other hand, banks settle their obligations promptly. Hence, there is a high correlation between the time of arrival of a bank's payment instructions and the time of their settlement, but across the network the timing of settlements is largely independent.

Renault *et al.* (2007) extend this framework to a setting in which two countries' large-value payment systems are linked via banks that participate in both systems. These banks use the foreign-exchange market to shift liquidity from one system to another. Again, banks are assumed to execute payment instructions immediately if they have sufficient liquidity available. In such a setting, liquidity conditions in one system can spill over to the other, particularly when systems are formally coupled by a settlement convention in the foreign-exchange market that synchronizes settlement of the two currencies. We describe this model further when we consider foreign-exchange settlement risk in Chapter 5.

While these studies demonstrate the dynamics of the link between liquidity levels and payment delay, liquidity levels are exogenously given. Galbiati and Soramäki (2008) go further by examining how banks may come to choose their level of liquidity in a set-up where banks learn their optimal behaviour over time. They simulate the operation of a payment system, supposing that a number of banks interact repeatedly over time. Each period, a bank sets an initial buffer of (costly) liquidity, trading off the opportunity cost against the expected cost of delay should the buffer be insufficient. A bank's pay-off therefore depends on its own and on others' liquidity choices.

Each period thus constitutes a simultaneous-move game, which is played repeatedly until an equilibrium is reached. The main novelty of the paper is that both the settlement process and intraday liquidity flows are explicitly modelled, generating delays and cascades, *à la* Beyeler *et al.* (2007). Hence, banks' end-of-day costs and profits are *derived*, rather than *exogenously* specified as a simple function of liquidity choices.

The authors describe the relationship between delay costs and banks' liquidity holdings, demonstrating that the higher are delay costs, the more liquidity banks hold *ex ante*. The authors are also able to show that the behaviour to which banks converge after many rounds of learning is a Nash equilibrium. In this respect, agent-based modelling can provide important insights to equilibrium behaviour in comparatively complex environments, while still allowing rationality to play some role when banks make their decisions.

4.1.4 *Empirical evidence on timing and funding and the flow of liquidity in RTGS*

Several studies consider the empirical trade-off between liquidity and delay costs. We first look at the US Fedwire system, where intraday credit is priced; and then the UK CHAPS and Swiss SIC systems, where intraday credit is free but fully collateralized.

Bartolini *et al.* (2008) investigate settlement delays in the US money market. They combine data on the time at which unsecured interbank loans are agreed with data on the timing of settlement in Fedwire. The authors find evidence for delays in settlement: senders of funds tend to cluster deliveries in the afternoon, even for trades conducted in the morning hours. Banks' decisions to delay appear to depend first and foremost on the value of the loan, rather than on the level of reserve balances. This provides some support for the notion that banks use simple rules of thumb for their liquidity management, and do not attempt a complete optimization. Agent-based models, discussed in the previous section, may therefore provide a good description of reality – provided that they use the correct rules of thumb.

Typically, however, data on the timing of the receipt of payment instructions is unavailable. Researchers can generally only observe the time of settlement. The stylized facts presented in such studies are still interesting. McAndrews and Rajan (2000) investigate the timing and funding of settlements in Fedwire, observing a peak in settlement activity towards the end of the day. The authors investigate the role of the Federal Reserve's pricing policy for intraday credit extensions in banks' timing and funding decisions. In particular, given that overdrafts are charged a zero interest rate for the first minute, and a positive rate thereafter, liquidity can be borrowed, used to settle as many transactions as possible, and then repaid within one minute at a zero cost. This offers incentives to co-ordinate the submission of payments during the most active period of settlement (see Section 4.1.2). To gauge the importance of this liquidity-recycling mechanism, the authors measure the percentage of outgoing payments funded by incoming payments received within a minute. According to this measure, co-ordination is very successful: incoming payments used by banks to offset outgoing payments that are entered within the same minute account for 25 per cent of the value of outgoing transfers during normal activity periods, and as much as 40 per cent during peak periods.

The transaction peak occurs relatively late in the day, at 16:30. One reason might be that settlement in an ancillary system, CHIPS, provides banks with information about their net balances at that point in time.[36] Armentier *et al.* (2008) observe that, in the years 2000–2004, the activity peak in Fedwire shifted to even later in the day. They infer that institutional factors are indeed important (e.g. changes in Federal Reserve policies and processes, and the timing of settlement of ancillary systems such as the securities settlement system, the Depository Trust Company (DTC), and CHIPS). For example, on days when DTC settles later, payments are submitted later than usual. Furthermore, the permanent shift in CHIPS settlement from 16:45 to 17:10 in 2000 appears to have led to a permanent delay in Fedwire settlement. By contrast, a change in the CHIPS settlement model in 2001, which provided intraday finality for payments, quickened the settlement of Fedwire payments throughout most of the day. Earlier finality in CHIPS seems to have enabled banks to settle their Fedwire payments earlier as well.

This observed profile lends some support to the thesis in Beyeler *et al.* (2007, see Section 4.1.3) that incoming flows to liquidity-constrained agents may trigger a cascade of settlements. In this context, the cascade would be triggered by flows from a linked system, rather than from within the system. The pattern identified by Armentier *et al.* (2008) would also be consistent with a hypothesis in which agents awaited resolution of uncertainty before settling queued payments. In this case, the source of uncertainty would be settlement obligations in linked systems.

The situation is different in the UK CHAPS system, in which intraday credit is not priced, but banks are required to collateralize their overdraft fully. For this system, Becher *et al.* (2008a) find that liquidity recycling is relatively stable throughout the day. Although volume peaks occur shortly after opening, and again late in the day, the payments profile is relatively smooth throughout the day. One reason for the difference here is that the opportunity cost of borrowing liquidity intraday is independent of its duration: virtually without exception, banks repo necessary collateral to the Bank of England at the beginning of the day. The higher level of recycling in CHAPS than in Fedwire may reflect not only differences in liquidity costs, but perhaps also the membership structure of the system. In particular, the CHAPS system has relatively few direct participants, with the bulk of payments concentrated among just four banks. Participants can therefore monitor each other easily and enforce co-operative behaviour throughout the day (see Section 4.1.2).

---

[36] McAndrews and Rajan (2000).

Finally, to gauge the effect of a change in the cost of liquidity on payment delays in a collateralized regime, it is worthwhile looking at the Swiss RTGS system, SIC. This system operated for a number of years without any arrangements for intraday liquidity provision. However, in October 1999, prompted by the increasing payment values processed by the system, the Swiss National Bank (SNB) introduced arrangements for collateralized intraday credit.

Heller *et al.* (2000) observe a significant reduction in payment delay in response to this change. During the first three quarters of 1999, the maximum value of payments queued in SIC awaiting settlement amounted to 55% of total turnover in 2000; this decreased to 40% following the introduction of intraday credit. Furthermore, over the same period, the volume of payments that had been settled by noon rose from less than one third to about half of the daily volume. This suggests that, faced with high liquidity costs, banks were indeed delaying their payments, and liquidity provision by the SNB relaxed this constraint considerably.

While important insights have already been gained in these studies, the rich data that central banks and operators of payment systems have available should provide many opportunities for applying more sophisticated econometric techniques. For instance, non-linear econometric methods developed for the analysis of high-frequency financial data are potentially a highly profitable avenue in the analysis of payment intensities and liquidity recycling through the day. The salient feature of (ultra)high-frequency data is that they are irregularly spaced. In the literature previously reviewed, the natural inclination for the econometrician has been to aggregate the data up to a fixed interval, with an associated loss of information.

In the financial econometrics literature, methods have been tailored to analyze irregularly spaced data. Engle and Russell (1998) develop a dynamic model that parameterizes the intensity of 'activity' as a function of the duration between events. Activity corresponds to transactions in the context of stock-market data, but the technique can be applied equally to payments. Alternatively, Gouriéroux *et al.* (1999) rely on kernel regressions to assess value- and volume-weighted durations between transactions. Similarly, multivariate volatility models developed to analyze the co-movements of financial returns (see, for example, Bollerslev *et al.*, 1988) may be used to evaluate time-varying dependencies between outgoing and incoming payments at the bank level.

4.2 Central banks' provision of liquidity in payment systems: the theory

As our discussion in Section 4.1 showed, the arrangements for intraday liquidity provision are a crucial element in the design of a successful real-time payment system: they determine the cost of liquidity and hence the incentive to delay. However, there remains intense, wide-ranging and ongoing debate about the optimal design of such arrangements. Some of the key insights are offered in this section. The models we discuss compare only a few policy instruments; in reality, central banks have a wide choice set. They can, for example, determine whether intraday credit should be collateralized and to what extent; they can vary the set of eligible collateral; they can impose lending caps, and charge penalty rates when these caps are exceeded. Section 4.3 explores their policy choices in practice. Readers unfamiliar with the topic might wish to first consult Section 4.3 before returning to the more theoretical discussion in this section.

4.2.1 Managing intraday credit exposures

An important design feature of arrangements for the provision of liquidity to users of a real-time payment system is the method by which the liquidity provider manages its credit exposures. In the first theoretical studies looking at the liquidity frictions arising in payment systems (e.g. Freeman (1996b), discussed in Chapter 2), the possibility of borrower default is excluded. Hence, provision of uncollateralized liquidity at a zero interest rate is optimal.

However, as demonstrated in Kahn and Roberds (2001a), the appropriateness of a policy of free intraday credit depends on the ability of the settlement agent (in their model, the central bank) to enforce repayment of its credit claims. Where it cannot do this with certainty, the provision of an unsecured overdraft can create credit exposures for the settlement agent. The main focus of academic work building upon Freeman's initial insight has therefore been to examine ways in which these credit exposures can be managed by central banks without imposing significant additional costs on payment-system users and thereby undermining the very benefits of intraday liquidity provision.

Freeman (1999) extends his earlier (1996b) model to incorporate the potential for an exogenous shock to trigger default. In this framework, a policy of free credit provision is still found to be optimal, but given the possibility that the central bank incurs credit losses, this policy can have an impact on the price level.[37]

A key feature missing from this reformulation is moral hazard: because the default shock is exogenous, the probability that it occurs cannot be altered by agents' behaviour. Both Martin (2004) and Mills (2006) extend Freeman's overlapping generations framework to incorporate the potential for endogenous default, finding that uncollateralized lending at a zero interest rate is no longer the optimal policy in this setting. However, there are differences in their policy recommendations.

Martin (2004) endogenizes default decisions by allowing agents to invest either in a safe production technology that yields a small positive return with certainty, or in a risky production technology with a lower expected return, but a small probability of a high return. Because agents are risk averse, investment in the risky technology is welfare reducing (but may be optimal from an individual agent's point of view). When the central bank provides free uncollateralized intraday credit, the author shows that agents overinvest in the risky production technology: the central bank's debtors rely on pay-offs from the production technology to repay their loan. If the project's pay-off is less than the loan, the debtor strategically defaults. Thus, the debtor's downside risk is limited, whereas he fully participates in the project's profit opportunities. Imposing caps on lending or charging a positive interest rate can reduce investment in the risky project, but only at the cost of reintroducing liquidity constraints in the payment system. However, the model shows that, if lending is against risk-free collateral and at a zero interest rate, no investment in the risky project occurs and the allocation is optimal.

Interestingly, the equilibrium overnight (as opposed to intraday) rate is, nevertheless, positive in Martin's model and, because overnight money growth is zero, it is equal to (the inverse of) consumers' discount factor – in line with the Friedman (1969) rule. Box 4.1 explores more generally the relative terms on which intraday and overnight liquidity are made available.

Full collateralization of intraday credit may, however, not be optimal when investments in collateral assets bear an opportunity cost (Mills, 2006). Indeed, it is often claimed that these opportunity costs are not negligible. RTGS systems have, therefore, been redesigned with a view to reducing liquidity demands, and hence the amount of collateral that is

---

[37] As these losses will prevent the central bank from retiring all the fiat money it printed to help debt markets clear.

Box 4.1: CENTRAL-BANK PROVISION OF INTRADAY AND OVERNIGHT LIQUIDITY

Central banks typically opt for arrangements in which intraday liquidity is offered on far more generous terms than those for overnight or longer-term lending. Should the provision of liquidity be equally generous for longer maturities? Friedman (1969) argues that the marginal benefit of holding additional liquidity is the decrease in transaction costs; given that the production of liquidity is costless for the central bank, it should accommodate any increase in demand.

Others disagree. If prices are sticky, monetary policy can influence real activity. The central bank may wish to vary the nominal interest rate accordingly. However, a 'tax' on money, that is, a positive nominal interest rate, may be more distortionary than other taxes, for example on consumption or income. The reader is referred to Kocherlakota (2005) for a recent overview of the literature.

In practice, even if the central bank finds it optimal to charge a positive interest rate for overnight and longer-term lending, it can accommodate money demand for settlement purposes intraday: a monetary policy action that is reversed intraday will not affect prices or real variables (Dale and Rossi, 1996; Millard *et al.*, 2007). Martin (2004) argues that because money has different functions – store of value and settlement asset – the central bank should vary its nominal interest rate with the maturity: in his model, he finds that it is optimal for money to be available at a zero interest rate when it is used as a medium of exchange. Yet, because it also functions as a store of value, it must have a positive return if it is to be held in equilibrium.

---

necessary to settle a given value of payments in a given time. (See Sections 4.4 and 4.5 for a discussion.) Mills (2006) argues that central banks can instead invest in their ability to enforce repayment of their loans, with the costs of this activity recovered via a positive intraday interest rate.

Both Martin (2004) and Mills (2006) are general equilibrium models and therefore able to trace the optimality of their policy instruments back to consumers' preferences. In contrast, Furfine and Stehm (1998) take banks' need to process payment instructions as given and analyze how different central-bank policies affect commercial banks' optimal use of intraday credit. This approach is simpler, but forces the authors to specify exogenously the central bank's objective function.

Furfine and Stehm (1998) assume that the central bank has three policy tools at its disposal: quantity limits on intraday credit; collateralized lending; and a positive intraday interest rate. Banks take the central bank's policy as given and choose how much intraday credit to take on. Banks seek to minimize their costs. These costs comprise: (i) the opportunity cost of holding any collateral required to obtain credit; (ii) any interest charge incurred from credit usage; and (iii) liquidity management costs incurred in reducing the liquidity need associated with making their payments (these costs encompass both direct delay costs of withholding payments, and the costs of acquiring the relevant systems and resources to manage intraday payment flows proactively).

The central bank's policy decision is considered in light of the cost implications for commercial banks, but also encompasses several sources of social costs that will not be internalized by individual banks: (i) the probability of payment-system gridlock occurring (which is inversely related to banks' liquidity postings); (ii) central-bank credit losses (dependent on levels of credit risk in the system and the central bank's collateralization policy); and (iii) the cost incurred by the central bank in implementing a particular credit policy.

The authors conclude that observed differences in central banks' credit policies are likely to be driven by the different weights attached to these sources of social costs. For example, where banks face low opportunity costs of posting collateral, full collateralization is likely to be desirable. However, if the opportunity cost of posting collateral is high and the likelihood of central bank credit losses is low, then a charging policy might be preferred.

In summary, there is a consensus that liquidity should be provided on generous terms intraday. However, no consensus has yet emerged on pricing and collateralization. What is clear is that the context within which an RTGS system operates – the creditworthiness of its members; the industrial organization of the banking system; features of domestic financial markets; and the wider role of the central bank – is crucial in establishing the optimal design of arrangements for liquidity provision.

4.2.2 *Mechanisms for the provision of intraday credit*

A related question is why intraday liquidity is generally provided via bilateral loans between the central bank and each settlement bank, and not via open-market operations, as is typically the case for central-bank provision of longer-dated liquidity. In principle, central banks could undertake an auction for intraday funds and rely on a private intraday money market – that is, on banks borrowing to and lending from each other – to redistribute these funds throughout the system.

Chapman and Martin (2007) extend the analysis in Freeman (1999) to address the choice between bilateral provision of liquidity and provision of liquidity via a market. They argue that a key benefit of the latter is the potential for market discipline amongst settlement banks. In their model the likelihood that default occurs is endogenous. In particular, the better the creditor monitors the debtor, the less likely the debtor is to default. Private banks know creditors' monitoring effort, but the central bank does not. Hence, it does not know the likelihood that a borrower will default.

The problem the central bank faces in Chapman and Martin (2007) is to find a policy that, first, supplies intraday liquidity to facilitate the settlement of debt, and second, ensures that creditors retain an incentive to monitor debtors. If the central bank simply fixed the rate at which it was ready to buy private debt from the market – i.e. if it operated a discount window – creditors would lose the incentive to monitor. If, instead, the central bank chose a limited set of banks at random and allowed them to bid for central-bank funds – i.e. if it conducted open-market operations – the incentive to monitor could be retained in equilibrium. The reason is that when banks obtain central-bank funds and then lend them on to other banks in the interbank market against private debt, they benefit from monitoring these institutions.

However, this begs the question as to how big the marginal benefit of an intraday market for liquidity is in the typical situation where overnight and longer-term interbank markets for liquidity are already established. Moreover, there remains a question as to how much the central bank could rely on an efficient redistribution of intraday liquidity if this were provided via open-market operations. Martin and McAndrews (2008a) suggest that there might be significant barriers to the establishment of a private intraday money market. In particular, they suggest that such a market would be prone to delays in settlement due to difficulties faced by banks in managing payment flows precisely; such delays could affect the broader functioning of the payment system. In addition, the potential benefits of lending intraday might be quite low, offering little incentive for agents to attempt to overcome this delay friction.

Finally, it is important to note that banks' intraday liquidity management is not only affected by how central banks provide intraday liquidity, but also by how they implement monetary policy (see also Section 2.2). In particular, the conditions under which the central bank offers liquidity at overnight and longer maturities may influence a bank's funding costs when it ends the day with a negative liquidity balance. This, in turn, will influence the size and timing of interbank loans it extends and draws down (both at overnight and longer maturities), and, as a consequence, the amount of liquidity it has available at a given time during the day.

The literature on this interaction is, however, sparse. One example is Berentsen and Monnet (2007). However, even here the authors take liquidity shocks as exogenous and derive the optimal monetary policy implementation framework in the presence of imperfect information about these shocks. Intraday payment behaviour is not modelled. Klee (2007) studies empirically how bank-level operational shocks affect interbank interest rates in the US; see Section 6.1 for a discussion.

4.3 Central banks' intraday credit policies in practice

Having considered the theory, this subsection turns to how in practice central banks typically manage the credit exposures arising from intraday credit extensions. A wide variety of approaches have been taken by central banks around the world, suggesting that there is no single optimal approach. Rather, the appropriate policy is likely to depend heavily on the particular characteristics of the local environment.

The majority of central banks provide intraday liquidity on a collateralized basis. Some central banks use intraday repurchase agreements (repos), crediting users' settlement accounts with the money loaned; others provide overdraft facilities against pledged collateral.[38] Economically, however, the precise legal details are of little significance, as long as the arrangements are legally robust and appropriate 'haircuts'[39] are imposed.

The cost imposed on system participants by collateralization depends on the opportunity cost of holding central-bank-eligible assets. As will be discussed at length in Section 4.4, several factors influence the magnitude of this opportunity cost, including: the range of collateral a central bank is willing to accept; the impact of liquidity regulation on the asset composition of the institution's balance sheet; arrangements for monetary-policy implementation; and the ease with which collateral can be delivered to the central bank.

Some central banks choose to only partially collateralize intraday credit. For instance, the US Federal Reserve currently uses a combination of policy tools. First, it charges an overdraft fee on the average unsecured overdraft incurred during the day, the level of which was an annualized 36 basis

---

[38] As discussed in more detail in CPSS (2005a), p. 15.

[39] The haircut refers to the difference between the market value of the collateral being posted, and the amount of credit the central bank is prepared to provide in exchange for the collateral. This will be less than the market value to protect against adverse price movements ahead of liquidation.

points at the time of writing.[40] It balances the need to give users an incentive to economize on credit usage, and the need to ensure that the cost imposed on institutions is not so large as to undermine the benefit of providing intraday credit. In addition, a net debit cap is imposed beyond which a participant is required to post collateral, though most institutions do not exceed this threshold.[41] Over time, however, participants in Fedwire have collectively increased their recourse to intraday credit from the US Federal Reserve. This has prompted the Federal Reserve to rethink its Payment Systems Risk Policy. Box 4.2 offers some detail.

Another method for reducing collateral costs is that applied by the Bank of Canada in respect of its LVTS system. An explicit guarantee of settlement from

---

Box 4.2: INTRADAY OVERDRAFTS IN FEDWIRE

In addition to incoming payments, banks operating in Fedwire can obtain central-bank money from two main sources: overnight balances held at the Reserve Banks; and daylight overdrafts. Over time, as the supply of central-bank reserves has fallen, demand for daylight overdrafts has grown, boosting both average and peak daylight overdraft levels. Peak daylight overdrafts rose from just above $60bn in 1986 to close to $160bn in 2007.[42]

One reason for the decline in the supply of central-bank reserves is the decline in required reserve holdings since the 1990s. In addition, since required reserves were not traditionally remunerated by the Federal Reserve, banks took increasing advantage of the ability to shift funds from accounts that were subject to reserve requirements to savings accounts, which are exempt. These so-called 'sweep balances' increased from around $10 billion in January 1995 to around $382 billion in February 2000. Over the same period, required reserve balances held in accounts at Federal Reserve Banks fell from around $22 billion to $6 billion.[43] Together with an increase in payments volumes and values in Fedwire, the decline in reserve balances significantly increased banks' reliance on daylight overdraft to fund their payments.

Several other factors may have contributed to the high demand for daylight overdrafts:

Generally, the relatively low degree of tiering in Fedwire implies that fewer payments are internalized – i.e. effected outside of Fedwire, across the books of correspondent banks (see Chapter 10). Consequently, higher volumes and values of payments feed directly through to greater demand for central-bank money.

(continued)

---

[40] This is calculated with reference to an institution's overdraft position at the end of each calendar minute of the day.

[41] Coleman (2002) explains how overdraft limits are set based on both the size and the creditworthiness of banks.

[42] Board of Governors of the Federal Reserve System (2008), Chart 1.

[43] Humphrey and VanHoose (2001).

Box 4.2: (Continued)

Securities settlement practices may also have played a role. Deliveries for less than the full amount of the trade obligation are typically returned to the sending institution. Consequently, dealers tended to stockpile securities before delivering them towards the end of the day, imposing higher liquidity requirements on purchasing banks. These were typically funded via increased recourse to daylight credit.[44]

Finally, heightened liquidity demands have been imposed on Fedwire by ancillary systems. A change in the design of CHIPS, the competing large-value system for US dollars, in 2001 required that CHIPS members pre-fund their accounts via transfers from Fedwire. And since the launch, in 2002, of the Continuous Linked Settlement (CLS) system to settle foreign-exchange transactions, banks have relied significantly on daylight overdrafts to fund their time-critical pay-ins.

Policy responses

Payments settled across Fedwire are final and irrevocable. Hence, payments settled using an uncollateralized overdraft expose the Federal Reserve to the default of the sender. Recognizing this risk, the Federal Reserve imposed net debit caps on daylight overdrafts in 1986,[45] followed in 1988 by the imposition of a $50 million limit on the par value of individual book-entry securities transfers over the Fedwire Securities Service. This policy was intended to discourage stockpiling of securities.[46] In 1994, the Federal Reserve began charging fees for daylight overdrafts.

Hancock and Wilcox (1996) analyze the effects of caps and fees. They estimate an error-correction model in which the change in daylight overdrafts depends on the past deviation of overdrafts from their long-run level. The model is used to analyze short- and long-run responses to policy changes. The authors find that caps and, to an even greater extent, fees reduced maximum and average daylight overdrafts. The initial introduction of fees – 10bp on an annualized basis at the outset – proved to have a strong effect: the authors estimate that the average daily maximum overdraft fell by about $90bn and the average total overdraft at any time during the day by about $40bn.

But overdrafts soon began to grow again. In addition, further increases in the fee led banks to co-ordinate their payments at particular times of day so as to achieve optimal recycling (see Section 4.1.4). In 2008, the Federal Reserve therefore proposed to waive fees if banks fully collateralized their intraday loans, and to increase the fee for uncollateralized overdrafts to 50bp.[47] Finally, from October 2008 the Federal Reserve started to pay interest on overnight reserves, reducing the need for banks to tap intraday sources of funds.

the Bank of Canada allows a subset of payments made through the system to be partially collateralized. The design of the LVTS system is described in Box 4.3.

Finally, New Zealand offers a good example of the link between banks' intraday liquidity management and the framework for central-bank monetary

---

[44] Board of Governors of the Federal Reserve System (2006).
[45] Emmons (1997).
[46] Federal Reserve Board (2007).
[47] Board of Governors of the Federal Reserve System (2008).

Box 4.3: PARTIAL COLLATERALIZATION IN THE CANADIAN LVTS

The Canadian Large Value Transfer System (LVTS) offers RTGS-equivalent settlement (See Arjani and McVanel (2006) for an overview.). That is, it provides unconditional and irrevocable gross settlement of payments intraday despite the fact that funds transfer across members' accounts at the Bank of Canada actually occurs on a multilateral net basis at the end of the day. Intraday finality is assured because the Bank of Canada guarantees settlement for payments made across LVTS. This guarantee alone would not suffice to reduce collateral posting requirements compared to a traditional RTGS system. However, the design of LVTS is such that, in effect, the Bank of Canada extends intraday liquidity on a partially collateralized basis.

The LVTS has two payment streams: Tranche 1 (T1) and Tranche 2 (T2). Banks can choose freely between the streams, as long as the payment passes the relevant risk controls. T1 payments must be fully funded either from incoming payments or collateral pledged to the Bank of Canada. If a default were to occur, the Bank of Canada would be entitled to realize the participant's collateral.

The intraday flow of T2 payments (which typically account for more than 90% of total LVTS flows by value) is conditional on bilateral and multilateral net debit caps applied to each bank. Bilateral credit limits (BCLs) represent the maximum positive bilateral exposures a participant is willing to assume on each of its counterparts. These BCLs are then used to calculate multilateral net debit caps for each participant: the sum of the BCLs it receives from other participants, multiplied by a fraction (currently 30%) called the 'system-wide percentage'. There is no cap on multilateral net credit positions.

To support its T2 activity, each participant must pledge to the Bank of Canada collateral equal to the largest BCL that it extends, multiplied by the system-wide percentage. This means that, while each individual bank is required to only partially collateralize its T2 payments, sufficient collateral will be pledged in aggregate to cover the single largest multilateral net debit position allowed in T2. The collateral requirement is calibrated such that, if a single bank were to default, the Bank of Canada could fully collateralize any intraday loans necessary to allow settlement to complete. The defaulting bank's collateral would be liquidated first, with any additional shortfall met from survivors' contributions, and with losses shared in proportion to the relative size of the BCL extended to the defaulter. This loss-sharing method is intended to encourage banks to monitor their intraday credit exposures in LVTS. Only if several banks defaulted on a single day – an extremely unlikely scenario – would the Bank of Canada be left with uncollateralized exposures.

---

operations. In 2006, the Reserve Bank of New Zealand ceased to supply intraday liquidity to settlement banks. At the same time, it increased its target level of banks' reserve balance holdings to around NZ$ 7bn, sharply up from NZ$ 20mn. This level of cash balances was perceived to be sufficient for settlement to continue unencumbered, despite the absence of intraday liquidity provision. To give banks an incentive to hold sufficient reserves, balances are remunerated at the policy rate. On the basis of a preliminary assessment in

2006, payments were on average processed earlier in the day in the RTGS system (see Nield, 2006).

4.4 Reducing the opportunity cost of collateralized intraday credit

When intraday credit is collateralized, a key determinant of opportunity cost is the central bank's policy on eligible collateral. Policies vary widely across central banks, with little evidence of convergence and, to date, limited discussion of the subject in the academic literature. A common feature is the acceptance of government debt denominated in the domestic currency. However, many central banks have in recent years widened the range of collateral they are willing to accept along three dimensions: currency; credit quality; and liquidity. And strains in the money markets at the time of writing have prompted several central banks to extend further their eligible collateral lists on one or more of these dimensions. In each case, such extensions are intended to reduce the opportunity costs of meeting collateral eligibility requirements.

Foreign-currency collateral. It is becoming more common for central banks to accept collateral denominated in a foreign currency when providing intraday credit. This is at least in part a response to the increasingly global structure of major banking groups and their participation in multiple large-value payment and settlement systems. Following a 2003 report by the New York-based Payments Risk Committee, the Basel Committee on Payment and Settlement Systems (CPSS) investigated existing arrangements for cross-border collateral (CPSS, 2006). The report examined barriers to the effective mobilization of foreign collateral, and discussed the costs and benefits of amending central banks' collateral policies to help dismantle them. For example, significant operational and legal frictions can inhibit banks' ability to rapidly move securities between locations, a crucial pre-requisite for allowing such assets to function effectively as collateral.

Manning and Willison (2006) demonstrate that cross-border use of collateral can alleviate mismatches between the location of a bank's liquidity demands and that of its available collateral. As long as liquidity demands are not correlated across countries, this will reduce liquidity risk, even if banks, in response, reduce precautionary reserves of collateral in each country. Should banks face high liquidity demands simultaneously across markets, a reduction in aggregate liquidity holdings may increase liquidity risk in at least one country. In recognition of this risk, central banks may choose to accept foreign collateral only in stressed circumstances, rather than routinely. Extensive testing of such arrangements is, however, important to ensure their availability as required in times of stress.

Lower-quality and illiquid collateral. Central banks may also choose to broaden their eligibility criteria by accepting assets that typically offer higher yields than government securities and therefore impose a lower opportunity cost. A central bank could accept less liquid assets – for example, bank loans are eligible within the Eurosystem – or assets of lower credit quality, such as corporate bonds or mortgage-backed securities. Indeed, in response to disruption to securitization markets in 2007/2008 and strains in interbank lending markets, several central banks extended their eligible collateral lists to include certain asset-backed (e.g. mortgage-backed) securities. Larger haircuts are typically applied to such assets, reflecting potential difficulties in liquidating such assets at short notice and higher price volatility.

Green (2007) advocates that central banks stand ready to extend short-term credit against illiquid collateral: in contrast to private banks, central banks do not face liquidity risk because they can issue liabilities at will. He argues that, in a fiat-money regime, creation of outside money by a central bank is constrained only by the requirement to maintain price stability. (See the discussion in Box 4.1.) This requires that money created through short-term lending to payment-system participants can eventually be reabsorbed when borrowers pay back their loans from the central bank, thereby not influencing the longer-term rate of money growth. If intraday loans were collateralized using illiquid assets, any additional money growth would be sterilized when the assets were sold.

Another potential influence on banks' opportunity costs of posting collateral is prudential liquidity regulation. In some countries, this takes the form of a 'stock requirement': banks must hold a prudential pot of eligible liquid assets, calibrated such that they could accommodate an extreme, but plausible, liquidity outflow over a short time horizon.

As discussed in Rochet (2007), the liquid assets held to comply with such regulation often take the form of government securities, which are also eligible as collateral in support of intraday credit from the central bank. Banks can therefore obtain liquidity intraday by utilizing assets that they are already required to hold for regulatory purposes, thereby lowering the opportunity cost associated with raising intraday liquidity.

This is currently the case in the UK, where domestic banks subject to the Sterling Stock Liquidity Regime – introduced in 1997 – are able to post assets intraday with the Bank of England that they are then required to hold overnight to meet the prudential requirement (see James, 2003).

4.5 Mechanisms to promote efficient recycling of liquidity

Another key determinant of intraday liquidity needs is the way banks manage their payments activity. Incoming payments can be an important source of intraday liquidity for banks in an RTGS system (as discussed in Section 4.1), creating the potential for strategic interactions between members of a payment system. If all banks maintain a good outflow of payments through the day, intraday liquidity will be recycled efficiently, potentially significantly reducing aggregate liquidity demands.

One approach to promoting efficient recycling is to introduce a central-ized co-ordination device, such as a throughput rule. That is, the system operator may require that banks send a certain proportion of their total daily payments by a particular intraday deadline. The imposition of such a rule, if adhered to, can reduce the aggregate liquidity needed for settlement.

Buckle and Campbell (2003) examine the optimal design of throughput rules. According to their model, increasing the number of throughput require-ments (stacked deadlines) increases liquidity efficiency, but at a decreasing rate. However, they qualify this finding by noting that, in practice, the arrival rate of payment instructions is uncertain. If requirements are too granular, banks might find themselves unable to comply, despite submitting all pay-ment instructions promptly on receipt. This highlights the difficulty in cali-brating throughput rules, suggesting that, alone, they may not be sufficient to optimize payment-sending behaviour.

A number of countries have throughput rules or guidelines in place to encourage co-ordinated submission of payments. For example, in the UK, two value-based throughput rules are imposed on members of the CHAPS system, requiring that, at a minimum, a bank sends 50% of its total daily payment values by 12:00 and 75% by 14:30. Evidence in Becher *et al.* (2008a) suggests that throughput guidelines do promote timely submis-sion of payment instructions, as a rise in values processed through CHAPS is seen ahead of both deadlines. In Hong Kong, too, throughput guidelines have been established, with participants required to submit 35% of pay-ments by noon, and 70% by 15:00. And users of the Canadian LVTS system face both volume- and value-based throughput guidelines at three points during the day (Arjani, 2006).

Elsewhere, other co-ordination devices have been developed. In some countries, market convention has evolved to co-ordinate banks' payments behaviour. For example, in Japan the vast majority of payments by value are processed in the first hour of operation, while in Norway sending is concentrated within a half-hour interval in the middle of the day. Market conventions in respect of the time at which overnight loans should be repaid can also encourage settlement banks to provide liquidity to the system early in the day.

In SIC, the Swiss large-value payment system, the per-unit processing fee rises in stages through the day, promoting early submission of instructions. However, a limitation to this approach is that, in practice, processing fees are typically low by comparison to the potential opportunity costs associated with generating liquidity.[48] Hence, this approach may alone fail to sufficiently encourage early settlement of payments, at least when they are large. For an overview of the different tariffs charged by the operators of large-value payment systems, see Box 10.1.

A final method for improving co-ordination is to facilitate the offsetting of payments within a central queue. Payment systems offering such functionality are referred to as 'hybrid' payment systems. We examine them in detail in the next section.

4.6 Hybrid payment-system design

As discussed in the preceding section, co-ordination of payments activity can significantly enhance the liquidity efficiency of an RTGS payment system. The past decade has seen a growing trend of adoption of so-called 'hybrid' payment-system designs for the settlement of large-value payments.[49] Hybrid designs have the potential both to improve liquidity efficiency and to speed up settlement within the day, without compromising

---

[48] For example, a rough calculation suggests that even if the opportunity cost of intraday liquidity were as low as 3.6 basis points on an annualized basis, or 0.0001% per day, the cost of providing liquidity to make a payment of value $100mn would be $100. By comparison, the tariff for processing a payment in most, if not all, systems, is likely to be significantly less than $1.

[49] According to calculations in Bech et al. (2008), only 3% of wholesale payments by value in G10 countries were settled over 'hybrid' systems in 1999. By 2005, the percentage had risen to 32%. This figure has continued to rise, with hybrid system designs introduced in several more countries since 2005.

the benefits of credit-risk mitigation and the immediacy of settlement offered by an RTGS design. The defining feature of a hybrid design is centralized queuing of payment instructions. This section outlines the key features of hybrid payment systems, offering some theoretical and empirical evidence on the impact of their introduction.

4.6.1 *Key features of hybrid payment systems*

As described in McAndrews and Trundle (2001), two main types of hybrid systems have emerged over recent years: queue-augmented RTGS (QART); and continuous net settlement (CNS). The key innovation of both designs is the introduction of a centralized queuing facility for payments. As discussed in detail in Section 4.1, costly intraday liquidity can discourage banks from submitting their payment instructions immediately to the central processor and thereby hamper liquidity recycling in the system. Centralized queuing gives banks good incentives to submit payment instructions early in the day, because by doing so they increase the probability that payments due to them will be released from the queues of other members.

Simultaneous settlement of offsetting payments can greatly reduce the system's liquidity needs. Queuing streams also typically continue to offer intraday settlement finality, ensuring that credit exposures between users do not build up within the system.

4.6.2 *Queue-augmented RTGS (QART) systems*

Queue-augmented RTGS (QART) systems have been adopted in a number of countries. Notable examples of such systems include TARGET2, the centralized large-value payment system of the Eurosystem, and RITS in Australia. A distinguishing feature of such systems is that they allow participants to prioritize and channel payments according to their urgency. That is, they typically offer participants a choice between submission of payments for standard RTGS – which will be appropriate for time-critical payments – and submission to a central queue for settlement by offset or other 'conditional release'. By allowing users to choose how to route each payment, QART aims to achieve an optimal trade-off between payment delay and liquidity efficiency.

The release of payments from the central queue of a hybrid system can operate in either a 'balance-reactive' or a 'receipt-reactive' manner. In a receipt-reactive system, payments are released for settlement conditional on the flow of incoming payments received by the bank. By contrast, in a balance-reactive system, payments are released conditional on the balance of funds available in the bank's account with the settlement agent. Both forms of queue release are discussed in more detail in Box 4.4.

Box 4.4: EXAMPLES OF QUEUE-RELEASE ALGORITHMS

This box presents worked examples to illustrate how typical balance- and receipt-reactive queue-release algorithms operate in practice. In each case, the algorithm described operates on a multilateral basis. However, it is also feasible for such algorithms to operate on a bilateral basis, or indeed for both bilateral and multilateral algorithms to be combined in one system.

Balance-reactive functionality

TARGET2, the RTGS system for euro payments, offers a range of liquidity-saving options. Here we will focus on one in particular: the ability to reserve liquidity for 'urgent' or 'highly urgent' payments: a balance-reactive facility.

This liquidity reservation functionality gives participants the option to assign 'urgent' or 'highly urgent' priority to individual payments. They can also choose how much liquidity they want to place in their urgent and highly urgent reserves. Liquidity can be moved into and out of these reserves from a bank's main settlement account at any time during the day. The entire balance on a participant's RTGS account is deemed to be available for highly urgent payments. The account balance less the amount reserved for highly urgent payments is deemed to be available for urgent payments. And the account balance less the amounts reserved for urgent and highly urgent payments are deemed available for 'normal' priority payments.

The numerical example in Figure 4.1 is intended to clarify how the liquidity reservation functionality works. To ease comparability with the receipt-reactive case, we assume, in this example, that only the urgent reserve is used.

Activity	Queued Payments	Account Balance	Urgent Reserve	Liquidity for Normal Payments
Start of Day	-	1000	800	200
Submit Normal payment 100	-	900	800	100
Submit Urgent payment 200	-	700	600	100
Incoming payment 50	-	750	600	150
Submit Urgent payment 500	-	250	100	150
Submit Urgent payment 300	300 Urgent	250	100	150
Incoming payment 100	-	50	0	50

Figure 4.1: Balance-reactive functionality

(continued)

Box 4.4: (Continued)

Receipt-reactive functionality

The receipt-reactive algorithm explored here, called receipt-reactive gross settlement (RRGS), has not been implemented in any payment system to date, but has been the subject of academic attention (as discussed in Section 4.6.5).[50] Under RRGS, all the intraday liquidity posted by a bank is reserved solely for making the payments it designates as being urgent. All other payments (with a normal priority assigned to them) are queued and only released (on a first-in, first-out basis) when sufficient liquidity has been received from incoming payments to fund them. This is intended to ensure that urgent payments are settled without delay, while non-time-critical payments are settled as efficiently as possible through liquidity recycling. The numerical example in Figure 4.2, using the same payment flows as in the balance-reactive example above, demonstrates how RRGS works:

Activity	Queued Payments	Account Balance	Liquidity for Normal Payments
Start of Day	-	1000	0
Submit Normal payment 100	100 Normal	1000	0
Submit Urgent payment 200	100 Normal	800	0
Incoming payment 50	100 Normal	850	50
Submit Urgent payment 500	100 Normal	350	50
Submit Urgent payment 300	100 Normal	50	50
Incoming payment 100	-	50	50

Figure 4.2: Receipt-reactive functionality

It should be noted that in principle both types of functionality could yield the same outcome. In this case, if 1000 had been set aside in the urgent reserve in the balance-reactive example, the same outcome would have been achieved as under RRGS.

4.6.3 Continuous Net Settlement (CNS) systems

While QART systems can be regarded as hybrids evolving from an RTGS design, Continuous Net Settlement (CNS) systems have evolved from DNS systems. Their key feature is that all payments are entered into a single centralized queue, where bilateral and/or multilateral algorithms search for groups of payments that can be settled without causing any bank to incur a net debit position on its account. When such a batch of payments is identified, they are settled net, with immediate finality. By running these algorithms continuously throughout the day, CNS systems enable a high proportion of payments to be settled net but in real time, reducing credit risk relative to DNS.

A notable example of a CNS system is the Clearing House Interbank Payments System (CHIPS) in the US. Participants are required to pre-fund

---

[50] RRGS is discussed in more detail in Johnson *et al.* (2004) and Ercevik and Jackson (2007).

their accounts at the start of CHIPS operations via transfer from Fedwire, the US RTGS system.[51] Additional transfers may also be made throughout the day, but a final end-of-day funding will usually be required from a subset of participants to ensure that any remaining payments (i.e. those that could not be offset during the day) are settled by the end of CHIPS operations.

CNS systems typically provide an alternative, liquidity efficient form of settlement, available alongside an RTGS system. In combination, an RTGS and CNS pair can be thought of as offering a similar package to a QART system. That is, users who have access to both systems have the ability to route individual payments on the basis of their time criticality, with the aim of achieving a more efficient overall outcome than that in which all payments are settled RTGS.

There is, however, an important difference. Users of a QART system post all incoming and outgoing payments to a *single* account in a single large-value payment system. By contrast, with separate CNS and RTGS systems operating in parallel, funds committed to the CNS system are segregated from the RTGS system.[52] The disadvantage of using separate accounts is that liquidity recycling can be reduced by 'splitting' the volume of trans-actions between the two systems: a surplus of liquidity in one system cannot necessarily be drawn down immediately to fund a deficit in the other, potentially increasing users' overall liquidity demands.

4.6.4 *Theoretical evidence on the impact of hybrid design*

The rise of hybrid systems in recent years reflects their perceived ability to mitigate the liquidity demands generated by RTGS systems without in-creasing credit risk.[53]

There has, however, been some concern that centralized queuing can introduce settlement delays, potentially also exposing a larger volume of as-yet-unsettled payments to an operational outage at any given time during the day. But, as discussed earlier in this chapter, costly liquidity can also trigger payment delays in RTGS systems. Hence, it is possible that queuing could *reduce* settlement delays if it encourages earlier submission of payments.

---

[51] Funds are transferred to the 'CHIPS Prefunded Balance Account' at the Federal Reserve Bank of New York. See CHIPS (2007) for more detail.

[52] Banks can also pre-fund their CNS accounts via correspondents, if they are not direct participants in the other LVPS.

[53] This is true as long as receiving banks do not anticipate payments they are due to receive in the queue and credit final beneficiaries' accounts before the payment has been settled/offset with finality. To avoid this, systems typically provide very limited information about payments in the central queue (payer, payee, value only) until finality has been achieved.

A number of theoretical and empirical papers have assessed the impact of hybrid system designs on liquidity efficiency and settlement delay. Willison (2005) uses a two-period multibank game-theoretic model to predict and compare equilibria under RTGS and a hybrid design. The form of hybrid design under scrutiny is a simple queue-augmented RTGS setup, in which payments submitted to the central queue can be settled via bilateral offsetting. The author examines the implications of running the payment-offset algorithm at different times of day – e.g. only in the morning; only in the afternoon; or throughout the day – and differing degrees of queue transparency. In Willison's model, banks cannot observe the time criticality of the payment instructions made by other banks. This creates uncertainty about the timing of the receipts from another bank in any given period.

Willison compares system designs based on two criteria: their liquidity efficiency; and the speed with which payments are settled. On the basis of these criteria, the author finds that, under certain circumstances, a queue-augmented RTGS system may be preferred to a pure RTGS alternative: when payments can be offset against each other in a central queue in the morning, settlement occurs early and liquidity demands remain low.

Martin and McAndrews (2008b) adopt a similar framework to study the payment-submission incentives of participants under RTGS and QART. However, they extend the approach in Willison (2005) in a number of ways, providing a richer analysis of the impact of hybrid design.

In particular, the authors assume that the payment system is also used by a 'non-strategic agent'. This agent is intended to represent an outside payment system, e.g. CLS or a securities settlement system. Each bank makes one time-critical payment to, and receives one payment from, the non-strategic agent. The introduction of this agent is a vehicle for modelling liquidity shocks: if a bank has to pay the agent in the morning, but only receives the return payment in the afternoon, this is a negative liquidity shock; if the converse is true, the shock is positive.

This paper is also the first theoretical work to compare balance- and receipt-reactive hybrid designs. The receipt-reactive arrangement analyzed is RRGS (see Box 4.4), while the balance-reactive functionality allows participants to queue payments with their release conditional on the incidence of a negative liquidity shock.

Welfare is defined in terms of the costs of liquidity and delay, with liquidity costs determined by agents' *ex-post* usage of intraday credit. This makes the results more applicable to payment systems in which intraday liquidity is provided for a fee, rather than systems in which intraday overdrafts are collateralized.[54] In the absence of liquidity shocks, both hybrid designs are shown to dominate RTGS and achieve the first best outcome when all payments between banks are submitted in the morning. This is as in Willison (2005).

However, when liquidity shocks are introduced, a *balance-reactive* hybrid system no longer dominates RTGS. Rather, the outcome depends on the particular characteristics of the payments processed through the system. A *receipt-reactive* system, on the other hand, always weakly dominates RTGS. Whether balance-reactive systems outperform receipt-reactive systems depends on parameter values. The paper concludes that, while the results point to QART systems having the potential to offer more efficient settlement performance than RTGS, the choice of which type of hybrid system design to adopt will depend on the particular circumstances in question.

4.6.5 *Empirical evidence on the impact of hybrid design*

Johnson *et al.* (2004) use simulation techniques to assess the impact of various types of queue-augmented RTGS designs on liquidity efficiency in the US Fedwire system. Using historical (rather than simulated) data of Fedwire payments, the paper finds that receipt-reactive gross settlement (RRGS, discussed in Box 4.4) can reduce participants' costs of obtaining intraday credit, while only modestly delaying the average time of settlement.[55] The authors also show that the benefits of RRGS are proportional to the amount of payments submitted to the central queue, with the introduction of RRGS functionality acknowledged to provide good incentives for banks to submit payments earlier in the day.

In a similar vein, Ercevik and Jackson (2007) apply a simulation approach to test the performance of RRGS, this time based on real payments data from the UK's CHAPS Sterling system (which operates as a simple RTGS system), as well as simulated data. Their simulations show that the introduction of RRGS can reduce banks' liquidity requirements and encourage earlier settlement of payments. However, both of these improvements are highly dependent on the characteristics of payment flows in the system.

---

[54] When intraday liquidity is collateralized, liquidity is typically generated in advance of the need arising. Hence, in such systems, banks typically generate some 'precautionary' liquidity. When liquidity is provided for a fee, on the other hand, it will typically be generated on demand.

[55] This cost reduction is based on the Federal Reserve's method of charging for intraday credit, which is a fee based on banks' average overdrafts calculated at the end of each minute, and may not necessarily apply to a system where intraday credit is free but collateralized.

The paper confirms that a key determinant of the impact of RRGS functionality is the level of liquidity recycling already being achieved under RTGS. This, in turn, is likely to be influenced by a number of factors including: the number of direct members of the payment system; the volume and value profiles of payments being processed in that system; the network structure; and the existence of co-ordination mechanisms encouraging early payment submission. CHAPS has a small number of members who typically post large excess reserves of liquidity in the system intraday. Furthermore, members are encouraged to co-ordinate via throughput guidelines. Hence, the potential incremental savings from introducing RRGS are relatively low. In a system with a larger membership, less plentiful intraday liquidity and no centralized co-ordination devices, RRGS might have a larger positive impact. Another relevant factor is the proportion of payments by value that banks can submit to the receipt-reactive queue.

The simulations also show that liquidity savings achieved through RRGS are distributed very unevenly, with the largest CHAPS banks seeing no benefits, while the smaller CHAPS banks make large savings. The distribution of the impact of RRGS across banks is important when thinking about incentives to invest in hybrid functionality. For banks already using liquidity very efficiently under RTGS, RRGS can actually disrupt liquidity recycling.

Finally, the authors consider the implications of earlier submission of non-time-critical payments. They show that, when a significant proportion of such payments would be delayed under RTGS, there may be benefits to early payment submission to a central queue. Under such circumstances, earlier average settlement times may be achieved under RRGS.

4.7 Optimal channelling of payments

Large-value payment systems are used to settle a wide variety of payments, exhibiting different properties and characteristics. When banks can choose the settlement venue, they will typically seek to channel payments to achieve the optimal (private) trade-off between immediacy of settlement and cost of liquidity. But the optimal choice from a private perspective may not be optimal from the perspective of a central bank that seeks to reduce systemic risk.

What characterizes the potential systemic externality that can arise from an individual payment? The *size* of a payment is clearly important. As we have seen, large payments have the potential to create sizeable credit exposures in DNS systems; and the failure to make a high-value payment can disrupt liquidity recycling in a real-time system. Another relevant characteristic is the *urgency* of a payment. A payment may be time critical because, if it is not made by a certain intraday deadline, the sender will be deemed in default. And, more generally, where activity in other payment systems or financial markets is dependent on the settlement of a payment, delay in one system can reduce the efficiency of settlement in another system. For example, if net pay-ins to a DNS system are made across an RTGS system, then the failure of a single bank to settle its pay-in can disrupt settlement in the DNS system.

The optimal channelling of payments depends on how different payment-system designs are equipped to mitigate specific externalities that might arise due to the size and urgency of particular payments. As discussed in Chapter 3, significant credit exposures can, under certain circumstances, arise in unprotected DNS systems. Therefore, such systems may not be suitable for the largest payments. And where payments are of an intermediate size, it may be preferable to embed protections in the DNS design, such as a collateral pool and net debit caps. DNS systems may also be inappropriate for the settlement of urgent payments if settlement occurs only infrequently. However, it is of course possible to design such systems with multiple settlement cycles during the day, thereby at least partially overcoming this problem.

CNS and the queuing streams of QART systems offer modes of settlement that can avoid the introduction of credit exposures (as long as banks do not credit their customers before settlement has occurred) while still delivering liquidity efficiencies. Such systems may therefore be suitable for large-value payments. However, to the extent that such systems cannot guarantee immediacy – because final settlement is dependent on conditional release from the central queue – they are unlikely to be suitable for urgent payments.

RTGS systems – as well as the urgent streams of QART systems, and systems judged to be RTGS-equivalent (such as the Canadian LVTS system) – both eliminate credit exposures within the system and provide immediacy of final settlement. These systems therefore offer the safest form of settlement for the largest and most urgent payments.

Figures 4.3 and 4.4 summarize this discussion, mapping payment types onto a 3 × 3 grid reflecting their size and urgency. The precise definition of

Size

	L	M	H	
H	Note issuance settlement	Interbank loans, central bank repos, wholesale market flows, FX transactions (outside of CLS)	Transfers to linked systems (CLS, SSS, other LVPS)	
M		Broker/dealer flows, OTC margins	Pay-ins to retail DNS systems, CCP margins	
L	Commercial flows	House purchases		
	L	**M**	**H**	**Urgency**

Figure 4.3: Classification by size and urgency of major payments types in LVPS

what constitutes high, medium and low size and urgency will vary according to the context in which a particular system operates. Clearly, it is possible that some categories will fall across types. For example, an interbank loan could be for either a very large or a very small amount. The approach adopted in Figure 4.3 is to place payment types in the highest category of size and urgency they might be expected to inhabit.

Interestingly, few payment types are both highly urgent and of large size. The bulk of payment types passing through large-value systems fall into the 'medium urgency' category.

Figure 4.4 maps payments of each size-urgency combination to the system design offering the optimal mix of risk and liquidity efficiency.[56]

Comparing Figures 4.3 and 4.4, it seems that only the relatively few sizeable and/or highly urgent payment types identified in Figure 4.3 would be optimally channelled via RTGS. This interpretation is consistent with

Size

	L	M	H	
H	Protected DNS / CNS	QART queuing stream	RTGS or equivalent	
M	Protected DNS	Protected DNS with multiple cycles / CNS	RTGS or equivalent	
L	DNS	DNS with multiple cycles	RTGS or equivalent	
	L	**M**	**H**	**Urgency**

Figure 4.4: Mapping payment-system design to the size and urgency of payments

---

[56] We assume that an 'unprotected' DNS system still has measures in place to mitigate the legal risk of netting being unwound.

the empirical regularity that the vast majority (typically >90%) of payment flows by value in a QART system are submitted to the central queue with non-urgent priority. This may also explain why hybrid settlement is becoming more commonplace internationally.

As discussed earlier, splitting payment flows across multiple systems is likely to inhibit settlement efficiency unless liquidity can be transferred seamlessly between systems. Therefore, the analysis in this section should not be taken to suggest that optimal design of payment arrangements can be achieved by having several different payment-system types operating in parallel, each processing the subset of payments that are best suited to its specific design features. Rather, the crucial message is that an important determinant of optimal payment-system design is the composition of the payment flows to be settled across the system. Therefore, any theoretical or empirical analysis seeking to consider risk management or efficiency in payment and settlement systems must be capable of reflecting the diversity of payment types processed by such systems.

5

Managing systemic risk in the clearance and settlement of foreign-exchange, securities and derivatives transactions

This chapter discusses specific risks arising in the clearance and settlement of foreign exchange, securities and derivatives transactions and the arrangements that have been developed to manage these risks. The risks considered are, respectively, foreign-exchange settlement risk; principal risk in securities settlement; and pre-settlement replacement cost risk.

Foreign-exchange settlement risk – often referred to as 'Herstatt risk', after a famous case in which such a risk crystallized – arises when the settlement of the two currency legs of a foreign-exchange transaction are not simultaneous. In such circumstances, a situation may arise in which one party to the transaction has settled, with finality, its payment obligation in currency A, but has not yet received currency B in return. That party then has an exposure to its counterparty to the full principal value of the currency it has paid away; an exposure that will crystallize if its counterparty fails before meeting its obligation. Foreign-exchange settlement risk can be mitigated by introducing co-ordinating mechanisms to achieve simultaneous exchange – so-called 'payment-versus-payment' – of the two currency legs.

In securities transactions, the failure to co-ordinate settlement of the securities and cash legs of a trade can give rise to similar principal risk exposures between the counterparties to the trade. Again, this risk will crystallize if one party defaults after it has received either cash or securities from its counterparty, but before it has fulfilled its corresponding obligation. Such risk can be mitigated by the implementation of 'delivery-versus-payment' arrangements.

Finally, derivatives transactions typically involve obligations to deliver cash or securities at a specified future date. By their nature, these contracts are characterized by long pre-settlement periods – typically of the order of several months – during which agents are exposed to 'replacement cost risk.' This is the risk that one party to the trade defaults prior to settlement, requiring that the trade be replaced, potentially at a loss. Central counterparties (CCPs) were first introduced in exchange-traded derivatives markets – and have progressively been introduced in other markets[57] – to manage such risk via collateralization, mutualization and the multilateral netting of exposures. Importantly, however, while such arrangements mitigate risk, they also concentrate replacement-cost risk within the CCP. Hence, it is critical that CCPs have robust procedures and adequate financial resources to manage this risk.

The chapter considers each of these risks – foreign-exchange settlement risk; principal risk in securities settlement; and pre-settlement replacement-cost risk – in turn.

5.1 Foreign-exchange settlement risk

Foreign-exchange settlement risk has attracted considerable attention over the past decade. Foreign-exchange settlement risk is a form of principal risk associated with foreign-exchange transactions, arising when the two currency legs of a trade are not settled simultaneously.[58] The absence of co-ordination in settlement introduces the risk that one party fulfils its obligation – say, by settling, with finality, a euro payment across TARGET2 – only to discover that its counterparty is unable, perhaps due to insolvency, to meet its corresponding obligation – for instance, a US dollar payment in Fedwire. Should such a risk crystallize, the bank that has fulfilled its obligation faces a loss to the entire value of its settled payment.

Box 5.1 describes three notable incidents in which foreign-exchange settlement risk crystallized: either triggering losses or disrupting settlement. More details of these and similar incidents may be found in CPSS (1996).

---

[57] They are now also common in cash securities and repo markets and have also emerged in OTC derivatives markets.

[58] In the pre-settlement period, FX transactions also carry both replacement cost and liquidity risk, regardless of whether settlement takes place simultaneously or not. However, the greater magnitude of principal risk has made it the main focus of efforts to reduce FX settlement risk.

Box 5.1: CASE STUDIES OF FOREIGN-EXCHANGE SETTLEMENT RISK INCIDENTS

This box describes three instances in which foreign-exchange settlement risk crystallized. In each case, a counterparty default either triggered losses or disrupted settlement.

Bankhaus Herstatt was a small bank in Cologne, active in the foreign-exchange market, which unexpectedly defaulted on 26 June 1974. At 3.30pm on the day of default, the German banking supervisor withdrew its banking licence and suspended all payments.[59]

By this time the German interbank payment system had already closed, and so was unaffected by the suspension. However, the US payment system had not long opened. Some US-based foreign exchange counterparties to Bankhaus Herstatt had already settled their Deutschmark obligations to Herstatt during German opening hours and were expecting to receive US dollars in return in the US system. However, following the default, Herstatt's New York correspondent bank froze all funds, leaving the US counterparties facing a principal loss.[60]

The case of Bankhaus Herstatt is one of the best-known examples of foreign-exchange settlement risk – in fact, such risk is often referred to as 'Herstatt risk'. The event was also one of the triggers for the formation of the Basel Committee on Banking Supervision.

BCCI was a major international bank that, on 5 July 1991, was closed by regulators on grounds of serious fraud. A British institution had entered into a transaction with BCCI on 3 July to buy US dollars. The UK firm had sent the sterling payment, but with BCCI's New York correspondent cancelling all BCCI trades due for settlement in the CHIPS system, it failed to receive the US dollar value in return. A major Japanese bank also incurred a 'Herstatt' loss, having paid away yen, but failing to receive the corresponding dollar leg of the transaction.

Drexel Burnham Lambert Trading Ltd (DBLT) was a foreign-exchange-trading London subsidiary of the US-based Drexel Burnham Lambert Group Inc.[61] Once the fifth-largest investment bank in the US, Drexel filed for Chapter 11 bankruptcy protection on 13 February 1990. One proximate cause was an insider-trading investigation, which had begun in 1986. Although Drexel settled with the SEC in 1989, the episode had damaged the firm's reputation. This, coupled with poor financial performance and its considerable exposure to the declining 'junk bond' market, led to Drexel's filing for bankruptcy protection.

Concerned that DBLT was insolvent, the firm's counterparties were reluctant to settle their obligations. Equally, DBLT was unwilling to pay away in advance, fearing that its counterparties would not honour their obligations but, rather, would offset them against claims against defaulted entities elsewhere in the Drexel group. The Bank of England was concerned about this impasse and the potential for systemic losses. Once satisfied that DBLT was indeed solvent, the Bank established escrow facilities

---

[59] See Danmarks Nationalbank (2000) for details.

[60] Failure to receive anticipated US dollars may also have exposed these parties to liquidity risk.

[61] To avoid confusion, we shall refer to the US parent as 'Drexel' and to the UK subsidiary as 'DBLT'.

into which both DBLT and its counterparties placed funds. This *de facto* 'payment-versus-payment' arrangement gave counterparties confidence in the smooth settlement of their foreign-exchange trades with DBLT. The arrangement lasted until DBLT was forced into administration.[62]

Responding to concerns raised by incidents such as those outlined in Box 5.1, G10 central banks undertook a survey in 1996 into the magnitude of foreign-exchange settlement risk. The survey revealed that potential exposures in the event of the default of a major player in the foreign-exchange market were indeed substantial. Private- and public-sector initiatives to manage such exposures were strongly encouraged.[63]

Over the past decade, great strides have been taken to mitigate foreign-exchange settlement risk, as revealed by a follow-up survey carried out by central banks in 2006 (see CPSS, 2007a).[64] Some of this reduction has been brought about by increased use of bilateral netting arrangements, but the major innovation has been the introduction and widespread usage of a payment-versus-payment (PvP) mechanism for settling foreign-exchange transactions in major currencies. In particular, in response to the 1996 survey (CPSS, 1996), a global infrastructure, the Continuous Linked Settlement system (CLS), was established in 2002 to ensure PvP settlement of foreign-exchange transactions. The design of the settlement mechanism in the system ensures that the two legs of a transaction are processed simultaneously.[65]

Box 5.2 describes CLS in more detail.[66] It explains that while principal risk is eliminated by using CLS, other components of settlement risk remain. Various techniques are employed by CLS to mitigate these residual risks.

Kahn and Roberds (2001b), writing before the launch of CLS, but at a time when its design had been established, analyze the incentives that the system places on banks making FX transactions, and compare them to the

---

[62] Escrow facilities are legal arrangements in which an asset is deposited into safekeeping (here, an account with the Bank of England) pending satisfaction of contractual contingency or condition. Once the condition has been met, the escrow agent delivers the asset to the relevant party in accordance with the contract.

[63] See CPSS (1996) for full details of the survey's findings and recommendations.

[64] While CPSS (2007a) reveals that great strides have been taken to mitigate foreign-exchange settlement risk, one third of foreign-exchange transactions continued to settle with principal risk in 2006.

[65] Before CLS was established, several bilateral and multilateral netting arrangements had been in place, e.g. ECHO and Multinet. See CPSS (1996) for details.

[66] For more details of CLS risk management see Annex 4 of CPSS (2007a).

Box 5.2: THE CONTINUOUS LINKED SETTLEMENT SYSTEM (CLS)

CLS facilitates payment-versus-payment settlement of FX transactions. Like other payment systems, CLS supports a tiered membership structure. Direct (or 'settlement') members submit trades to CLS Bank (CLSB) on behalf of themselves and their customers, and are responsible for funding them. Indirect (or 'user') members can also submit trades directly to CLSB, but rely on a settlement member to fund settlement. Finally, 'third parties' select a settlement or user member to submit trades on their behalf. We focus on settlement members in our description of the risks in FX settlement.

Trades must normally be submitted to CLSB by the start (midnight Central European Time, CET) of the settlement day. From 07:00 CET onwards, trades settle gross on the members' accounts at CLSB: CLSB simultaneously debits the settlement bank's account by the amount of the 'sell' currency and credits the purchaser's settlement bank's account by the amount of the 'buy' currency. In the process, settlement members accumulate negative balances in those currencies in which they and their customers are predominantly sellers, and positive balances in those in which they are predominantly buyers. Settlement of all trades submitted is normally completed by 09:00 CET.

While FX trades are settled on a gross basis, members provide funds to CLSB on the basis of the multilateral net short positions they are expected to have across all trades and currencies held in their accounts. This reduces the liquidity demands on settlement members. Nevertheless, principal risk remains (virtually) eliminated by the requirement that the sum of each member's overall account balances is positive. When aggregating the balances of different currencies, CLSB guards against adverse changes in exchange rates by undervaluing the member's long positions, and overvaluing its short positions. (Technically speaking, CLSB applies 'haircuts'.) In addition, CLSB limits the sum of a member's negative balances across all currencies, ignoring any currencies in which the member has a positive balance.

Liquidity demands on settlement members are further reduced by the use of so-called 'in/out swaps'. A member with a negative balance in one currency in CLS buys this currency against a currency in which it has a positive balance in CLS. This trade settles *outside of* CLS. The member now concludes exactly the opposite trade for settlement *in* CLS. Because the trades exactly offset, the member's overall FX position remains unchanged, while the net balance in CLS is reduced. However, in/out swaps reintroduce some principal risk as one leg of the swap settles outside of CLS.

---

alternative means of settlement through correspondent banking networks. They show that CLS may act as an 'escrow agent', able to impose greater penalties for non-performance than could be imposed through bilateral arrangements. Thus, in their model, CLS reduces banks' incentives to (strategically) default between the day of transaction and the settlement date (typically two days later) should the value of the trade turn against the trader. The mechanism is also shown to reduce the potential for co-ordination failures where expectations of failure to settle become self-fulfilling (e.g. as highlighted in the Drexel case described in Box 5.1). In addition, by introducing arrangements whereby all of a bank's trades can be rejected, it removes any incentive to default selectively on a subset of trades.[67]

Renault *et al.* (2007) investigate the degree to which PvP settlement links the execution of payments in the participating national payment systems. Their model consists of two symmetric RTGS systems, each settling payments in a different currency. The two RTGS systems are linked through a few large 'global banks' that are direct participants in both systems and trade foreign exchange with each other. Each RTGS system processes its own local currency payments, as well as the local-currency legs of the foreign-exchange transactions executed by the global banks.

Payment flows are modelled as links between participants. The assignment of links is random. The arrival of payment instructions to the banks is modelled as a Poisson process, and is a function of a bank's deposit base. In one version of the model, the settlement of foreign-exchange transactions is uncoordinated. In the second version, PvP settlement is imposed; that is, the settlements of each of the two associated currency flows occur simultaneously.

When settlement of foreign exchange is on a non-PvP basis, intraday credit exposures arise between the global banks active in foreign-exchange settlement. If both systems are liquidity rich, all transactions, including those associated with foreign-exchange trades, settle immediately, and the duration of the credit exposures is negligible. The lower the liquidity in a system, the later settlement occurs, and the longer the exposures last. The authors show that this duration can be reduced when higher priority is given to the settlement of foreign-exchange transactions. Of course, no credit exposures arise when PvP settlement is imposed.

Another measure of the link between the two systems is the degree to which payment instructions are queued because banks do not have sufficient liquidity to settle them. When settlement of foreign-exchange transactions is uncoordinated, there is no correlation between the sizes of the queues in the two systems. In contrast, when PvP settlement is imposed, correlation arises when liquidity is scarce in at least one of the systems:

---

[67] Kahn and Roberds (2001b) also examine the incentives CLS gives to banks when deciding whether to trade with risky counterparties. By eliminating principal risk, PvP makes banks less concerned about the risk profile of their counterparties (provided they are also CLS members). However, in a PvP system without a central counterparty replacement-cost risk remains. Hence, some incentives for monitoring are preserved.

settlement can only occur if sufficient liquidity is available in *both* systems to settle the associated payments. Again, higher priority of foreign-exchange transactions reduces the importance of this link because, quite independent of the available liquidity, foreign-exchange transactions are not queued.

Thus, Renault *et al.* (2007) show that, notwithstanding its important risk reduction benefits, the introduction of CLS has contributed to greater interdependencies between participating national payment systems. Looking ahead, such interdependencies pose a key challenge for payment-system overseers (see Chapter 11).

5.2 Settlement risk in securities settlement systems

The processing of securities trades can create similar credit exposures to those arising in the settlement of foreign-exchange transactions. As both parties to a securities trade are typically required to fulfil an obligation, with one delivering a quantity of a specific security and the other making a cash payment, both principal and replacement cost risk can arise in the event of a failure to settle. The importance of the risks arising from settlement of securities trades was highlighted when the worldwide collapse of equity prices in October 1987 exposed weaknesses in the settlement arrangements for securities markets. This prompted both industry groups and central banks to recommend enhancements to the management of settlement risk in securities settlement systems.

The key risk-mitigating innovation within securities settlement systems has been the introduction of delivery-versus-payment (DvP). A DvP mechanism aims to create the strongest possible link between the securities and cash legs of a transaction, thereby eliminating principal risk in a manner analogous to a PvP mechanism for FX transactions.

CPSS (1992) identifies three distinct models of settlement that can be adopted by securities settlement systems to provide DvP for securities transactions. These models are:

- **Model 1:** systems that settle transfer instructions for both securities and funds simultaneously on a trade-by-trade (gross) basis;
- **Model 2:** systems that settle securities transfer instructions on a trade-by-trade basis, but settle funds-transfer instructions on a net basis at the end of the processing cycle;

- **Model 3:** systems that settle transfer instructions for both securities and funds on a net basis, with final transfers of both securities and funds occurring at the end of the processing cycle for equities.

In systems using Model 1 or Model 3, DvP is achieved by ensuring simultaneous processing of both cash and securities legs. By contrast, under Model 2, a more complex design is needed to enforce a link between the gross securities legs and the net cash payment leg. CPSS (1992) discusses these approaches in detail and concludes that all three can eliminate principal risk, but each approach can still potentially give rise to other forms of settlement risk. This arises from the need (and potential inability) on the part of participants to fund either or both the securities and the cash leg of the transaction: i.e. liquidity risk. Moreover, DvP settlement does not eliminate replacement-cost risk, the risk that a counterparty defaults prior to settlement and the other party is forced to forgo any unrealized gain on the unsettled trade.

Below, we discuss some of the key risk-management challenges arising from each model of DvP settlement.[68]

5.2.1 *DvP Model 1*

The requirement to settle both legs of a securities transaction individually and in real time can impose significant liquidity demands on banks. In response, banks might delay the settlement of securities. In the extreme, an instruction may not settle at all. To avoid these problems, securities settlement systems usually have arrangements in place to economize on liquidity usage.[69] The frictions that need to be overcome in designing these arrangements are similar to those in RTGS systems (discussed in detail in Chapter 4).

Banks have several sources of (cash) liquidity to settle their transactions, the first two of which have direct equivalents in large-value payment systems. First, at the start of the day, banks typically pledge collateral to the central bank in exchange for intraday funds. Second, security sales generate cash inflows, corresponding to incoming payments in payment systems. The third source, a process called 'auto-collateralization', is specific

---

[68] It should be noted that a number of major systems employ more than one settlement model. For instance, a system might run day-time settlement on a Model 1 basis and night-time settlement on a Model 3 basis.

[69] Liquidity is usually provided by the settlement agent, typically the central bank. However, in certain systems that settle in commercial bank money, for example the ICSDs, Euroclear and Clearstream, the provider of intraday liquidity will be the private settlement agent.

to securities settlement systems. When a bank has insufficient liquidity, the securities settlement system can automatically activate a repurchase agreement with the central bank, according to which the liqudity-short participant sells (or pledges) eligible securities to the central bank, which, in return, provides the participant with central bank funds. Auto-collateralization is made possible by the fact that banks' central-bank eligible collateral typically resides in accounts held at a securities settlement system. Under a variant of this mechanism, banks can use securities they are about to acquire as collateral with which to obtain funds to settle the purchase.[70] In some systems, intraday liquidity is generated automatically whenever an eligible transaction is settled, irrespective of the balance on the buyer's account. This is known as 'supply-driven' auto-collateralization. An alternative approach is to limit the creation of intraday liquidity to the settlement of those transactions for which additional liquidity is required – i.e. a 'demand-driven' approach.

But in securities settlement, liquidity constraints can also arise on the securities side: a party needs to have the securities in place in order to be able to fulfill its delivery obligations. If a party has entered into a trade, the settlement of which is contingent on the receipt of securities from a third party, the failure of that contingent trade to settle will have a knock-on effect. For example, a bank may have sold a security that it did not own, intending to borrow it before it had to deliver the security to the buyer in the securities settlement system. Or a trader might have bought and sold securities on the same day, in the expectation that both trades would settle on the intended settlement date. Failure to receive securities on the intended settlement date may result in the trader's inability to deliver securities, triggering a knock-on failure to settle. Such constraints may be particularly acute in a Model 1 system, in which the securities leg settles in real time, although the problem that a 'chain' of failures may arise from a single failed delivery is common to all models.

Devriese and Mitchell (2006) observe that a shortage of securities is potentially more difficult to overcome than a shortage of cash liquidity. The authors use a simulation approach to analyze the potential impact of the failure of the largest participant in a securities settlement system.[71] The study reveals that such a failure can trigger a persistent decline in

[70] This is the principle behind the self-collateralizing repo ('SCR') mechanism employed in CREST in the UK.
[71] As discussed earlier in this volume, several studies have analyzed the impact of such a default event on cash payment systems, but the issue has received less attention in the context of securities settlement.

settlement efficiency, lasting days or even weeks. An important source of persistence is the time lag between trade date and settlement date – typically two or three days for equities.

A key conclusion of the work, then, is that intraday provision of liquidity to participants in a securities settlement system can only go so far in promoting settlement efficiency, because it cannot alleviate problems caused by a shortage of securities.

The findings of Devriese and Mitchell are corroborated by empirical evidence presented in Fleming and Garbade (2005), which looks at the US Treasury securities market in the months following September 11, 2001. The World Trade Center attacks caused major disruptions to trading in the Treasury securities market, with greatly increased levels of settlement fails being observed for several weeks following the attack.[72] The data show that a single settlement failure in a particular security can generate a long and persistent chain of fails in that security.

To address this tendency, securities settlement systems often themselves rely on securities borrowing to alleviate securities shortages. Such borrowing may be centralized within the securities settlement system or may rely on the decentralized securities lending market. An intrinsic difficulty here is that the elasticity of supply of securities is much lower than that of cash liquidity. Issuers may retain a fraction of a securities issue, to be lent out with a view to alleviating a shortage, but this cannot be done on the same scale as intraday expansion of a central bank's balance sheet. In practice, most securities lending is carried out by custodian banks, drawing on large portfolios of securities held on behalf of their customers. The credit exposures generated through this lending then need to be managed, typically through collateralization by either cash or other securities.[73]

Securities borrowing – or in some cases buy-in – arrangements often form part of a broader settlement discipline regime, which may also entail financial penalties for participants failing to deliver on the intended settlement day.

Finally, recognizing that many trades are contingent and that the order in which trades settle can be important, DvP Model 1 systems today

---

[72] Here, an additional contributory factor was the fact that several actively traded securities were trading 'special' in the repo market following the attacks, meaning that incentives to borrow securities to avert a failure were greatly diminished.

[73] Securities lending transactions typically settle on a shorter cycle than standard exchange-traded transactions, often on the same day. When settled against cash or securities collateral, similar principal risk issues arise. To address such risks, cash-collateralized transactions should settle DvP and securities-collateralized transactions ideally DvD (delivery-versus-delivery). Some of these issues are considered in CPSS (2001b).

increasingly incorporate sophisticated queue-management and optimization functionality. This may involve the application of 'offsetting' algorithms that search for groups of linked transactions and settle them in a batch. Such functionality can significantly reduce disruption and delay arising from a shortage of cash or securities.[74]

5.2.2 DvP Model 2

Many of the frictions decribed above associated with real-time delivery of securities apply equally in Model 2 systems.

The ability to settle cash on a multilateral net basis at the end of the settlement cycle can in principle go some way towards reducing liquidity pressures on the cash leg of securities transactions in Model 2 systems. However, to ensure that the securities are indeed transferred with finality intraday – and hence that DvP is achieved – watertight safeguards need to be in place to guarantee that net settlement can be completed even in the event that a member fails to meet its funding obligations. Therefore, in practice, the impact of this model of settlement on liquidity frictions depends on the costs imposed by these safeguards.

The methods used to ensure the completion of net settlement in the event of a failure are the same as those discussed in detail in Section 3.2: that is, a combination of 'defaulter pays' (requiring *ex ante* posting of collateral to partially collateralize net debit positions), 'survivor pays' (establishing loss-sharing agreements, backed by a default fund) and the use of net debit caps to control the size of potential exposures. The securities settlement system may also establish lines of credit to alleviate any liquidity issues arising from delays in liquidating collateral in the event of a default.

5.2.3 DvP Model 3

Where both securities and cash transfers settle net at the end of the settlement cycle, liquidity pressure is lower and DvP is achieved through simultaneous settlement. However, to ensure that settlement can complete, safeguards similar to those discussed above for the Model 2 systems may be required for both the cash and securities legs of transactions

---

[74] Central queuing does not play exactly the same role as in hybrid payment systems (described in Chapter 4), because most transactions processed by an SSS are typically known at the start of the day, (e.g. equities are usually settled $T + 2$ or $T + 3$). Therefore, there is little benefit to be gained from offering incentives for earlier submission of payment instructions.

processed through the system. Alternatively, procedures for the back-out and rescheduling of a defaulter's transactions may be established, with these applied in such a way that the knock-on effects to other participants' liquidity demands are minimized.

5.3 Management of replacement risk in clearinghouses

A clearinghouse acts as a 'central counterparty' (CCP) when it interposes itself as a legal counterparty to both sides of transactions in a market, becoming the guarantor of the contractual commitments made by both counterparties. This contrasts with bilateral or decentralized clearing, where participants retain credit exposure to their trading counterparties until the settlement of all obligations is complete.[75]

CCPs initially emerged to support trade on futures (and other derivatives) exchanges. Moser (1998) traces the origins of futures clearing houses that exhibited all key aspects of modern CCPs to Europe, where they had been developed to support trading on commodities exchanges. In France, the so-called '*Caisses de Liquidation*' were established in the nineteenth century to support trading on commodities exchanges at Le Havre, Lille and Roubaix, as well as the sugar exchange in Paris. This model was first copied in the US by the Minneapolis Chamber of Commerce in 1891. As observed in Chapter 1, these arrangements were preceded by *interbank* clearinghouses, which were used to settle claims between banks arising from the provision of payment services.

For derivatives contracts (the general term for forwards, futures, swaps and options), counterparty default is especially important because the contracts defer the performance of a significant part of the obligations. For example, a futures contract obligates the seller (the short) to deliver the underlying (commodity or security) at a future date. And it obligates the buyer (the long) to deliver the agreed amount of cash at the future date in return for the underlying asset.[76] Since these contracts are, by their nature, subject to long pre-settlement periods, agents are exposed to 're-placement-cost risk', the risk that, before final settlement, the counter-

---

[75] We understand clearing to entail identifying and reconciling the obligations created by trades of two counterparties (either bilaterally or facilitated by an exchange), and administering any actions that need to be executed prior to final settlement as well as those needed to effect final settlement, e.g. through relaying instructions to securities settlement systems.

[76] In practice, futures contracts based on securities are sometimes settled in cash, so that only the difference between the price of the underlying and the futures price are exchanged between the parties.

party defaults and the trade has to be replaced – potentially at a loss. For exchange-traded contracts in particular,[77] agents may not be willing to carry such counterparty risk and hence central counterparty clearing emerged as a vehicle by which, through novation, the clearinghouse interposes itself as the buyer to every seller, and the seller to every buyer. In this way the CCP is able to guarantee the performance of the contract for both parties, who each retain a credit-risk exposure only to the CCP (Bernanke, 1990).

A further key benefit of a CCP is that it facilitiates 'settlement by offset'. This means that a firm can extinguish a position by entering into an equal and opposite trade with any other market participant. In the absence of settlement through the central counterparty, entering into an offsetting contract can neutralize market risk; but unless the offsetting contract is struck with the original counterparty, this comes at the cost of creating additional counterparty risk. With a central counterparty, settlement by offset allows both market risk and credit risk to be extinguished. Relatedly, by providing for multilateral netting of contracts, CCPs can help market participants to economize on the total cost of credit-risk protection compared to the cost of providing equivalent protection in bilaterally cleared markets (see Baer *et al.*, 2004).

Over time, central counterparties have expanded their operations beyond futures and options to a broader set of markets. For example, in the last decade CCP services have become commonplace for exchange-traded equities, and have also emerged for government debt, repos, interest-rate swaps and other over-the-counter (OTC) derivatives.

Indeed, the financial market stresses of 2007/08 revealed issues around the transparency of OTC derivatives markets and highlighted concerns arising from systemic dependence on a small number of highly interconnected market participants. Calls therefore intensified for greater centralization of the infrastructure supporting this market, including central counterparty clearing for a wider range of OTC products, such as credit derivatives.[78]

In September 2008, SwapClear, a central counterparty for interest-rate swaps operated by LCH.Clearnet, successfully managed the orderly default of one of its participants, Lehman Brothers Special Financing Inc., winding down a $9 trillion portfolio via a risk-neutralization and competitive

---

[77] When securities are traded on an exchange, market rules will typically allocate trades according to price and then time priority, irrespective of the identity and credit standing of the participants. Thus, exchanges facilitate anonymous trading, ensuring that each participant is equally willing to trade with each other participant of the exchange.
[78] Financial Stability Forum (2008). See Chapter 11.

auctioning process among SwapClear members. This episode underlined both the potential benefits of central counterparty clearing in the OTC derivatives market, and the importance of sound and well-tested default processes in less-liquid, bespoke markets.

A number of studies describe in more detail the key features of alternative clearing arrangements, and their historical evolution (Moser (1998); Hills *et al.* (1999); Kroszner (1999); Ripatti (2004), and Moser and Reiffen (2008)). They also identify the risks that arise in clearing arrangements, and describe the infrastructural innovations that have emerged to deal with them.[79] We discuss some of these issues below.

5.3.1 *Risk-management tools employed by CCPs*

The starting point is that, since the CCP takes on obligations to both the seller and the buyer in any transaction, it concentrates replacement-cost risk and therefore needs to have robust mechanisms in place to manage this risk. Empirically, these risk-management tools appear to have been successfully applied: cases of failures of central counterparties have been extremely rare (see also Box 5.3).

A central plank of the management of replacement-cost risk by CCPs is margining: the collateralization of the CCP's exposure to past and prospective future price movements.

The collateralization of prospective future price moves occurs via the imposition of an 'initial margin' requirement upon establishment of the trading position. Initial margin is typically set in relation to the price volatility of the contract traded and ensures that a daily price change will exhaust the initial margin only with a very low probability. Figlewski (1984) provides an early empirical study of the degree of coverage afforded by the margin levels set on stock and stock index futures. Day and Lewis (2004) follow a similar approach but recognize more explicitly how the margin structure determines endogenously the value of a trader's option to default strategically.[80] Various complications may arise in setting initial margin to achieve a set minimum level of coverage, including non-normal price-change distributions and non-linear portfolios of contracts (e.g. involving options). The various statistical approaches developed to deal with these issues are surveyed by Knott and Mills (2002).

---

[79] CPSS (2004) also gives a comprehensive overview of risks and risk-management issues arising in CCPs.

[80] That is, the authors assume that the trader could walk away from the trade if it were deemed profitable to do so.

Initial Position: contract value $1000   Price falls to $950 per contract

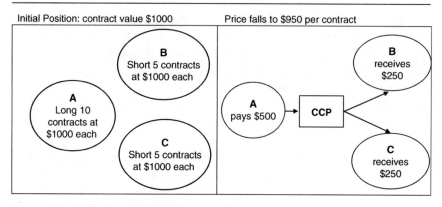

Figure 5.1: Collection and distribution of variation margin by a CCP

Past price movements are covered by the collection and distribution of 'variation margin', whereby CCP participants' positions are 'marked-to-market.' Participants with loss-making positions are required to pay in funds to the CCP, with these funds then distributed to those with profit-making positions.

For example, as shown in Figure 5.1, a trader (and member of the clearinghouse) (A) might be long 10 stock index futures that each obligate A to pay $1000 in exchange for a specific stock index in three months' time; two other members might be short 5 contracts each. If there is a price change such that the price of the index future falls to $950, the clearinghouse will collect $500 from trader A, whose position has lost $50 per contract, and disburse $250 each to members B and C, who have each gained $50 per contract. The payments collected and disbursed in this fashion are referred to as 'variation margin'. In this example, were A to default on its obligation to pay 500, the CCP would close out A's position and would itself be liable to make the payments to B and C. It would therefore be exposed to the cost of replacing the positions held by A, amounting to $500 in the example.[81]

---

[81] The procedure for settling daily gains and losses differs across CCPs. Some call automatically for variation margin and pay these funds to profit-making members. Others let the balance in a member's account adjust to reflect gains and losses until the balance in the account hits a 'maintenance margin level'. The member then receives a margin call and is instructed to restore the account back to the maintenance level, usually within a specified grace period. Failure to provide funds is typically deemed an event of default, resulting in the close-out of the member's position. See Knott and Mills (2002).

Another element of managing the replacement-cost exposure of the CCP is to mark positions to market relatively frequently, such that price movements that might occur in between markings are likely to be relatively small. However, marking to market carries administrative costs, such as valuing positions, notifying members of payment obligations and processing margin payments. In practice, marking is typically done once a day, with intraday margin calls occurring only in response to increased price volatility. Fenn and Kupiec (1993) offer further analysis of the trade-offs involved in setting the frequency of marking-to-market.

The CCP may also impose certain access conditions, for example requiring that any firm seeking to become a clearing member meets a threshold standard of creditworthiness. If such minimum standards are imposed, a tiered clearing structure may emerge, which will typically involve a chain of financial guarantees. For example, clearing members are obliged to guarantee the contracts entered into by their customers (Figlewski, 1984). The clearinghouse may further require both that margin be posted to the clearing member and that the clearing member post margin with the clearinghouse. Under such arrangements, the clearing member becomes the legal counterparty to the non-clearing member and the clearinghouse becomes the legal counterparty to the clearing member (Moser and Reiffen, 2008).

The final layer of protection against replacement-cost risk is typically for the CCP to require its members to make contributions to a default fund. Using these funds as an insurance pool, the CCP can mutualize its losses should margin prove insufficient and replacement-cost risk crystallize. The default fund may rely on clearing members' *ex-ante* contributions. It may also call on clearing members to make further contributions in the event of the default of a clearing member, should available resources be insufficient to cover the replacement costs. Losses may be shared equally, related to the trading volume of each participant, or – to encourage market discipline – weighted towards those that had traded most with the defaulting member (Hills *et al.*, 1999).

In the context of the clearing of multiple assets through a single CCP (e.g. multiple futures contracts based on different underlying securities), the pooling of margin may have important additional risk management benefits. These can be derived when an agent's margin payments in respect of multiple positions can be pooled, such that, in the event that the participant defaults on any one position, the CCP can draw on any residual margin in the pool (either from profitable or only modestly loss-making positions) to cover any margin shortfall arising on the loss-making position (Gemmill, 1994; Jackson and Manning, 2007b).

5.3.2 Risk-management trade-offs in central counterparty clearing

A number of studies examine analytically the trade-offs involved in managing replacement-cost losses and how these trade-offs in turn might be shaped by the type of clearing arrangement that is in place. Starting with Telser (1981), Figlewski (1984) and Fenn and Kupiec (1993) most of these studies recognize that protection against replacement-cost losses comes at a cost. In particular, posting of margin carries a positive opportunity cost for the trader. Moreover, a number of authors point out that, because margin carries opportunity costs, participation and liquidity in markets might fall when margins are excessively high.[82] Telser (1981) shows formally how an exogenous increase in the margin reduces the volume of trade and hence market liquidity. Hardouvelis and Kim (1995) provide

---

Box 5.3: FAILURES OF CENTRAL COUNTERPARTIES

Cases of failures of central counterparties have been extremely rare. Those documented by Hills *et al.* (1999) are the insolvency of Caisse de Liquidation (1974), the failure of the Kuala Lumpur Commodity Clearing House (1983) and that of the Hong Kong Futures Guarantee Corporation (HKFGC) (1987).

The latter case occurred during the stock market crash of 1987, when both the Hong Kong stock and futures exchanges were closed for four days. It was clear that the value of long positions in the Hang Seng index future would fall dramatically when the futures exchange reopened, which prompted fears that participants would default on margin calls. Indeed, the fear that the scale of losses would exceed the total reserves of the guarantee fund prompted the government and private institutions to prepare a rescue package for the fund.

Risk-management failings on the part of the clearinghouse were subsequently analyzed and addressed by a technical committee. This committee recommended that a central counterparty be re-established with at least a proportion of its risk resources comprising contributions by clearing members. This would give clearing members appropriate incentives to monitor the risk-management procedures of the CCP: so-called 'skin in the game'.

---

[82] Kupiec (1998) surveys a sizeable theoretical and empirical literature on the relationship between margin levels, trading volume and price volatility in the context of US Federal regulation (Regulation T), introduced in 1934 and extended in 1992, that gives power to the US authorities to prescribe minimum margins on leveraged purchases of securities as well as on margins set on stock index futures.

evidence that an increase in initial margin reduces the volume of trade. By examining 500 initial margin changes on eight metals futures contracts on the New York Commodity and Mercantile exchanges and the Chicago Board of Trade, Hardouvelis and Kim (1995) found that a 10% increase in initial margin reduced average volumes traded by 1.4%.

Baer *et al.* (2004) develop a model in which margin setting in bilateral clearing and the formation of clearinghouses are both motivated by the need of market participants to balance deadweight losses due to counterparty default against the opportunity cost of posting margin. They first argue that because one party's monetary losses from default are offset by monetary gains on the part of the defaulting party, only the deadweight losses of default (such as the cost of finding a new trading partner, drawing up a new contract, etc.) should enter the calculus. It is assumed that these costs are a constant fraction of the defaulted amount.

The authors are then able to establish that (initial) margin amounts are optimal when the opportunity cost of margin is equal to the probability of default times the deadweight loss of default. With normally distributed price changes, the coverage ratio, defined as the ratio of margin to the standard deviation of price changes, is a constant and should not itself vary with volatility. Moreover, when trades are cleared through a CCP, margin levels per unit of exposure will be the same as under bilateral clearing. However, under CCP clearing, multilateral netting of exposures means that margin needs to be applied only to the multilateral net exposure. This is shown to reduce the total amount of margin posted. Equally, since net exposures tend to be smaller than bilateral exposures, the total expected deadweight loss from default is smaller. In sum, the creation of a clearinghouse leaves no participant worse off and, if there are offsetting positions, lowers margin requirements and deadweight default costs, at least for some participants. Thus, the creation of the clearinghouse is Pareto improving.

In an extension, Baer *et al.* also show that, because of these benefits, and when traders expect to trade in more than one period, CCPs may credibly threaten to expel a member who strategically defaults on a contract.[83] This threat lowers traders' incentive to default opportunistically and can cause a trader to honour its contract even when the price change exceeds the posted margin. However, the authors point out that margin may still be

---

[83] Baer *et al.* (2004) point out that, in the nineteenth century, expulsion from the exchange was the principal mechanism for ensuring contract performance. Defaulters were barred from trading with any exchange member until they had settled with their creditors.

needed to protect against replacement-cost losses when default occurs for other non-strategic reasons.[84]

Building on the model by Baer *et al.* (2004), a study by Jackson and Manning (2007b) attempts to quantify the benefits of forming a CCP. This exercise may be important when the establishment of a CCP involves significant set-up costs, so that the CCP no longer always Pareto dominates bilateral clearing. In contrast to Baer *et al.* (2004), Jackson and Manning consider default to occur exogenously, with a probability that is independent of the value of the position of a trader. As in Baer *et al.* (2004), however, margin per unit of exposure continues to be a function of the opportunity cost of margin and the replacement-cost losses in the event of default.

Within this framework, Jackson and Manning show how the benefit of establishing a CCP varies with the number of traders. When trading positions are drawn from a normal distribution – so that for each pair of traders the bilateral position between trader i and trader j is as likely to be long as short – the netting ratio, defined as the ratio between the sum of all bilateral positions and the sum of the multilateral net positions across traders is increasing in the number, N, of traders, but at a decreasing rate. Since, as in Baer *et al.* (2004), the margin per unit of exposure is the same under bilateral clearing as under multilateral clearing, the collateral savings from multilateral netting are likewise increasing in N, but at a decreasing rate. In fact, under bilateral netting the expected total margin posted is larger than that under multilateral netting by a factor that is shown to equal the square-root of the number of any trader's trading parties $(N–1)$.

In an extension, Jackson and Manning also consider the implications of a product-specific CCP taking on the clearing of a second asset (e.g. a second futures product). In this case, margin posted by a trader on his position in one asset can be drawn upon when the trader defaults on his position in the other asset. Their simulation results demonstrate that the resulting margin-pooling benefits are substantial when the asset returns are uncorrelated, but that these benefits otherwise also depend on correlations in positions taken across the two assets.[85] Finally, Jackson and Manning (2007b) allow trader credit quality to vary and analyze agents'

---

[84] Indeed, the value traders attach to a continued operation of the CCP will make it possible for the CCP to extract from members *ex-ante* contributions to a default fund, which (unlike margin) may be independent of trading volume in any particular period. Very few studies analyze trade-offs that might arise in choosing the optimal mix of margin and default-fund contributions.

[85] The diversification benefits of margin pooling were foreshadowed in an earlier study by Gemmill (1994).

individual incentives to adopt particular clearing arrangements. They show that tiered clearing arrangements, where risky traders are not able to become members of the CCP, but must clear their trades through a more creditworthy member, may emerge naturally. Chapter 10 provides further discussion of tiered membership in central counterparties.

6

Other sources of systemic risk: operational and business risk

While the literature has tended to focus primarily on credit and liquidity risk in payment and settlement processes, it is clear that other sources of systemic risk – namely, operational and business risks in system providers – might also be important. Costs arising from crystallization of these risks can be particularly high if the provision of infrastructure is concentrated and rerouting of payments to a substitute system is not possible in the event of a failure. But costs can also be high if member-level responses affect activity and risk exposures in dependent markets; or if outages occur during stressed or high-volume periods, exacerbating nervousness in markets and triggering further uncertainty. This chapter focuses initially on the effects of operational shocks and how their impact might be contained. It closes with a brief discussion of issues around business risk and potential mitigants.

6.1 Operational risk

Operational risk can be defined as the risk of loss resulting from inadequate or failed internal processes and systems, from human error, or from external events, such as terrorist attack. The consequences of an operational shock will depend on its particular nature, and on which part of the network infrastructure fails.[86] We argued in Chapter 2 that settlement in (electronic and paper-based) payment systems improves welfare relative to cash-based systems: production and storage costs are lower, and they are

---

[86] See McPhail (2003) for a broader discussion on managing operational risk in payment, clearing and settlement systems.

less susceptible to theft. Payment systems also sustain the use of inside money, which can be put to productive use by the banking system. However, to reap these benefits, users need to be convinced that these payment systems are resilient to operational shocks.

The impact of an operational outage at the infrastructure level depends on a number of factors: whether other infrastructures are available as substitutes (and the settlement arrangements in these substitute systems); the response of market participants and the relevant authorities; and the degree of interlinkages with other systems. We will focus here on the first two issues; see Chapter 11 for a discussion of system interdependencies.

6.1.1 *Availability of substitutes*

The provision of infrastructure (computer hardware and software, network infrastructure, and messaging services) is subject to strong forces towards concentration. The higher the market share of an infrastructure provider, the more attractive its product becomes to potential new participants.

A similar network effect is observed in the software industry, among others. And it is also powerful for communications technology, as evidenced by the rise of the SWIFT messaging service used to transmit payments information.[87] Financial institutions participated in the development of the SWIFT messaging standards during 1974–1975, with SWIFT's messaging service then going live in 1977. At the time of writing, SWIFT is dominant, with a customer base of around 8000 users in 200 countries. Operational problems at SWIFT could severely disrupt financial markets. Box 6.1 discusses SWIFT's risk-control measures and central-bank oversight arrangements.

A second reason for concentration is that the provision of infrastructure services is characterized by increasing returns to scale and scope. Marginal costs are close to zero, and costs of increasing capacity relatively low, so competition among compatible providers can be fierce, at least in a transitory phase before a competitor exits the market.

Concentration and a lack of substitutes to an infrastructure provider's services create single-point-of-failure risk, increasing the potential impact of an operational shock on financial markets. In some circumstances, concentration may also increase the likelihood of operational or business risk. Fish and Willison (2008) investigate investment in the resilience of a system's network infrastructure. They maintain that an external, monopol-

---

[87] SWIFT is the Society for Worldwide Interbank Financial Telecommunication.

Box 6.1: OPERATIONAL RISK AND CENTRAL-BANK POLICY FOR PAYMENT
NETWORK INFRASTRUCTURES: THE EXAMPLE OF SWIFT

Payment and settlement systems rely on messaging services to transmit transaction-
related information – e.g. information on the payer, the payee, and the amount to be
transferred – quickly and reliably. SWIFT's market dominance can be explained by the
global reach (most financial institutions have a SWIFT connection) of the service, and
its high security and availability (99.996% in 2006), particularly in a business exhibiting strong network externalities. Large-value payments, securities transactions, and a
large proportion of foreign-exchange trades all rely heavily on SWIFT.

To ensure high resilience against operational shocks, SWIFT runs two operating
centres on different continents, one in the US and one in the Netherlands. Each is
capable of processing all SWIFT traffic. All messages on the most widely used SWIFT
service are replicated between these sites to minimize the risk of data loss. As insurance against a deliberate physical attack on both centres, SWIFT maintains a third site,
the location of which is confidential, which could be operational within 12 hours.

SWIFT is neither a payment nor a settlement system and, as such, is not formally
regulated by central banks or prudential supervisors. Nevertheless, it is recognized as
a 'single point of failure' in the global payments infrastructure: if its messaging
services became unavailable, the financial markets would be severely disrupted.
Consequently, the central banks of the G10 countries have agreed that SWIFT should
be subject to co-operative oversight by central banks, with a focus on the security,
operational reliability, business continuity and resilience of the SWIFT infrastructure.

As SWIFT is incorporated in Belgium, the National Bank of Belgium (NBB) is the lead
overseer. The NBB monitors SWIFT on an ongoing basis and identifies relevant issues
via the analysis of documents provided by SWIFT, supported by discussions with
SWIFT's management. The NBB also chairs the senior policy and technical groups
that facilitate the co-operative oversight and monitors the follow-up of any decisions
taken.

---

istic private system might choose to operate the payment system at a
higher level of risk than would be socially optimal. The authors show
that when the users of the system have different (and unknown) characteristics, a profit-seeking monopolistic provider might be unable to discrim-
inate between them, and hence also be unable to recover its expenditures on
system resilience. Consequently, it may invest too little in risk-mitigation
technology relative to the social optimum.[88] Such considerations motivate
the public sector's involvement in the oversight of systemically important
infrastructure providers (see Chapters 8 and 9).

Typical approaches to mitigate single-point-of-failure risks include: high
standards for project management, in particular when systems undergo an

---

[88] A (partial) solution to the problem is the emergence of a contestable market for payment
services. The threat of rival payment systems can induce the monopolist to increase investment in the quality of its product, i.e. in risk-mitigation technology.

upgrade; stringent risk-management procedures; and appropriate business-continuity plans to deal with external events.[89]

To guard against IT outages, back-up systems or other workarounds are typically required. However, contingency arrangements will often be unable to fully replicate the design and resilience features of the primary system.

For example, CHAPS, the UK's large-value payment system, ordinarily operates as a real-time gross settlement system, eliminating unintended credit-risk exposures arising in the settlement process. However, the contingency system, 'CHAPS By-Pass Mode', settles on a deferred net basis, thereby reintroducing the potential for credit exposures between settlement banks. And with a higher degree of manual intervention in these contingency arrangements, there is also increased risk of human error.

Member-level workarounds might also reintroduce risks that a system, in its normal operations, seeks to mitigate. For example, were the CLS system for foreign-exchange settlement (see Box 5.2) unavailable, banks would revert to bilateral arrangements via their correspondent banks. As a consequence, Herstatt risk (the principal risk arising when settlements in domestic and foreign currency do not occur simultaneously) would be reintroduced; i.e. the very risk that CLS was designed to mitigate. This would be particularly problematic if system outages were correlated with member fragility or distress.

Crisis-management exercises are increasingly seen as useful vehicles to explore *inter alia* the consequences of the operational failure of key infrastructure providers. One of the main benefits of such exercises is that they reveal whether existing contingency arrangements are adequate; whether they are adequately communicated; and whether they are based on realistic assumptions about member-level responses to the shock under consideration.

Box 6.2 provides some detail on a market-wide exercise conducted in the UK in 2006, which simulated the consequences of a flu pandemic: that is, an operational shock hitting human capital, rather than physical or financial capital. Financial infrastructure providers, such as payment and settlement service providers, appeared to be highly resilient to the particular characteristics of this crisis scenario, reflecting the high level of automation in their processes. Other countries, including the US and Australia, have since run similar exercises.

---

[89] See, for example, the European Central Bank's expectations regarding systemically important payment systems' business continuity planning in European Central Bank (2006).

Box 6.2: SIMULATION OF THE EFFECTS OF A PANDEMIC:
A MARKET-WIDE EXERCISE IN THE UK

The United Kingdom's prudential banking supervisor, the Financial Services Authority (FSA), leads the assessment of resilience and recovery among the key UK market participants and financial market infrastructure providers. One of the main conclusions of a survey of operational resilience in 2005 was the need for more co-ordinated testing. Institutions naturally find it easier to run exercises internally than to plan joint exercises with competitors, so the Bank of England, the FSA and the Treasury took a role in encouraging and delivering co-ordinated exercises.

One of the main business continuity initiatives in 2006 was a market-wide exercise, simulating 22 weeks of a flu pandemic. (See Bank of England *et al.* (2006) for details.) Seventy organizations from across the financial sector took part, including some that extended the exercise to include their overseas offices; in total around 3500 people were involved. The key objectives of the exercise were: first, to improve the sector's preparedness by providing each of the participants with an opportunity to review, test and update their plans for managing a pandemic threat; and, second, to assess whether there were any sector-wide issues that might need to be addressed collectively in order to improve the ability of the financial sector to cope with a pandemic.

The distinguishing feature of a pandemic is that its main impact is upon the availability of personnel rather than on physical assets. In order to simulate that impact, the scenario modelled a gradual increase in the overall level of absenteeism, rising from 15% at the start of the exercise to a peak of 49% at the height of the pandemic – with 'clusters' of absence taking the peak rate up to 60% in some business units. The main impact of these absence levels was to move firms' personnel-management policies to centre stage and subject them to increasing stress as absence levels rose. Firms were forced to examine a range of issues, such as: repatriation of staff from overseas locations; quarantine rules; certificates of sickness; use of vaccines; absence due to caring for children (following the closure of schools and crèches); voluntary absence (the 'fear factor'); bereavement counselling; dealing with financial hardship; and the fungibility of staff across business units. The home-working strategies of firms were also tested and many issues surfaced in relation to ensuring effective compliance and control over remote activity. IT security and support capabilities and health and safety issues came to the fore in this regard. The exercise also raised the question of whether the telecoms infrastructure would be able to support large-scale home working for a prolonged period when staff shortages in the telecoms sector also progressively eroded maintenance capability.

Across the financial sector as a whole, not surprisingly, the heaviest impact of the simulated pandemic was upon the more labour-intensive parts, notably the provision of customer-facing retail financial services, such as the distribution of cash. Although no overall cash shortage emerged during the exercise, there were bottlenecks. In addition, growing staff shortages forced the high-street banks to close an increasing number of branches, which reduced the availability of retail banking services to the public. Market infrastructure services, such as payment and settlement services, were less affected because they are highly automated. For example, the UK's large-value payment system, CHAPS, continued to function normally. There was pressure on market infrastructure providers to shorten the trading day and extend clearing and settlement times.

Regarding debit and credit cards, some participants were able to extend expiry dates as a workaround to the difficulty of issuing new cards due to postal delays. And in the wholesale markets, firms responded to the growing shortages of staff by reducing trading volumes. Proprietary activity, in particular, was sharply cut back as firms concentrated their resources on fulfilling customer-driven business and maintaining strong liquidity positions.

Case studies can also be informative about the consequences of an outage, as long as the design of the affected system – and the broad environment in which it operates – has not changed materially.

6.1.2 Simulation studies of participant-level operational outages

The way in which market participants respond to an operational outage is an important determinant of its ultimate systemic impact. This is particularly true when an outage occurs at participant level. For instance, when an individual settlement bank experiences difficulties in submitting payment instructions to the system, but can still receive payments, it can quickly become a 'liquidity sink' (i.e. liquidity becomes trapped in its account), potentially significantly disrupting liquidity recycling in the system.

A number of studies have attempted to simulate such 'outage' scenarios, making various assumptions about the identity of the stricken bank, the timing of the outage, and the responses of other participants in the system. These studies translate essential design features and simple behavioural rules into a simulation engine, measuring the impact of a participant-level operational shock using metrics such as the percentage of payments remaining unsettled at the end of the day (volume and value), the length of any delay to settlement, and the amount of additional liquidity ultimately required to effect settlement.

As discussed in Box 6.3, simulations may be run using either simulated or actual historical payments data. For studies of operational disruption, researchers have generally tended to work with historical data, thereby allowing them, for instance, to determine (*ex post*) the worst-case scenario (e.g. which bank, and at what time of day).

A number of central banks have conducted such studies. Bedford *et al.* (2004) provide the seminal paper for RTGS systems (see Box 6.3). They find that, in CHAPS Sterling, the United Kingdom's large-value payment system, an operational shock to one bank is unlikely to lead to the crystallization of liquidity risks at other banks. The key explanation is that CHAPS Sterling is sufficiently liquidity-rich to enable healthy banks to continue to make their payments. Schmitz *et al.* (2006) and Ledrut (2007) obtain similar results for the Austrian and Dutch large-value payment systems, respectively. Each of these papers uses historical data, the scenarios differing in terms of the number of banks affected by an operational shock, and in the responses of the stricken bank's counterparties.

Box 6.3: SIMULATION OF THE EFFECTS OF OPERATIONAL OUTAGES: BEDFORD *ET AL.* (2004)

Bedford, Millard, and Yang (BMY) apply a simulation approach with exogenous payments behaviour based on historical data from the UK's CHAPS Sterling system. In common with many other studies, they make use of the Bank of Finland's Payment and Settlement System Simulator. Important inputs for this programme are: the settlement mode; a set of payment instructions; and upper limits of liquidity available to each bank. Payment instructions can be random or imported from other sources. BMY do not have information on the time at which banks received their settlement instructions. They opt instead to use actual payment flow data as a proxy, essentially assuming that settlement banks submit payments as soon as they receive instructions from their clients.

The programme then checks whether each bank can settle its payments with the liquidity available, respecting the sequence of payments. Importantly, the pro-gramme allows the user to simulate a member-level operational outage by specifying that, from a certain point in time, a bank is unable to make further payments.

In a first step, BMY establish a benchmark simulation against which the results of simulations of operational events may be compared. For the purposes of establishing benchmark liquidity levels, the simulation permits all (twelve) CHAPS Sterling settle-ment banks to draw on unlimited amounts of intraday credit from the Bank of England (having started each day with zero account balances).

If no bank was liquidity constrained, the outage of a single bank would never prevent any other bank's payments from settling. Thus, all subsequent simulations are performed using a range of upper liquidity bounds. The largest upper bound corresponds to the amount of intraday credit a settlement bank needed in the benchmark simulation in order for all its outgoing payments to settle immediately upon their submission to CHAPS Sterling. The smallest upper bound refers to the amount required for the settlement bank just to cover its net outflow of funds across the day as a whole.

BMY consider a number of different scenarios. In each case, the operational failure is assumed to be both unanticipated and permanent; that is, of sufficient severity to preclude resumption of normal payment processing operations before the end of the business day concerned.

In the first scenario, a single bank is hit by an operational shock at the moment its account balance with the Bank of England reaches its peak, and is unable to make (but still able to receive) any payments thereafter. This is clearly a worst-case scenario: because the stricken bank is unable to make any further payments, other settlement banks, who may have relied on incoming payments from the stricken bank to finance their payments, may become unable to make their own remaining payments. BMY find that, unless settlement banks' upper liquidity bounds are low, non-stricken banks can still settle most of their payments.

In their second scenario, BMY assume that several settlement banks are simultaneously affected by an operational disruption. As might be expected, they find that the remaining banks are able to settle fewer payments by comparison with the first scenario.

In their third scenario, BMY assume that the central payment processing infrastructure is hit by an operational shock. In this case, payments are settled using a deferred net settlement system, subject to intraday credit caps to limit exposure to a single settlement bank's failure. In their simulations, the credit caps prevent the settlement of a single large payment. This, in turn, prevents the settlement of several other payments.

By contrast, Glaser and Haene (2008) find that the effect of an operational disruption can be large. They assume that a major participant in the Swiss RTGS system, SIC, is hit by an operational shock that lasts until the end of the settlement day, and that other participants continue to send payments to the stricken bank for the first two hours of the operational outage. As a result, on an average day, 22% of payment values would not be processed. This reflects a number of factors, including: the high degree of concentration in the Swiss system (the two largest participants account for roughly 50% of the value processed); the relatively low level of precautionary liquidity held by participants (in the absence of operational shocks, participants are able to settle about 14 Swiss francs worth of payments with a single franc of liquidity by recycling liquidity efficiently); and the assumption of a lagged response to the stricken bank's outage.

Under similar assumptions (outage lasting for the entire day, healthy banks reacting only two hours after the shock occurred), Lublóy and Tanay (2007) also find that a relatively large proportion of payments (about a third) would remain unsettled in the Hungarian large-value payment system. This is despite the fact that the system is liquidity-rich: the turnover ratio in VIBER is only 2.5.[90] Indeed, the authors find little change in the share of unsettled payments had healthy banks not reacted at all to the operational outage. Such variations in the assumptions on the behavioural response provide useful robustness checks in simulation studies: how banks might react in practice to extreme outages is uncertain, precisely

---

[90] See Magyar Nemzeti Bank (2005).

because they are only very rarely, if ever, observed. Particularly for these scenarios simulation studies can add substantially to insights gained from other empirical methods, such as econometric analyses.

Bech and Soramäki (2005a), in a study of the Danish large-value payment system, consider the application of gridlock-resolution mechanisms to mitigate disruption in the event that a large participant suffers an outage. When liquidity is scarce and sequential settlement is not possible, such procedures may be invoked to settle as many payments as possible simultaneously. The authors find that a gridlock-resolution mechanism is able to somewhat reduce the value of unsettled payments.

In another study by the same authors, Bech and Soramäki (2005b) offer an overview of the methods used to analyze risks in DNS systems. An example here is Mazars and Woelfel (2005), who conduct a study of the consequences of operational risk in the Paris Net Settlement (PNS) system. Based on historical payment flows, they assume that on a given day, the largest net debtor is unable to settle any payments at all. The authors consider a number of responses by other participants in the system. In particular, the authors consider alternative bilateral limits between participants. The size of bilateral limits determines the amount that a bank would pay away to a stricken bank before it ceased to make further payments. The authors conclude that, while the size of bilateral limits may have a negligible effect on settlement efficiency in normal times, low limits can significantly reduce the likelihood that a liquidity sink develops when a bank suffers an operational outage.

6.1.3 Market implications of operational outages

The importance of the responses to operational shocks goes beyond the response of participating settlement banks in large-value systems. Indeed, depositor confidence in a bank might be affected when the bank is unable, for operational reasons, to effect payments. When the stricken bank's retail customers are uncertain about the duration of the outage, good public relations management becomes key to avoiding the risk that customers attempt to withdraw their deposits from the stricken bank as soon as systems are back up again.

Participant-level operational problems that disrupt payment system activity may also have implications for dependent financial markets. For instance, Klee (2007) investigates the link between participant-level outages on the level and volatility of rates in the US Federal Funds market. As is true for many central banks, the Federal Reserve's deposit rate lies below its lending rate,[91] creating an active market for overnight funds. Participant-level outages that disrupt the flow of liquidity within the system therefore have the potential to affect the Fed Funds rate (the rate at which banks lend their reserves with the Federal Reserve to other banks). Disruption to payment flows may also increase uncertainty about end-of-day positions, affecting both the level and the volatility of the Fed Funds rate.

Klee does not have direct information about operational outages at settlement banks. Instead, she takes unusually long intervals between payment outflows from a bank as a proxy. Using observations from the period 1998–2005, Klee finds that both the level and volatility of the effective Federal Funds rate increase in response to operational problems. The increase in the rate is larger, the longer the duration of the outage, the later the outage occurs during the day, and the more active is a participant as a member of the system in normal times.

As noted, operational shocks at the central infrastructure can also affect conditions in other dependent markets, such as securities markets. Indeed, outages affecting key components of the infrastructure can have particularly severe consequences when uncertainty in financial markets is already high. In such situations, traders rely particularly heavily on: (i) the absence of credit risk in settlement; (ii) the quick execution of their orders; and (iii) up-to-date pricing information. To the extent that they cannot rely on these three elements, their willingness to trade may be reduced, potentially further amplifying price changes. Box 6.4 illustrates how otherwise minor operational problems may have exacerbated the stock market slide in October 1987.

6.1.4 *The authorities' response to operational disruption*

The simulation studies described in Section 6.1.2, above, assume that the central bank's behaviour remains unchanged in the face of an operational shock. This may not be so. Because the central bank determines the terms on which it will make central-bank liquidity available to system participants, its response is crucial to the ultimate outcome.

---

[91] The Federal Reserve used to pay a zero rate on deposits, since it was prohibited by law to pay positive interest on funds. This rule has changed from October 2008, when the Federal Reserve started to pay interest on reserves at the target rate – still below the rate it charges when lending overnight through its discount window.

Box 6.4: BLACK MONDAY 1987

On Monday 19 October 1987, the US stock market experienced the largest one-day decline in its history. In a single day, the Dow Jones Industrial Average fell by 22.6%, while the S&P 500 futures index declined by 29%. Trading volumes were much higher than usual and key infrastructures hit their capacity limits. More than a tenth of trades remained unmatched, twice more than usual.

Uncertainty increased when Fedwire, the US RTGS system, had to shut down for a period on the following day due to a programming error. On both days, rapid market movements made it difficult for institutions to judge the solvency of their trading counterparties. Twice as many trades as normal were queried as a result.

The adverse price movements led to successive intraday margin calls from central counterparties as they revalued their positions using current market prices. However, many customers found themselves short of funds, with banks reluctant to lend. Consequently, margin calls were met several hours behind schedule, leaving central counterparties uncovered.[92]

Kleidon and Whaley (1992) argue that a series of technical failures at the NYSE meant that orders were only processed more than an hour after being submitted. Prices did not therefore reflect the prevailing state of demand and supply, further increasing uncertainty.

The crash came to a halt when the US Federal Reserve injected funds. The Fed also encouraged banks to lend, promising support if necessary. In the end, three clearing-house members defaulted in the US, resulting in about $9mn of losses – a relatively small amount, considering the magnitude of the shock.

For instance, the central bank may extend the opening hours of the payment or settlement system to allow operational problems to be fixed. Or, if the problems persist, the central bank may reduce the cost of overnight borrowing, or relax collateral requirements (see Chapter 4), to facilitate the settlement of outstanding payment instructions by healthy banks.

By way of example, Box 6.5 describes the different measures employed by the Federal Reserve in response to operational disruption arising from the attacks on the World Trade Center in September 2001.

McAndrews and Potter take a closer look at how the disruption affected the degree of co-ordination of payments in Fedwire. The authors' starting point is that, as far as possible, banks seek to make their payments using incoming funds rather than daylight credit from the Federal Reserve: that is, banks seek to co-ordinate their payments (see Section 4.1). The authors show that co-ordination declined on the days following the terrorist attacks: the coefficient on incoming payments was much lower than in a benchmark period. This might be explained by two factors. First, banks may have faced greater uncertainty about their counterparties' payments

[92] See, e.g., Eichenwald (1988) for details.

Box 6.5: PAYMENT SYSTEM DISRUPTIONS AND THE RESPONSE OF THE FEDERAL RESERVE FOLLOWING THE ATTACK ON THE WORLD TRADE CENTER ON 11 SEPTEMBER 2001

Lacker (2004) investigates the monetary and payment system consequences of the attack on the World Trade Center on 11 September 2001. The following facts are drawn from his paper.

Both US large-value payment systems, the Federal Reserve's Fedwire Funds Transfer System and the Clearing House Interbank Payments System (CHIPS), continued to function. Nevertheless, payments occurred significantly later in the day, and intraday overdrafts were significantly larger. This appears to have reflected two specific factors: operational problems at the Bank of New York (BoNY), which usually processes a substantial portion of the payments that flow across Fedwire, and increased uncertainty about incoming payments.

Because payments are initiated by the sender of funds in Fedwire, BoNY's connectivity problems only affected its ability to send payments; it could still receive. This led to an increase in its account balance with the Federal Reserve. At one point during the week after 11 September BoNY was publicly reported to be due to make $100bn worth of payments. Balances in the rest of the banking system were correspondingly lower.

In addition, several Federal Funds brokers were disabled in the attacks and could not resume operations until the following Monday. Hence, banks with excess balances found it difficult to locate borrowers. About 800 banks experienced a noticeable increase in their account balances. The general disruption in payment flows would also have increased uncertainty for many banks as to when scheduled incoming payments would be received. Overall, the volume of payments processed over the Fedwire funds transfer and securities systems fell sharply on 11 September.

Response by the Federal Reserve

The Federal Reserve eased the availability of both intraday and overnight credit in the days following 11 September.

McAndrews and Potter (2002) argue that the design of the Federal Reserve's intraday credit policy gives settlement banks an incentive to co-ordinate their payments to a specific time of the day (see Section 4.1). Under greater uncertainty about other participants' ability to make payments, settlement banks may have preferred to delay or even withhold payments in order to avoid charges for intraday credit – and for overnight credit should other banks have failed to fix their operational problems before the end of the settlement day. (If banks fail to cover a negative reserve account balance with the Federal Reserve by the time Fedwire closes this account balance becomes an overnight overdraft and a penal rate of interest is charged.)

The Federal Reserve's policy response in the aftermath of the attacks reduced this incentive to delay payments. In particular, intraday overdraft fees, and the penalty on overnight overdrafts for depository institutions, were waived from 11 September through 21 September. In addition, the Fed extended Fedwire closing times on the days following 11 September.

(continued)

Box 6.5: (Continued)

Two other measures also helped to facilitate access to overnight credit: an injection of liquidity via repurchase agreements; and an extension of credit via the discount window. Both are essentially forms of collateralized lending to the banking sector but differ in their dependence on individual banks' operational availability. Repurchase agreements are concluded with (primary) dealers in US government securities. Settlement takes place on the books of BoNY or JP Morgan Chase (JPMC), since all of the primary dealers clear through one of those banks. An injection of funds thus increases the banking system's balances in the first instance by increasing the account balances of BoNY or JPMC. Those new balances are then reallocated throughout the banking system during the day as banks send payments to other banks and borrow and lend in the interbank fed funds market.

The distribution of liquidity through repurchase agreements to the banking sector relies on the functioning of the interbank market, and in particular primary dealers' (operational) ability to pass on the liquidity to other banks. In contrast, the Federal Reserve's second policy tool, lending through the discount window, enables banks that find themselves short of liquidity to borrow directly from the Federal Reserve.

Banks made extensive use of the facilities provided by the Federal Reserve. On 12 September, the Fed added $38bn via overnight repos, rising to $70bn and $81bn on the following two days. Overnight borrowing via the discount window reached $37bn on 11 September, and $46bn and $8bn on the following two days, before falling back to zero on September 14. The total balances of the banking system increased from $13bn on September 10 to $121bn on 13 September before falling rapidly back to around $15bn in the following week.[93]

---

behaviour. Second, more flexible credit policies by the Federal Reserve may have reduced the incentive to co-ordinate payments.

6.2 Business risk

As is the case with every other private-sector company, payment and settlement systems in private ownership are subject to business risk. Business risk may crystallize under a number of circumstances, including that in which a payment system provider is engaged in other – perhaps unrelated – business activities and suffers losses in those activities. Ultimately, the crystallization of business risk can result in the closure of the payment system, potentially imposing costs on both system participants and the wider economy via a disruption to transactions.

For systemically important infrastructures, private incentives to control business risk may not be perfectly aligned with social incentives. Moreover, important system providers may perceive themselves to be 'too

---

[93] See McAndrews and Potter (2002), Table 1, for details.

systemic to fail': their incentives may be skewed if they expect to be able to rely on public intervention in the event that they run into financial difficulties. The perception of implicit insurance by the public sector may encourage infrastructure providers to engage in riskier business activities than would be socially optimal, a problem that may be particularly acute if the providers are also engaged in activities unrelated to payments, in respect of which they may be under less regulatory scrutiny.

A number of controls may be put in place to increase resilience against business risk:

• Imposition of a capital-adequacy requirement to ensure a buffer against financial losses.

• Legal separation of the key assets necessary to operate the infrastructure from other parts of the provider's business so as to prevent access by creditors should those other parts of the business fail.

• Imposition of regulatory restrictions on the business activities of the infrastructure provider outside the provision of infrastructure services. An example here is CLS Bank (see Section 5.1). CLS Bank is subject to strict regulation imposed by a co-operative of overseers led by the Federal Reserve Bank of New York as regards the business activities in which it can engage outside the provision of settlement services for the foreign exchange market.

Should an infrastructure provider, notwithstanding risk-control measures taken, fall into financial difficulties (or otherwise be unable to continue to provide its service), it is important that the continuity of services is ensured. So-called 'step-in rights' can permit the payment scheme[94] to direct the infrastructure provider to take a particular action. It might also be possible to transfer the existing systems to a new institution and support it with a capital injection. Such a transfer may be facilitated if the necessary legal arrangements are already in place, and financing of the new institution has been secured in advance. Finally, payment-system participants may be willing to agree *ex ante* to extend a capital line to a new infrastructure provider.

Thus, capital can not only reduce the probability of insolvency, but also mitigate the impact of insolvency by ensuring continuity of payments and settlement during the transition to installation of a new provider. Capital

[94] A payment scheme is the body that defines and enforces the payment system's rules (e.g. membership requirements) about how payments are processed. It is typically separated from the (technical) infrastructure necessary to execute the payments. See Chapter 8.

requirements may be complemented by liquidity requirements to cover operating costs during the transition period.

An example in this regard is the 'New Bank' proposal. Major participants in the US government securities market depend critically on two commercial banks (Bank of New York and JP Morgan Chase) to settle trades and facilitate the financing of positions. In 2005, the Federal Reserve endorsed a recommendation for the creation of a dormant bank (New Bank), which could be activated to clear and settle US government securities in the event that one of the incumbent providers was forced to exit and no well-qualified bank stepped forward to purchase the exiting bank's business. The scenarios triggering exit include a credit or legal problem that undermined confidence in the bank's ability to continue providing its services. Upon activation, all critical clearing-bank functions would be performed by New Bank under a service-level agreement with the exiting clearing bank.

Part III

Public-policy intervention in payment and settlement systems

In Part II we discussed a number of examples of public-policy intervention in payment and settlement systems, in the context of the mitigation of specific risks arising in such systems. In Part III, we first rehearse the general motivation for public intervention in payment and settlement systems and then go on to discuss a variety of forms public-sector intervention may take.

First, Chapter 7 discusses how the provision of infrastructures may be subject to market failures, such as systemic externalities and inefficiencies in pricing and quality of service.

Chapter 8 then reviews the different forms public intervention may take in response and what this implies for the general governance of payment systems. In particular, the following alternative forms of intervention are considered: public ownership; targeted intervention or 'oversight'; and mutual ownership with a high degree of self-regulation. These models vary in terms of the intensity of public intervention and each creates its own practical challenges.

Finally, Chapter 9 discusses central-bank oversight arrangements, describing how these have come to be guided by commonly accepted international standards. The chapter closes with an overview of central-bank oversight in practice.

7

Market failures in payment and settlement systems

Given the importance of payments and financial market infrastructure for the real economy, it is unsurprising that public authorities have taken a close interest in their development. This chapter briefly reviews the market failures that have led to close public-sector involvement in the provision of financial market infrastrucure, some of which have been examined already in Part II of this book. The various forms of public-sector intervention are then described in more detail in Chapter 8.

7.1 Market failures: implications for systemic risk

We defined systemic risk in Part II as 'the risk that the failure of one participant in a transfer system, or in financial markets generally, to meet its obligations will cause other participants or financial institutions to be unable to meet their obligations (including settlement obligations in a transfer system) when due' (CPSS, 2003c). We went on to explore in detail the circumstances in which payment and settlement systems may be the source of systemic risk, observing that such risk is rooted in externalities that arise when agents do not fully consider the costs imposed by their actions on other agents within the financial system.

Millard and Saporta (2007) and Jenkinson and Manning (2007) consider potential sources of systemic risk externalities arising in payment and settlement systems. They identify externalities arising from (operational) failure at the level of the system itself and externalities arising from the beliefs or behaviours of participants within the system, which might themselves be influenced by the design of the system. Building on these contributions, these externalites may be broadly categorized as follows: (i) externalities arising from interactions between participants within a system; and (ii) externalities arising from interactions either between systems or between a system and the rest of the economy.

In respect of interactions between participants of a payment system, the precise way in which systemic risk may manifest itself depends crucially on the design of the system and the environment in which it operates. For instance, the design may give rise to settlement-related risk exposures between participants; with limited liability, a bank may not take into account the consequences of its own insolvency on system participants when deciding on its balance-sheet structure and level of business risk. Such issues are considered in Chapter 3.

Equally, system design may generate incentives for liquidity-driven strategic interactions between participants, which may have implications for system-wide liquidity risk. If the benefit that incoming payments convey on the recipient remains unremunerated, making a payment constitutes a positive externality (see Chapter 4).

Finally, as discussed in Chapter 6, operational shocks at the level of a payment-system participant can disrupt the flow of liquidity within a payment system, potentially delaying the settlement of payments even between healthy banks. But these costs are external to the stricken bank and, since it is difficult to quantify the costs of such delays and therefore to design an appropriate financial penalty, there is a risk that settlement banks may undervalue the successful and timely transmission of payments and underinvest in the resilience of their internal systems to operational shocks.

As regards interactions between systems, the (financial or operational) failure of a single payment or settlement system can have consequences for other related payment systems, and for financial markets more generally. For example, as described in Chapter 2, securities settlement systems typically achieve ultimate cash settlement in the large-value payment system. And if the securities settlement system ceased to function for a prolonged period, trading in financial markets at large would be affected. Chapter 11 discusses in more detail the effects of increased system interdependencies.

The severity of the impact of a payment system failure, and hence the extent of systemic risk, depends critically on whether substitutes are readily available to allow payment flows to be rerouted via another system. As discussed in Chapter 6, the economics of payment services tends to favour concentrated provision where few if any competitors will be viable.

One reason is that the provision of payment and settlement services is characterized by high fixed costs and low marginal costs – and hence increasing returns to scale. Hancock *et al.* (1999) estimate that a 1% increase in the number of Fedwire transfers leads to an increase in the total cost of Fedwire operations of at most 0.5%. Moreover, the greater the volume of trade settling through a particular system, the greater the opportunities for netting and liquidity recycling.

Put differently, there are postitive network externalities. Together, these characteristics imply a tendency towards concentrated provision of payment and settlement services. This in turn reduces the availability of substitutes and can lead to 'single-point-of-failure' risks. Faced with a prolonged disruption (or frequent disruptions) to the operation of a single provider of payment and settlement services in a particular market, there is unlikely to be an alternative provider to which users will readily be able to reroute volume. Trades may then remain unsettled for a period, either imposing direct losses (for instance where the intended recipient of funds was relying on timely settlement, perhaps to meet another obligation), or creating unintended credit or market exposures. Alternatively, users may seek workarounds, reverting to other – perhaps bilateral – settlement arrangements, with attendant costs and risks.

7.2 Market failures: implications for efficiency

Market failures may not only manifest themselves in systemic risk externalities. Rather, they may more generally impede efficient provision of services. Such considerations may attract public-policy interest, though where intervention is deemed appropriate, this will often fall to the competition authorities rather than the central bank.[95] In this regard we will provide only a brief overview and refer the reader to more detailed surveys such as Joskow (2007).

---

[95] Australia is one country in which the central bank has clear statutory responsibility for competition and efficiency in payment systems. This responsibility is executed via the Payments System Board, which was established in 1998. In accordance with the Reserve Bank Act 1959, the Payments System Board determines the Reserve Bank's payments system policy so as to: control risk in the financial system; promote the efficiency of the payments system; and promote competition in the market for payments services. In establishing the Payments System Board, the Government also afforded the Reserve Bank additional powers under the Payment Systems (Regulation) Act 1998 to pursue its efficiency mandate.

As noted above, payment and settlement systems are typically characterized by increasing returns to scale and the presence of network externalities. Both characteristics can increase the market power of the incumbent provider, leading to inefficiencies in the pricing and quality of service and stifling innovation. Network externalities can also discourage compatibility between different networks.

Increasing returns to scale and network externalities make it difficult for new payment services to enter the market. By definition, new entrants do not (yet) have a large enough market presence to be attractive to users. And they must fear being unable to recoup their set-up costs, if they fail to attract a large enough customer base. Since this barrier to entry may be difficult to overcome, an existing customer base confers market power to incumbents. If this market power is exploited, economic welfare may fall. An increase in market power may not only raise the price of payment services, but may also reduce the quality of services provided. Lower quality can in turn lead to higher risk. In this sense, high market power can be detrimental to both efficiency and financial stability (see Allen *et al.*, 2007).

Second, payment-service providers may have an incentive to protect their market power and ensure that barriers to entry remain high. This may leave a payment-service provider with a reduced incentive to ensure interoperability and compatibility between its own system and potentially competing systems. Interoperability can have two opposing effects on providers' profits (Matutes and Padilla, 1994). If users can – through interoperability – benefit from a larger total pool of liquidity, users' valuation of and willingness to pay for the service may increase. On the other hand, with compatibility, any particular provider cannot derive market power from the size of its own customer base or extract an economic rent, which is likely to drive down profits. If the latter effect dominates, payment-system providers may oppose compatibility and obstruct interoperability even when these would be welfare enhancing. Indeed, it is easy to see that compatibility and interoperability will tend to increase welfare, for two reasons: first, precisely because it reduces payment providers' market power; and second, because it reduces single-point-of-failure risks.

The third consequence of network externalities is that they may discourage innovation. The reason is organizational in nature. Innovations often require investments not only to the central infrastructure, but also to banks' access infrastructure. In practice, negotiations about the distribution of investment costs can be complicated and may sometimes delay the implementation of innovations.

8

Ownership, governance and regulation of payment systems

The likely existence of market failures in payment and settlement systems, discussed in Chapter 7, implies that some form of public-sector intervention may be needed. But the optimal intensity of such intervention is considerably less certain.

In this chapter, we discuss the alternative governance and regulatory models that might be brought to bear to address market failures in the provision of payment services. We interpret the term 'governance' relatively widely as the distribution of rights and responsibilities of the board, managers, shareholders and other stakeholders, including the rules and procedures for making decisions on organizational matters.[96]

We consider three broad governance and regulatory models: public ownership (Section 8.1); regulation and oversight (Section 8.2); and private mutual ownership (Section 8.3). The reader is also referred to Millard and Saporta (2007), who provide an assessment of the costs and benefits of various forms of central-bank intervention in payment systems. We then offer, in Section 8.4, some thoughts as to which public authority might be best placed to intervene. Challenges for public-sector intervention emanating from the evolution of the payments landscape are discussed in Chapter 11.

---

[96] The corporate governance structure can thus be interpreted as a solution to a principal-agent problem, in which multiple principals (shareholders, creditors, clients, employees) have different preferences over the firm's manager's actions, and in which the manager has private information and his actions are only imperfectly observable. Becht *et al.* (2002) provide an overview of the literature on corporate governance; Tirole (2001) discusses the issues more formally.

8.1 Public ownership and subsidization of payment systems

Public ownership is the most direct vehicle for public-sector influence over risk mitigation in payment systems. Through investments in risk-mitigating technology, a public owner can fully internalize systemic risk externalities, avoiding the agency problems – e.g. asymmetric information – associated with monitoring a regulated entity. Occasionally, authorities perceive public ownership as an intermediate step to establishing a system that, perhaps due to co-ordination failures, the private sector has failed to provide. Box 8.1 provides an example.

But the scope of public ownership will generally be limited to the common components of the payment system: settlement banks typically remain responsible for their own access systems and for the quality of their liquidity management more generally.

Box 8.1: PUBLIC-SECTOR INVOLVEMENT IN THE CREATION OF A NEW SECURITIES SETTLEMENT SYSTEM IN THE UNITED KINGDOM

Norman (2007) argues that CREST was built to overcome a co-ordination failure in the private sector. In 1993, the London Stock Exchange announced that it was abandoning its project to build a new securities settlement system, Taurus. The *Financial Times* reported that the project had cost 'hundreds of millions of pounds', and asked: 'The short-term self-interest of particular groups helped to turn the Taurus project into a technologist's nightmare. Where is the leadership in the City to prevent the same thing happening again?'[97]

In response, the Bank of England created a task force that recommended the creation of a new settlement system. The system, which later became CREST, was to offer electronic book-entry transfer across the market, operating with a short rolling settlement cycle. According to Norman (2007), the Bank was well placed to develop this new system, given its experience with previous settlement projects, and because it could use its authority and influence to establish consensus among market participants.

The Bank of England declared that it had no intention to own or operate the system, since it believed that CREST 'should be a utility service and would best be owned by its users'.[98] The Bank preferred ownership to be 'broadly based to preclude dominance by any sector or single organisation within the industry'.

In 1994, 69 shareholders from across the equity market provided the initial capital for CRESTCo that funded the development of CREST. In order to maintain control during the development phase, the Bank of England held the only voting shares until the launch of the system in 1996. In 2002, CRESTCo joined the Euroclear Group.

---

[97] *Financial Times*, 19 March 1993, p. 11: 'Sudden death of a runaway bull – The Taurus project was blighted by misjudgment, mismanagement and neglect'.
[98] Bank of England (1994), p. 130.

Also, public ownership may not always be feasible, even if it is desirable. For instance, public ownership of a system may not be an option where the system operates across borders. One example in this regard is CLS, the cross-border settlement system for foreign-exchange transactions.[99] The regulatory alternative applied in this case is co-operative oversight; the Federal Reserve Bank of New York leads the oversight of CLS and reports to a central-bank committee on which all issuing central banks of CLS-eligible currencies are represented. Similarly, co-operative oversight is applied in the case of SWIFT, which provides messaging services to financial institutions and market infrastructures in over 200 countries. Here, the National Bank of Belgium is in the lead (see also Chapter 6).

There are, however, examples of joint public ownership. For example, TARGET2 is jointly owned by the central banks of the Eurosystem. While firmly rooted in the public sector, decision-making powers are distributed across various public-sector institutions. The ECB Governing Council is responsible for the management and control of the payment system. Participating central banks have a subsidiary competence for some issues. They also advise the Governing Council in all matters relating to TARGET2. The three central banks (the Banque de France, the Bundesbank, and the Banca d'Italia that built the system) are also responsible for its future development. Users are involved via public consultations, in national user groups, and in working groups and task forces at the European level. The oversight of the system is conducted by the ECB.

When a system is publicly owned, an important question arises – as with any public-sector provision of services – as to whether and how the costs associated with service provision should be recovered from users. A number of academic contributions examine this question in the context of the specific market failures associated with payment-service provision.[100]

Holthausen and Rochet (2006) assume that the public sector aims to maximize welfare subject to recovering its operating costs but does not know the benefit banks derive from routing their payments via the public system. The authors conclude that, irrespective of whether the public system faces competition from a private system, marginal fees in the public system should decline as volume increases. With low fixed costs of operating the system, the cost-recovery constraint is not binding. However,

---

[99] See Box 5.6: The CLS System, for details.

[100] In addition, direct participants face the (often substantial) costs of accessing the payment system. The sum of these costs is one of the factors influencing the choice of whether or not to participate directly in payment systems; see Chapter 10.

with high fixed costs, full cost recovery may be incompatible with the unconstrained first-best tariff. Thus, full cost recovery may be incompatible with efficiency.

Another argument against full cost recovery is presented by Holthausen and Rochet (2005). If a public owner chooses to invest more in system resilience than would a private owner, the operating costs of the public system are likely to be higher than settlement banks deem necessary. Settlement banks might then respond to a policy of full cost recovery by building an alternative, cheaper or more convenient private system. In the United States, CHIPS competes with the publicly owned Fedwire; and in the euro area, Euro1 competes with TARGET2. Of course a privately owned system may in some cases be cheaper simply because it operates more efficiently. And a private system that operates in several jurisdictions may be able to take advantage of economies of scale and scope not typically available to a public owner.

But where a publicly owned system is more expensive, not because it is less efficient, but because it offers higher resilience, it may be justified to offer a subsidy – or to tax the use of the privately owned system to reduce the price differential. Holthausen and Rochet (2005) make this point in a model of spatial competition in which there are two payment systems located at opposite ends of a spectrum: one privately owned; and one publicly owned. Both systems provide a private good (transfer of payments) at equal cost. Additionally, the publicly owned payment system produces a public good (e.g. reduction of systemic risk) and derives economies of scope from the simultaneous production of the private and the public goods. Production of the public good is costly, but, by definition, it cannot be sold separately. Thus, the public payment system operates with a larger cost base, enabling the private system to capture a larger share of the market for the private good. The optimal level of production of the public good can be restored by subsidizing the public system. The subsidy enables the public system to capture a larger share of the market for the private good, thereby reducing the average cost of providing the public good.

In practice, moral hazard may be an important obstacle to identifying the right level of subsidy. In an extension of their model, Holthausen and Rochet consider the possibility that the public system's efforts to improve efficiency cannot be observed. The operators of the public system may then untruthfully claim that efficiency improvements are difficult to achieve, purely to reap a larger subsidy. The competition between the private and the public systems would then be distorted. The authors conclude that the optimal subsidy must leave a rent to the public system so as to maintain a sufficient incentive to improve efficiency.

Empirically, public operators differ in their charging practices (see also Box 10.1), and in their willingness to subsidize their system. For example, the Federal Reserve is required to charge *above* its costs for Fedwire, the US large-value RTGS system. This provision was made to encourage private-sector competition with the public system.[101] The Bank of England fully recovers costs in its operation of CHAPS. The Eurosystem, by contrast, aims to achieve 'a high level of cost recovery'[102] for TARGET2; that is, it allows for some subsidization.

8.2 Targeted intervention ('oversight')

Targeted intervention addresses particular market failures with specific policy instruments. An example of such intervention is the prudential regulation of banks, one objective of which is to limit the probability and impact of bank failures. The key application of targeted intervention in the payments sphere is oversight of payment systems, practical aspects of which are described in more detail in Chapter 9. Such targeted intervention responds flexibly to an assessment of specific risks in payment systems. It can address operational risks and business risks and can affect fundamental system design choices. Indeed, perhaps the most prominent examples of targeted intervention were initiatives to reduce settlement risk through bringing in changes in system design: the introduction of RTGS in large-value payment systems; the introduction of DvP in securities settlement systems; and the introduction of PvP in the settlement of foreign-exchange transactions.

In practice, as discussed in more detail in the next chapter, overseers increasingly base their actions on accepted international standards: the 'Core Principles for Systemically Important Payment Systems',[103] and equivalent 'Recommendations for Securities Settlement Systems'[104] and 'Recommendations for Central Counterparties'.[105] The Core Principles are

---

[101] The Monetary Control Act of 1980 (MCA) requires the Reserve Banks to recover fully, over the long run, the cost associated with the provision of most financial services they provide, including a private-sector adjustment factor.

[102] European Central Bank (2007, p. 4).

[103] CPSS (2001a).

[104] CPSS (2001b).

[105] CPSS (2004).

designed specifically to address market failures in systemically important systems, thereby acknowledging that the intensity of intervention should be proportional to the systemic importance of the system.

Overseers and other regulators attempt to influence outcomes in a variety of ways. For instance, they may seek to promote changes in the design of the overseen system itself, to tackle directly some of the sources of risk identified and described in Part II.[106] Alternatively, they might seek to influence the behaviour of system participants, perhaps in respect of the robustness of their connectivity to the system.

Other market failures – discussed in Chapter 7 – that affect either the price or quality of payment services may be addressed using the tools developed in competition policy for regulating other network industries, such as telecommunications, electricity, or the railways.[107] In these industries, control of the (uncompetitive) shared network infrastructure is typically separated from the control of (competitive) service provision. Basic building blocks of regulation of the uncompetitive component are: 'cost-of-service' regulation, under which the regulated firm is allowed to earn a certain profit margin above its cost; and 'price-cap' regulation, under which the firm's profit margin is derived endogenously, given the price cap.

However, this level of intervention may be too intrusive for payment systems, where the joint infrastructure is far cheaper than in other network industries. In contrast to railways and the utilities, only an electronic network needs to be created and maintained. Hence, notwithstanding the network externalities, barriers to entry should be lower (and, as Chapter 11 suggests, may be falling), increasing contestability.[108]

As with outright ownership, a public overseer may find it difficult to identify the best design, establish the optimal standards, and set the appropriate prices. But there are other disadvantages of targeted intervention, relative to public ownership. For example, targeted intervention involves agency issues: Can the overseen firm's behaviour be sufficiently closely monitored? How can required actions be enforced? Can appropriate incentives be designed to encourage a private owner to behave as the public authority desires?

---

[106] For instance, they may promote changes in the settlement model to facilitate more efficient liquidity recycling; or perhaps call for additional contingency measures.

[107] Gönenç *et al.* (2003) and Joskow (2007) provide an overview.

[108] In a 2003 review, the United Kingdom's competition authority, the Office of Fair Trading, concluded that potential benefits from increasing competition were too low to justify the creation of a new regulator: total expenditures of the three main UK payment systems (CHAPS, C&CC and BACS) were only GBP 3.6mn (about USD 5mn) in 2001. See Office of Fair Trading (2003).

One approach to reducing the informational asymmetry between regulator and regulated company has been to move towards a form of 'internalized regulation', or self-regulation. This amounts to a change in the governance arrangements of the regulated company, and may be most appropriate when market failures are not too severe. More specifically, the idea is to give external stakeholders a sufficiently strong voice in the company's strategic decisions perhaps through a seat on the board. Under such arrangements, the regulator's role may be reduced to arbitrating in cases of substantial disagreement between these external stakeholders and the company's management.

Of course in some cases targeted intervention or oversight may not be necessary at all: depending on the system's governance, a system might have sufficient incentive to agree to at least partially internalize any externalities without third-party intervention.[109] If properly designed, mutual ownership of the payment system may be sufficient to facilitate such agreements.

8.3 Mutual ownership and integration of external stakeholders

Whether or not mutual ownership can counteract some of the market failures arising in payment systems depends critically on its design. Important factors include: the scope of the co-operative; admission criteria; voting rights; and the role of external stakeholders. The following paragraphs discuss each of these topics in turn.

8.3.1 Scope

First, what should be the scope of the co-operative(s)? Should it cover the entirety of national payment systems? Or should there be a separate co-operative for each individual payment system?

If there were a single co-operative for the entire national payment system, or if ownership of individual payment systems overlapped significantly, the co-operative should ensure the internalization of external effects arising from the interaction between systems.[110] With a single co-operative, issues around incompatibility between payment services should

---

[109] Coase (1960) argued that such agreements can completely internalize external effects.
[110] However, even in this case, internalization might only be partial, as the dependence between payment systems *internationally* has risen.

also be addressed. However, competition might suffer and the speed of innovation could fall, in particular because existing members of the co-operative could erect barriers to entry. Thus, at least in theory, competition and innovation should be higher with separate co-operatives.

Hausman *et al.* (2003) investigate these issues in the context of credit-card schemes, i.e. the bodies that set, control and enforce the system's rules.[111] Here, overlapping ownership of scheme companies is referred to as 'duality'. The authors assume that companies are horizontally differentiated, i.e. that they offer the same quality of payment transmission but are distinguished by other features, such as branding and loyalty schemes. Visa and MasterCard may be thought of as examples. Hausman *et al.* find that under external private ownership, when ownership is not linked to use of the system, duality reduces competition between two schemes and reduces welfare. In contrast, under mutual private ownership, duality delivers the socially optimal outcome. Thus, while overlapping ownership is often seen as hindering the efficient provision of payment services, it may, when schemes are mutually owned, be a positive feature.

8.3.2 *Admission criteria*

Second, how should admission criteria be designed? Membership at the level of the individual end-user of payment services, or even of all financial institutions, would be impractical because of their large number. One may therefore wish to restrict membership, perhaps to only wholesale users and providers of payment services. Indeed, if membership were too broad, members' interests might be too diverse to allow efficient decision making.

Hart and Moore (1996) formalize this point. They model a co-operative that makes decisions by simple majority vote, with each member having one vote. Members' preferences can be sorted along a single dimension, such that the outcome will be determined by the vote of the median member. However, if members' preferences are skewed, the median preference will not coincide with members' mean preference. In this case, decisions taken by the co-operative would not maximize the sum of all members' welfare. By way of example, preferences could be skewed if many members preferred an investment project with low fixed and high

---

[111] A scheme is the body that defines and enforces the payment system's rules (e.g. membership requirements) about how payments are processed. It is typically separated from the (technical) infrastructure necessary to execute the payments.

variable costs (the preferred option of members with small payment volumes), whereas a few members (those few with high payment volumes) preferred an investment project with high fixed costs and very low variable costs. Indeed, Hart and Moore show that external private ownership might be preferable in such a case, even if the external private owner would have market power.

Another source of heterogeneity among members in practice is the age of their IT infrastructure. Members with newer systems will be disinclined to contribute to a system-wide upgrade of the payment infrastructure. Equally, those with older systems may face higher upgrade costs due to difficulties in accommodating new interfaces required by the system upgrade. In some countries, overseers have observed that this type of heterogeneity, coupled with consensus decision making, has tended to stifle innovation.

If membership is voluntary, existing members have a tendency to apply excessively tight admission criteria. Settlement banks benefit by offering their (clearing) services to non-members; profit they would lose if they allowed their clients to join the co-operative. The industrial organization literature examines this problem in a different context. Consider an oligopolist who sells a good both to the end-customer and to an intermediary who resells the good to the end-customer. An example might be electicity-generating firms that own their network, but resell some of their electricity to distribution firms. Were the intermediaries permitted to join the co-operative, they would acquire the good at cost. Correspondingly, settlement banks would lose the margin above cost earned from providing services to non-members when these firms were excluded from the co-operative.

Lai *et al.* (2006) argue that, in payment systems, the incentive to exclude members may not be as high as in other industries. The authors show that any increase in settlement fees charged will be accompanied by a reduction in an indirect member's profits, reflecting both a decline in margins and a decline in end-consumers' demand for payment services. But the lower the indirect member's profits, the greater its susceptibility to financial difficulties – consequent failure would then impose a loss on the settlement bank unless it fully collateralized intraday credit provided to the indirect member.[112]

---

[112] See Chapter 10 for a discussion of the risks arising in the relationship between a settlement bank and its clients.

In practice, settlement banks can use various methods to restrict membership. They can, for example, impose strict credit or capital criteria, or high admission fees. For example, one of the membership requirements for the main UK clearing schemes is that members have to be financial institutions.[113] This excludes many wholesale users of payment services, such as utilities, from becoming settlement members. Of course, some membership requirements reflect legitimate risk-control objectives. For example, high credit standing among settlement members reduces the likelihood that transactions will have to be unwound in a deferred net settlement system due to member default.

High admission fees are often seen as restricting membership to bolster the market power of existing members. However, one could argue that without admission fees, no investment would take place in the co-operative at all. New members could join the co-operative immediately after a sizeable investment, thereby benefiting from its introduction while contributing nothing to its cost. They could then compete with existing members in the provision of payment services to end-users from a lower cost base.

Analysis of the downstream market can give some indication of the extent to which tight admission criteria do indeed boost system members' market power. In the case of the United Kingdom, the Office of Fair Trading (2003) found that competition for correspondent services was intense, indicating that members' market power was relatively low.[114]

8.3.3 *Voting rights*

Third, how should voting rights be distributed among members? Settlement banks differ widely in terms of their customer base (which determines whether they are net suppliers or net recipients of liquidity in the system), their size, and their general business strategy. Therefore, if decisions had to be made unanimously, many innovations or system enhancements could be delayed, in some cases undermining system resilience. On the other hand, unanimity can protect individual financial institutions from being burdened with an unreasonable share of the costs of innovation.

An alternative is majority rule, whereby each member is allocated a given share of the vote and a majority threshold is specified. Such a system still faces practical challenges. For instance, if voting power were allocated

---

[113] Office of Fair Trading (2003), §9.46.
[114] Office of Fair Trading (2003), §9.78.

purely on the basis of payments volume, small institutions might be vulnerable to having to finance innovations that would not be commercially viable for them. Setting sufficiently high voting thresholds for specific decisions might offer a compromise.

All this implies that voting rules tend to be a key issue in the bargaining process when establishing a co-operative. In the United Kingdom, members controlling higher payment volume tend to enjoy a larger share of the voting rights. Nevertheless, members still usually aim for unanimity in their decisions. Economic theory provides only limited guidance so far. Barbera and Jackson (2004) provide an elegant framework in which a group of potential members of a co-operative decides on the 'first-order' majority requirement necessary to pass governing board decisions, and on the 'second-order' majority requirement necessary to change the first-order majority requirement. They argue that a first-order simple majority requirement and a second-order unanimity requirement are the likely outcomes. The authors assume that each member has an equal voting share, and there is no equivalent to a membership fee in their model. But in reality, membership fees and voting requirements are determined jointly in a bargaining process, with the usual outcome that those members contributing more to the co-operative's expenses also obtain a greater share of voting rights.

8.3.4 *External stakeholders*

Fourth, how should external stakeholders participate in the decision-making process? External stakeholders are individuals or companies directly or indirectly affected by a payment system's decisions, but who are otherwise independent of the operators of the system or its direct participants. The greater their influence, the higher the chance that the system will take external effects into account when making its decisions.[115] The options range from granting external shareholders a right to suggest payments innovations (combined with an obligation on the scheme's part to consider them), via formally establishing interest groups (overseen by a member of the scheme's governing board), to appointing independent directors to the governing board.[116] Independent directors need to have

---

[115] See Allen *et al.* (2007) for a formalization of this idea.

[116] Where independent directors have the fiduciary duty to act in their company's best interest, their addition to the board can contribute to the internalization of the scheme's external effects only if the scheme's objectives are sufficiently broad (for example, if they include the objective to ensure that the scheme's services meet the needs of the wider economy).

Box 8.2: GOVERNANCE ARRANGEMENTS IN THE UK

Governance arrangements in the United Kingdom offer an example of a relatively light form of intervention. In the United Kingdom, payment systems are owned and operated by major financial institutions. The ownership of payment schemes – that is, the bodies that set, control and enforce the rules of the systems – overlaps substantially. External stakeholders' interests are voiced by three public-sector institutions: the Bank of England oversees payment systems, focusing on their resilience to shocks; the Financial Services Authority oversees system participants as part of its wider mandate to promote efficient, orderly and fair financial markets; and the Office of Fair Trading ensures that systems and participants comply with competition law.

The aim of a governance reform in 2007 was to increase the emphasis on collective self-regulation in the payments industry. The key change was the creation of a new body, the Payments Council (PC), which has a contractual relationship with the main payment schemes, binding all parties to accept its decisions. External stakeholders are represented on the Payments Council.

The Payments Council's objectives are broad and overlap with those of the public institutions interested in payment systems. In particular, the PC seeks to do the following: lead the future development of co-operative payment services in the UK; ensure the integrity of payment services (i.e. their resilience to shocks); and identify and sponsor innovative solutions, while facilitating competition within the sector. Full membership of the PC is open to all payment-service providers. Full members are, with some exceptions, bound by the PC's board's decisions, and most large UK banks have joined the PC. The PC's influence is complemented by contracts between the PC and major payment schemes, which set out respective rights and duties towards each other.

The PC is headed by a governing board comprising a (non-voting) independent Chair, four independent directors and 11 representatives from the banking sector. The largest five members each appoint one director to the board; smaller members elect a total of six directors. The governing board aims for unanimity but decides with a qualified majority rule. The majority requirement ensures that no decision can be passed against the collective opposition of either the five largest members, or the four independent directors. In addition, full members without direct representation at the governing board can apply for a waiver from the governing board's decision.

Involvement of external stakeholders is not limited to the presence of independent directors. The board is expected to consult with key stakeholders before determining the PC's strategy, and before making important decisions. Non-members can set-up user fora, each chaired by an independent director. Monitoring of the PC's work is facilitated by the requirement to publish an annual report, with a separate contribution by the independent directors, and the publication of board minutes.

The establishment of the PC complements rather than substitutes for the powers of the regulatory bodies with an interest in payments. Successful self-regulation may, however, lead to a less interventionary involvement of the regulatory authorities going forward. For example, the PC took over some of the work of a task force on payment systems previously led by the Office of Fair Trading.

sufficient resources at their disposal to be able to contribute meaningfully to the scheme's decisions, in particular if they lack extensive industry experience. Nevertheless as members of the governing board, they may offer their specific experience and a broader strategic vision. They may also help to balance a number of conflicting objectives in the governance of payment systems: social welfare maximization and private business interest; co-operation and competition between systems and between service providers; and finally, transparency and confidentiality. Box 8.2 provides details on the role of independent directors in the high-level governance of the UK payments industry.

Interest groups, in the form of associations of users, are probably the most frequent form of external stakeholder representation in other network industries. In the UK railways sector, for example, 'Passenger Focus' is a statutory body with the task of ensuring that the views of passengers are communicated to industry representatives, and mediating in respect of unsettled disputes between passengers and train companies.[117]

Another interesting example can be found in the UK telecommunications sector. A committee of the Board of British Telecom (BT), the incumbent, has been established to monitor whether BT abuses its market power. This committee, staffed by a majority of independents with extensive industry experience, is obliged to report non-trivial abuses of market power to the regulatory authority (in this case, the Office of Communications, OfCom). Less important issues are taken up with BT's board directly.[118] Such an arrangement may be appropriate when day-to-day involvement of a public regulatory authority cannot be justified.

8.4 Which authority should intervene?

As we have seen, central banks, by virtue of their provision of the ultimate settlement asset and their objectives of safeguarding monetary and financial stability, have a strong interest in addressing systemic externalities arising in payment and settlement systems.

Figure 8.1 reveals that, in discharging this interest, many central banks own or operate some components of the national large-value payment

---

[117] See www.passengerfocus.org.uk/ for details.

[118] For more information on the 'Equality of Access Board', cf. http://www.btplc.com/ Thegroup/Theboard/Boardcommittees/EqualityofAccessBoard/EqualityofAccessBoard.htm.

Country	Domestic LVPS(s)	Owner	Operator	Overseer
Canada	LVTS			✓
Japan	BOJ-NET	✓	✓	✓
UK	CHAPS*		✓	✓
US	Fedwire	✓	✓	✓
	CHIPS			✓
Euro area	TARGET2	✓	✓	✓
	EURO1			✓

Figure 8.1: International models of intervention in payment systems

Note: TARGET2 is owned by the Eurosystem, operated by the central banks of Germany, France, and Italy, and jointly overseen by the national central banks in the euro area.

Source: Central banks' websites.

system (Figure 8.1).[119] There are some examples of a pure oversight model, even for large-value systems, but these tend to occur where private and public large-value systems co-exist: the public Fedwire Funds Transfer System coexists with CHIPS in the US; the public TARGET2 co-exists with Euro1 in the euro area.

Differences in the degree and form of central-bank involvement will often reflect historical evolution, but may also be related to cultural differences and differences in risk tolerance. For example, some central banks argue that *only* the central bank should be allowed to change book entries on its own accounts: the central bank should therefore own, or at least operate, the corresponding part of the joint infrastructure of any system that settles in central-bank money. Other central banks outsource the operation of their accounts to the private sector, for example to facilitate the simultaneous transfer of securities and funds in a privately owned securities settlement system.

But not necessarily all of the market failures described in Chapter 7 are best addressed by the central bank. The exact boundary of central-bank interests will vary across countries, reflecting differences in the central bank's mandate and the division of responsibilities between the central bank and other public authorities.

For example, in the US the mandate of the Federal Reserve includes 'efficiency' in the provision of financial services. However, in practice the Federal Reserve works closely with the Security and Exchange Commission (SEC) and the US Department of Justice as the relevant competition

[119] When a central bank also owns the system, oversight may be considered a form of internal audit, or an internal control function.

authority, when it comes to the efficiency of payments and securities settlement arrangements. In Australia, the Reserve Bank has an explicit mandate to promote competition and efficiency and has powers, enshrined in statute, to designate payments systems and set standards and access regimes in designated systems. In the UK, the mandate of the Bank of England is to safeguard monetary and financial stability, giving it a particularly strong interest in the mitigation of systemic risks that might arise from the operation of payment systems. In respect of efficiency considerations, however, the Office of Fair Trading (OFT), as the relevant competition authority, would take the lead.[120]

---

[120] In the United Kingdom, the Office of Fair Trading chaired a Payment Systems Task Force to address concerns regarding the efficiency of the provision of payment services. See Office of Fair Trading (2007).

9

Central-bank oversight of payment and settlement systems in practice

As private-sector involvement in the provision of core payment and settlement services has expanded, central banks have increasingly sought to exercise control and influence via assumption of an oversight role. This is defined by CPSS (2005b) in terms of the promotion of safety and efficiency by 'monitoring existing and planned systems, assessing them against these objectives and, where necessary, inducing change.' Over time, this role has become more formalized.

9.1 Oversight objectives

The scope of oversight is typically set to achieve a central bank's monetary and financial stability objectives. It therefore reflects an assessment of the importance of particular payment and settlement systems to financial stability and to the functioning of the economy as a whole. Several factors are weighed in gauging 'systemic importance', including: the values and volumes processed by the system; the design of the system; and the availability of substitute payment media should the system fail (Haldane and Latter, 2005). Figure 9.1 illustrates, in a stylized way, how the direct influence sought by a central bank varies in respect of different components of the financial infrastructure.

The strongest interest will typically be in the large-value payment system (LVPS). With such systems typically settling transaction-by-transaction in central-bank money, central banks tend to exert considerable influence as settlement agent. They often also operate major components of the supporting infrastructure.

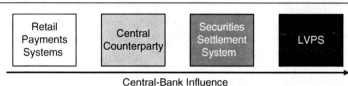

Figure 9.1: Central-bank influence on financial infrastructure

Central banks are often also closely engaged with the securities settlement process, although oversight of other aspects of the activities of national depository and settlement systems, such as the issuance and depository functions, often falls within the remit of the securities regulator.[121]

The central bank typically has more limited influence over central counterparties. While final settlement of margin typically passes across central bank accounts, the payment arrangements embedded in a CCP are only one (small) component of CCPs' overall activities. A CCP's risk-management activities, policies and processes and the broader operational framework are also critical for financial stability, but are typically outside the sphere of the central bank's direct influence – again often falling within the supervisory scope of the securities regulator.[122] Similarly, for retail systems, while net settlement between members tends to take place via the large-value payment system, central banks' influence over other elements of the value chain is typically more limited.

While the main objective of oversight is to assess and, if necessary, mitigate systemic risk in payment systems, efficiency considerations (e.g. whether a system processes payments in a timely and reliable way, at reasonable cost) need also to be weighed to some degree. For instance, it would be counterproductive to create a risk-proof payment system that was so expensive that no-one was prepared to use it, encouraging flow to other, perhaps riskier, alternatives.

---

[121] The degree of a central bank's direct operational control over settlement depends on whether an 'interfaced' or 'integrated' model is operated by the securities settlement system. If an 'interfaced' model is adopted, security records are under control of the CSD, but cash transfers are under the direct control of the central bank. An 'integrated' model, on the other hand, allows the SSS, for a period, to control both the securities and cash records in the system, thus reducing the central bank's direct control. Nevertheless, in practice, an 'integrated' model is typically accompanied by a strong monitoring and control regime in respect of movements across central-bank money accounts.

[122] The central bank does sometimes also assume a direct role here, at least in respect of system stability. In Australia, for instance, the Reserve Bank of Australia has statutory responsibility for the stability of clearing and settlement systems, reporting annually, via the Payments System Board, to the relevant government minister on the systems' compliance with a set of Financial Stability Standards.

Central-bank oversight of payment and settlement systems in practice

Criteria	Canada[a]	Japan	UK	US[b]	Euro area[c]
Oversight responsibility defined in statute	✓	✓	✓		✓
Systems are obliged to provide information to the central bank	✓		✓	✓	
System participants are obliged to provide information to the central bank			✓	✓	
Payment systems must be licensed / authorized by the central bank				✓	
Central bank must approve, or can impose, payment systems' operational rules	✓		✓	✓	
Central bank can set conditions for membership of payment systems[d]			✓	✓	
Enforcement powers (ability to issue regulations, fines, civil or criminal sanctions)	✓		✓	✓	✓

Figure 9.2: Central banks' statutory powers of oversight of payment systems

Notes:

(a) Central-bank statutory powers apply only to a subset of payment systems, for example those considered systemically important.

(b) The Federal Reserve Board has various supervisory responsibilities with regard to certain payment and settlement systems, such as those chartered as banking organizations. For other systems, the Board has no such jurisdiction. The Board oversees systems that settle over US$5 billion gross per day, and those *vis-à-vis* which it has legal or operational responsibilities. The Board also has statutory authority to oversee and supervise Federal Reserve member banks. The powers that apply therefore depend on the organizational character of a payment or settlement system, operational relationships with the system, and whether the system is owned or operated by the Federal Reserve.

(c) The ticks apply to the ECB. The treaty establishing the European Community gave the ECB the right to 'make regulations, to ensure efficient and sound clearing and payment systems'. Policies defined at the NCB level apply within the framework of the objectives and core principles defined at the Eurosystem level. For details, see European Central Bank (2000).

(d) This is distinct from access conditions for central-bank settlement accounts.

Oversight responsibilities have been explicitly formalized in statute in many countries. In others, the central bank's role in this area remains informal and oversight relies more on operational influence and persuasion (see Figure 9.2). Some central banks also have other publicly stated oversight objectives.

By way of example, Eurosystem central banks have among their stated objectives 'safeguarding the transmission channel for monetary policy'. Some central banks also consider the control of money laundering and the avoidance of anticompetitive practices to fall within their oversight function.[123] Whether a particular public-policy objective falls within

---

[123] See CPSS (2005b) for additional examples.

central-bank oversight depends on how a country chooses to define 'oversight' and how it allocates responsibility for various public-policy objectives between the central bank and other authorities.

9.2 Implementation of oversight

Central banks around the world have adopted common principles as a guide for their oversight activities. In respect of large-value payment systems, these 'core' principles are codified in a report published by the CPSS (2001a). The ten Core Principles, listed in Box 9.1, provide a set of

---

Box 9.1: CORE PRINCIPLES FOR SYSTEMICALLY IMPORTANT PAYMENT SYSTEMS

  I The system should have a well-founded legal basis under all relevant jurisdictions.

  II The system's rules and procedures should enable participants to have a clear understanding of the system's impact on each of the financial risks they incur through participation in it.

  III The system should have clearly defined procedures for the management of credit risks and liquidity risks, which specify the respective responsibilities of the system operator and the participants and that provide appropriate incentives to manage and contain those risks.

  IV The system should provide prompt final settlement on the day of value, preferably during the day and at a minimum at the end of the day.

  V A system in which multilateral netting takes place should, at a minimum, be capable of ensuring the timely completion of daily settlements in the event of an inability to settle by the participant with the largest single settlement obligation.

  VI Assets used for settlement should preferably be a claim on the central bank; where other assets are used, they should carry little or no credit risk and little or no liquidity risk.

  VII The system should ensure a high degree of security and operational reliability and should have contingency arrangements for timely completion of daily processing.

  VIII The system should provide a means of making payments that is practical for its users and efficient for the economy.

  IX The system should have objective and publicly disclosed criteria for participation, which permit fair and open access.

  X The system's governance arrangements should be effective, accountable and transparent.

Source: CPSS (2001a).

---

minimum standards, covering legal risks (Core Principle I), financial risks (Core Principles II to VI) and operational risks (Core Principle VII), as well as efficiency (Core Principle VIII), access criteria (Core Principle IX) and governance (Core Principle X).

Hence, in addition to the consideration of risks arising from system design, oversight also involves assessment of the legal framework within which a system operates and its rules, operating procedures and operating environment, as well as review of changes to a system's (and its members') risk-management procedures.

In light of the outcome of their assessment against the Core Principles, central banks may propose changes to the rules, design and operation of a system, or to the legal framework, in order to eliminate, reduce or better manage any settlement, business or operational risks identified.

Despite these common standards, the form and effect of oversight differs across countries: the standards only define high-level principles, in general terms, and they may be interpreted and applied differently to different systems. Though guided by the Core Principles, central banks adopt a variety of approaches to the assessment of risks and prioritization of risk-mitigating actions. Box 9.2 sets out one quantitative approach, used by the Bank of England.

Box 9.2: ASSESSING AND MANAGING RISKS THROUGH OVERSIGHT

As part of their oversight responsibilities, central banks undertake systematic assessments of risks in payment systems. One, qualitative, approach is to apply the CPSS Core Principles. A Core Principles assessment may, however, be supplemented by a more quantitative approach to estimating credit, liquidity, business and operational risks – in particular, by estimating the probabilities of certain scenarios that would trigger these risks, and calibrating the impacts if they should occur.

Specifically, under such a quantitative approach, for each risk event, two sets of calculations may be undertaken:

- first, an estimate may be made of the probability that a given risk event occurs;
- second, a conditional loss distribution may be estimated – that is to say, an estimate of the distribution of losses conditional upon the occurence of that risk event.

Data constraints – in particular, in relation to material business and operational risk events (which tend to occur relatively infrequently) – may in practice hamper the process of quantification. If so, then in order to derive a numerical assessment, it may be appropriate to make approximations in the estimation process, for instance by relying on stylized facts such as that many conditional loss distributions tend to be approximately log-normal in shape. This is to say that if a risk event occurs, it will tend to

---

have a modal impact that is relatively small, but a (long) tail of larger impacts that could occur, albeit with a decreasing probability as the impacts increase. Figure 9.3 contains a stylized representation of a log-normal distribution.

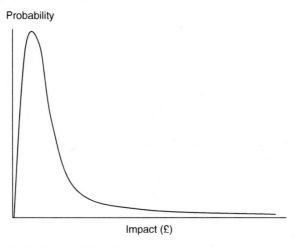

Figure 9.3: The log-normal distribution

As the following example of credit-risk estimation demonstrates, it is possible in some cases to be more precise, combining the probability of the risk event occurring with the conditional loss distribution to produce a reasonably robust quantitative risk estimate. Quantitative estimates across several payment systems and risk types can guide the intensity of oversight among the different systems – thereby ultimately helping to deliver more proportionate, risk-based regulation.

A (fictitious) example of a quantitative estimate of settlement risk

This example is of a payment system settling at the end of the day on a deferred net settlement (DNS) basis. As described in Chapter 3, credit risk can therefore arise as the system's participant banks build up exposures when receiving their payment instructions from each other. In the event of a participant default, the credit risk crystallizes in the amount of the (net) exposure of the surviving banks to the defaulting bank. This amount is a measure of the potential impact – and can be expressed as a monetary amount (which in turn facilitates comparison with other estimates). The institution that effects settlement (typically the central bank) can build up a dataset of these net settlement amounts, to form a (frequency) distribution of the end-of-day exposures in the system.

This gives the central bank all the information it needs about the conditional loss distributions in this credit-risk example. The probability that the banks in a payment system default in the first place may be inferred from credit ratings as assigned by agencies (Fitch, Moody's, Standard & Poors), or from market prices. Based on these rating estimates, an approximation that at least one participant bank defaults may be constructed simply by summing the probabilities of each participant defaulting.

Tables 9.1 and 9.2 contain illustrative exposure and probability of default data for a (fictitious) payment system comprising four participant banks.

(continued)

Box 9.2: (Continued)

Table 9.1: Rating agencies' annual probabilities of default for participants in the payment system

	Credit rating	Annual default probability (%)
Bank 1	Aa3	0.138
Bank 2	A1	0.358
Bank 3	A2	0.358
Bank 4	A3	0.358
Pr(a participant defaults)		1.212%pa

Table 9.2: Central bank's record of distribution of net debit positions to be settled

	Net debit position (£m)			
	0–100	101–500	501–1000	>1000
Frequency (%)	1	85	14	-

In this example, the annual probability that one of the participant banks defaults leaving the surviving banks facing a crystallized exposure of between £0mn and £100mn is approximately $0.01212 \times 0.01 = 0.0001212$. Similarly, the annual probability that one of the participant banks defaults leaving the surviving banks with a crystallized exposure of between £101mn and £500mn is approximately $0.01212 \times 0.85 = 0.010302$. Finally, the annual probability that one of the participant banks defaults leaving the surviving banks with a crystallized exposure of between £501mn and £1000mn is approximately $0.01212 \times 0.14 = 0.001697$.

A measure of the aggregate credit risk in this example can be derived by simply multiplying these annual probabilities by their respective impacts. Using this approach, an aggregate measure of annual credit risk in this system (which could be compared with equivalent estimates for other systems) can be approximated by $[(0.0001212 \times £50mn) + (0.010302 \times £250mn) + (0.001697 \times £750mn)] = £3.854mn$.

The CPSS – working with the International Organization of Securities Commissions (IOSCO) – has also developed Recommendations for Securities Settlement Systems and Recommendations for Central Counterparties.[124] As in the case of payment systems, these guidelines emphasize the need for a sound legal basis and adequate risk controls, including in respect of credit and operational risk.

Specifically, for securities settlement systems, the CPSS and IOSCO recommend control of, *inter alia*, pre-settlement risk (e.g. prompt sending of trade confirmations and scheduled settlement no later than three days

---

[124] CPSS (2001b) and CPSS (2004).

after the trade occurred), settlement risk, and operational and custody risk. Regarding settlement risk, recommendations include the adoption of a delivery-versus-payment model and safeguards to ensure timely settlement when the participant with the largest payment obligation is unable to meet its scheduled obligations. The role of securities borrowing and lending is acknowledged in this regard. Principal responsibility for ensuring compliance with these recommendations lies with the designers, owners and operators of the securities settlement system. However, depending on their mandate, public authorities are also encouraged to assess the system's compliance, and promote the implementation of the recommendations by the system.

For central counterparties, CPSS-IOSCO place particular emphasis on the robustness of risk-management processes and procedures. Recommendations 2 to 5 cover the soundness of participation requirements, the measurement and management of risk exposures, and the adequacy of margins and other financial resources available to the central counterparty. In respect of financial resources, CPSS-IOSCO recommend that the central counterparty ensure that it has sufficient financial resources to withstand the default of the largest participant 'in extreme but plausible market conditions'.[125] Central counterparties are again encouraged to conduct a self-assessment against these recommendations, but with public authorities also expected to assess CCPs' observance.

Oversight practices necessarily evolve through time to reflect changes in the pattern of payment flows and changes in the environment in which payment systems operate. For example, in light of the increased dependence on information technology and telecommunications networks, overseers have placed particular focus on operational risk. Since 11 September 2001, increased concerns regarding terrorist attacks have added impetus to this shift in focus. As we saw in Chapter 6, operational vulnerabilities in payment systems are important because they can exacerbate existing credit and liquidity risks and lead to disruption in the financial system. And increasing linkages between systems may amplify the consequences of operational shocks (see Chapter 11).

Another source of change in oversight practices is the increased reliance on payment and settlement systems operating across borders. This creates a need for co-operation between central banks responsible for oversight of such systems. Co-operation in the oversight of cross-border systems helps to avoid gaps and duplication of activity and minimize the risk that

---

[125] CPSS (2004).

different central banks impose conflicting requirements on a system. CPSS (2005b) lays out a set of principles for co-operative oversight.

Co-operation is particularly well developed amongst the central banks of the G10 countries and the central banks of the European Union. For example, in 1994, the European Central Bank's predecessor, the European Monetary Institute, co-ordinated the development of an agreement on information sharing by all EU central banks and financial regulatory authorities.

In addition, there has been increased international emphasis on the need for transparency in oversight arrangements. In September 1999, the International Monetary Fund's interim Committee of the Board adopted a 'Code of Good Practices on Transparency in Monetary and Financial Policies: Declaration of Principles'. Transparency provides a basis for others to judge the effectiveness of the central bank's policy and thus for the accountability of the central bank for the performance of its oversight. It also enables payment and settlement-system operators to understand and observe applicable policy requirements and standards. In practice, transparency can be achieved via the production of oversight reports, which set out the central bank's framework for oversight, including the process and procedures adopted, and present system assessments.[126]

Because payment systems do not work in isolation, co-operation is also sought domestically between central banks and other authorities, such as securities regulators and banking supervisors. Members and users are affected by the operations of a payment system; likewise, a payment system is affected by the activities, risk-management policies and practices of its members and their customers. This calls for close co-operation between the central bank and authorities in charge of regulating individual banks, including their participation in payment systems.

---

[126] The Bank of England, for instance, published its first Payment Systems Oversight Report in 2005, and has since published annually (see *http://www.bankofengland.co.uk/publications/ index.htm*). There has also been a notable trend towards publication of assessments against either the Core Principles of Recommendations for Securities Settlement Systems or Recommendations for Central Counterparties, either by the overseer or the system itself.

Part IV

Future policy challenges
for central banks

At the time of writing, the wholesale market infrastructure is undergoing significant change driven by the combined forces of technological progress, financial innovation, globalization and regulatory change. Furthermore, as the full effect of the financial market stress of 2007 and 2008 is realized, changes in financial firms' structures and business practices will surely also condition the future evolution of the supporting financial infrastructure. This final part of the book draws out some of the key themes and trends and, with an eye to the future, poses some important questions likely to exercise the minds of central banks and other policymakers over the coming years.

The high fixed costs and low marginal costs that characterize the provision of infrastructure give rise to economies of scale and scope that, when combined with powerful network effects, imply a pronounced tendency towards concentration. But technological and regulatory change, and market participants' increasing demands for cross-border services, are stimulating fresh competition in both trading and the provision of post-trade services – both among incumbent providers, and between these providers and potential or actual new entrants. And with financial innovation spawning new niche infrastructure needs, the landscape is becoming more complex.

It remains to be seen whether markets can support multiple providers of trading, clearing and settlement infrastructure in the long term. If the forces towards concentration remain sufficiently strong, we may simply be witnessing a transitional process as competing providers vie for dominance in markets hitherto defined on a national scale but now redefined with wider reach. During this transition, however, this competition may manifest as fragmentation at the national level. If, on the other hand, the forces towards concentration have been weakened by technological advances and regulatory change, then perhaps, at least at certain points in the value chain, fragmentation may be able to persist.

Both fragmentation and globalization may over time afford an ever greater role for banking firms in the provision of infrastructure. Banks have a long history of involvement in settlement of other banks' – often overseas banks' – claims across their own books, in the form of correspondent banking. And due to their global reach and consequent ability to connect into multiple systems, banks may become an increasingly important link in the overall infrastructure landcape. Part III starts by exploring these aspects in more detail, in Chapter 10, before moving on to a discussion, in Chapter 11, of the forces that are shaping the evolution of this landscape.

10

Banks providing infrastructure services

A bank may choose not to participate directly in all of the large-value payment systems for currencies in which it needs to make and receive payments. In some cases, even if it has a domestic presence, a bank may choose to access a payment system indirectly via another bank. The ratio of indirect to total participation in a payment system is often referred to as the degree of 'tiering'.

When a settlement bank becomes sufficiently large it becomes, in essence, a system itself, performing the same functions for its customer banks as a payment system provides for its direct members. Thus, the services provided by settlement banks can generate similar risks to those discussed in previous chapters in relation to dedicated systems. For instance, credit exposures build up between a settlement bank and its customers; and customers are dependent on the operational and financial resilience of their settlement bank. Public authorities seek to mitigate these risks in dedicated payment systems through system design and oversight. Bank regulators might also need to give further consideration to the mitigation of equivalent intraday risks in tiered settlement arrangements.

Accordingly, this chapter explores public authorities' interest in the risks that arise from settlement banks' provision of payment services. The issues raised apply both in respect of settlement services for clean payments and settlement services for the cash leg of securities transactions.

The chapter begins with a description of the role of a settlement bank, considering why some banks might prefer to participate in a system indirectly, rather than opt for direct participation (Section 10.1). The risks associated with tiered arrangements are then outlined and compared with those considered in Part II (Section 10.2). The chapter concludes with a description of other examples of firms providing infrastructure services for which similar risks and regulatory themes arise (Section 10.3).

10.1 The provision of wholesale payments services

Chapter 2 explained that direct participants in a payment system hold accounts with the settlement institution through which they settle claims on each other. These participants in turn provide accounts and payment services to their own customers, comprising not only individuals and non-financial firms, but also other banks.

An arrangement in which one credit institution (the service-providing bank) holds an account for another credit institution (the customer bank) and makes and receives payments from/to that account under instruction from that credit institution, is known as a correspondent banking arrangement.[127] Figure 10.1 provides a stylized illustration of such an arrangement.

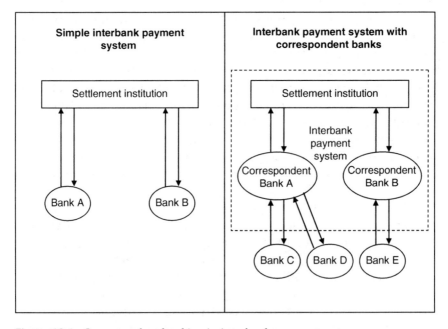

Figure 10.1: Correspondent banking in interbank payment systems

[127] CPSS (2003c).

The terms nostro (from the Italian, ours) and vostro (yours) are used to describe the ownership of the account through which correspondent banking transactions are made. For example, a German customer bank will refer to its US dollar account with a bank in New York as its nostro account. Correspondent banks are therefore often referred to as 'nostro agents'. The same account in the New York bank's books would be referred to as a vostro account.

With the internationalization of the financial industry in recent decades, international correspondent banking relationships have become increasingly important. The expansion of cross-border financial flows has resulted in an increasing demand for correspondent services to facilitate the settlement of payments (including in relation to foreign-exchange transactions[128]) in those jurisdictions in which a bank does not have a domestic presence or direct access to the local payment system.

But even in a domestic context correspondent banking can be an important feature. A correspondent bank – often referred to in this context as a settlement bank – can sometimes offer a smaller domestic institution or the domestic branch or subsidiary of a foreign institution a more efficient channel for the settlement of its large-value payments and securities transactions. Indeed, correspondent banking initially emerged in this context, with small, local banks relying on a clearing bank or 'money centre' bank to settle on its behalf in the national payment system.

10.1.1 Motivations for indirect participation

There are several reasons why it may be more efficient and cost effective for local banks, whether foreign or domestically owned, to access the payment system indirectly.

First, direct membership can be expensive. There are relatively high fixed costs associated with setting up the necessary infrastructure and IT systems. There are also staff costs, because a direct member will need to maintain a dedicated payment system and liquidity management team, whereas correspondent bank customers can rely on their settlement bank to perform this function. Moreover, the fee structure for payment systems often involves both fixed fees and regressive per-transaction

---

[128] See Chapter 5 for details on how foreign-exchange transactions are settled. Not all CLS members are direct members of all of the necessary national RTGS systems, so they use a correspondent to access systems in which they are not direct members.

Box 10.1: PRICING STRUCTURE IN LVPS

The tariff structure of payment and settlement systems is an important determinant of a bank's decision as to whether to become a direct system member, and hence of the degree of tiering in the system. One-off entry fees are meant to compensate existing members for sunk investments in the shared infrastructure. But not all systems charge entry fees. For example, LVTS in Canada and CHAPS in the UK charge entry fees (as of 2008, the fees are respectively CAN$ 60,000 and £70,000; interestingly, the CHAPS fee was reduced from £1 million in 2001 to encourage direct participation[129]). In contrast, Fedwire (US), BOJ-NET (Japan) and SIC (Switzerland) do not charge for entry.

Periodic fees and transaction fees are meant to recover the (comparatively high) fixed and the (usually low) variable cost of operating the system. Only some systems charge annual fees, including EURO1, CHAPS and LVTS. For example, EURO1 clearing banks have to pay the EBA Clearing Company an annual fee of €10,000.[130] Fedwire does not levy such fees.

Transaction fees can vary with the quantity of payments a settlement bank submits. Sometimes, users have the choice between different pricing schedules. For example, in TARGET2, users can choose between a pricing schedule with a low monthly fee (€100) and a volume-independent transaction fee (€0.80), or a higher monthly fee (€1250) and a regressive transaction fee falling to €0.125 for transaction above a monthly volume of 100,000.[131] In Fedwire, fees are only based on the volume of transfers, and, in 2007, ranged from $0.18 to $0.58 per transfer.

Transaction fees are sometimes only charged to the originating institution (e.g. CHAPS in the UK, and TARGET2 in the euro area), or to both the originating and the receiving institution (e.g. Fedwire and SIC). Occasionally, they vary with the time of day to encourage early settlement, particularly of large payments. For example, the Swiss Interbank Clearing System, SIC, charges the originating institution SFr 0.01 for payments submitted and settled before 8am (independently of their value), but costs rise over the day to SFr 3.00 for large payments submitted and settled after 2pm.[132]

Chapter 8 also provides some background on the optimal tariff structure and subsidization of large-value payment services. Chapter 4 discusses some of the reasons why banks may have an incentive to delay payments in RTGS systems.

(volume-based) fees, so direct membership becomes relatively cheaper for banks with larger flows. Box 10.1 provides an overview.

Second, the settlement bank may be able to process a customer bank's payments more efficiently than could the customer bank itself, exploiting

---

[129] Canadian Payments Association, LVTS Rule 3, Access to LVTS. Available at http://www.cdnpay.ca/rules/pdfs_rules/lvts_rule_03.pdf.
[130] CPSS (2003b).
[131] European Central Bank (2007).
[132] CPSS (2003b). Figures are from 2002.

economies of scale in processing high volumes and values of payments. By attracting business from other banks, a settlement bank is often able to lower the average liquidity it needs to settle a given value of payments. This cost saving can, in turn, help it to attract further customers.

Jackson and Manning (2007a) highlight two channels via which the overall liquidity demands of a RTGS system may be reduced when banks access indirectly, rather than directly. The channels include the following:

- *Internalization of payments*: internalization refers to the settlement of payments between the settlement bank and a customer bank, or between two customer banks of the same settlement bank, internally across the settlement bank's books. For example, transactions between banks A and B in Figure 10.1 could be settled across the books of correspondent A, without recourse to the settlement institution. Internalization allows payments to be made without the need to draw on reserves of liquidity (or raise it from the settlement agent).

- *Liquidity pooling*: to the extent that liquidity generated by payment inflows to one customer bank can be used to fund outflows from its own account, or that of another customer, a settlement bank enjoys a diversification, or liquidity-pooling, benefit. That is, it can meet its and its customers' payment needs from a smaller aggregate reserve of liquidity than would be required were each customer bank to participate directly and fund its needs from a segregated pool of liquidity.

Lasaosa and Tudela (2008) attempt to quantify the effects of internalization and liquidity pooling in an empirical study of the UK's CHAPS system. The authors employ a simulation approach, using the Bank of Finland payment and settlement system simulator (BoF-PSS2), based on payment-by-payment data from CHAPS. To gauge the liquidity impact of changes in the degree of tiering, the authors simulate a reduction in the number of direct participants in the system, sequentially simulating indirect participation of each of the (seven) smallest participants (by value settled). Each new indirect participant's transactions are allocated to one of the three largest CHAPS banks. Assuming no change in the timing of payments upon becoming an indirect participant, but allowing for payments between the new indirect participant and its settlement bank (which include payments to the settlement bank's other customer banks) to be internalized, the authors monitor the change in liquidity required to settle all of the payments in the system.

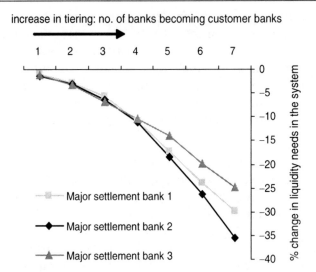

Figure 10.2: Increase in tiering and liquidity needs in CHAPS £

Source: Lasaosa and Tudela (2008).

As shown in Figure 10.2, reproduced from Lasaosa and Tudela (2008), there can be a substantial system-level liquidity saving associated with indirect participation, reflecting internalization of payments between each new indirect participant and its new settlement bank and the increased liquidity pooling enjoyed by the new settlement bank. The authors attempt to decompose the total liquidity saving into these two elements, finding that the liquidity-pooling effect dominates.[133]

From the perspective of an individual bank, indirect participation may further reduce the cost of participating in a payment system, if: (i) the settlement bank's liquidity costs are lower than its own;[134] and (ii) if the settlement bank is able to better monitor the customer bank's creditworthiness compared to the settlement agent, and can thus substitute monitoring for costly collateralization.

Kahn and Roberds (2005) explore (ii), showing that, where monitoring reveals private information about the reliability of agents, intraday credit extensions need not be fully collateralized. To the extent that the settle-

[133] This decomposition cannot be achieved with precision but, on average, the authors find that internalization accounts for 1–22% of the total saving, and liquidity pooling the remaining 78–99%.

[134] In a competitive market for payment services, this lower cost will be reflected in the price of such services.

ment agent, often the central bank, cannot carry out this monitoring effectively, a tiered structure can enhance welfare. Good monitoring is shown to enforce 'reliable' behaviour among second-tier banks: if a second-tier bank is deemed unreliable, it will have to collateralize fully, but if deemed reliable, the cheaper alternative of monitoring will suffice (with collateralization only in 'stressed' states of the world). And, by assuming credit exposure on its customer banks, first-tier banks have an incentive to monitor effectively.

The attractions of indirect participation may, however, be limited because the use of a settlement bank can place the customer bank at a competitive disadvantage. A consequence of indirect participation is that its settlement bank will acquire inside knowledge of the customer's payment activity, information the settlement bank may then exploit to its own advantage.

Lai *et al.* (2006) investigate the proposition that a settlement bank will strategically price its wholesale payments service so as to gain a competitive advantage over customer banks with which it competes in the retail-payments arena. The authors find that although a settlement bank may indeed have an incentive to strategically price its wholesale payments services, this incentive may be limited by the potential consequences for its credit exposure to its customer banks. In particular, such an action could undermine its customer banks' profitability, increasing the probability of default and, in turn, the likelihood that the settlement bank sustains a loss on any uncollateralized credit extensions to its customer banks.

10.1.2 Determinants of tiering in large-value payment systems

While the decision as to whether or not to participate directly in a payment system is a private choice for each individual firm, these private choices collectively determine the overall structure of the payment system. Although tiering is a feature of most systems, the degree of tiering varies widely across payment and settlement systems internationally. In a highly tiered structure, a few settlement banks settle directly at the central bank and a larger number of customer banks process their payments through the direct members. Table 10.1 provides an indicator of the degree of tiering in different systems. This is, however, only an approximation, for in some cases domestic banks may be required to hold accounts

Table 10.1: Tiering in large-value payment systems

Country	System name	Number of settle-ment banks[a]	Number of credit institutions	Settlement banks/ Total credit insti-tutions
United Kingdom	CHAPS Sterling	13	420	0.04
Germany[b]	RTGS Plus	93	2,370	0.04
France[b]	TBF	156	1,067	0.15
Belgium[b]	ELLIPS	16	109	0.15
Canada	LVTS	14	45	0.31
Netherlands[b]	TOP	106	155	0.68
Japan	BOJ-NET	371	506	0.73
United States	Fedwire	7,736	8,130	0.95
Switzerland	SIC	307	327	0.99

Source: Lasaosa and Tudela (2008).

Notes:
(a) Includes central banks. Data for 2003.
(b) These national LVPS have now migrated to TARGET2.

directly with the settlement institution, but may still have a cost incentive to direct (the bulk of) their flow via a settlement bank.

In seeking to understand the structure of different systems, the payments literature has reached out to work on the structure and functioning of networks in the field of physics. Payment systems can be thought of as a complex network of relationships and payment flows between payers and payees. Soramäki *et al.* (2007) study the network of interbank payment flows in Fedwire, with a particular emphasis on the impact on payment flows of the events of 11 September 2001. Lubloy (2006), Inaoka *et al.* (2004) and Becher, *et al.* (2008b) examine the networks of the large-value interbank payment systems of Hungary, Japan and the United Kingdom, respectively.

These topological studies provide insight into the implications of tiering for the network of payment flows in different payment systems. Figures 10.3 and 10.4 compare the network topologies for Fedwire and CHAPS sterling, where lines represent *links* (i.e. payment flows) between the different *nodes* (i.e. banks) within the *network* (i.e. payment system). The width of each line represents the value of payments passing across that link. It is clear that CHAPS is much more highly tiered, with a large number of indirect participants making payments through a small number of direct members. As such, payments are concentrated between settlement banks (CHAPS settlement banks are indicated by circles). By contrast, with a large proportion of institutions accessing Fedwire directly, payment flows are much less concentrated.

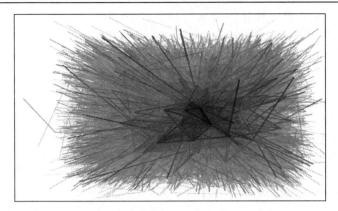

Figure 10.3: Fedwire interbank payment network
Sources: Soramäki *et al.* (2006).

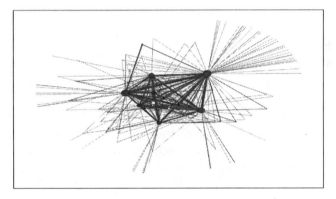

Figure 10.4: CHAPS sterling interbank payment network
Sources: Becher *et al.* (2008b).

In recognition of this divergence in structures, the literature has also sought to model and explain the factors that determine the structure of different payment systems. The aforementioned benefits in terms of cost efficiency would imply pressures towards concentration in the provision of wholesale payment services. Adams *et al.* (2009) model the effects of internalization and liquidity pooling on the structure of a payment system and observe how that structure evolves towards an equilibrium. In their model a given number of banks face an exogenous stream of payment requests and choose between settling payments directly and becoming the customer of a settlement bank (for a fee).

The authors find that the cost of liquidity is a key determinant of the evolution of the structure of the system; tiering is more likely to arise when the cost of generating liquidity is relatively high and when payment-system participants face differential costs of liquidity. For instance, we saw in Chapter 4 that the opportunity cost of collateral may be low for banks subject to a prudential liquidity regime that requires that they hold a stock of eligible collateral assets. Posting these assets as collateral for intraday payment liquidity thus imposes few additional costs. Where some banks in a system are subject to such a regime but others are not, those with the higher opportunity cost of liquidity may find it cost effective to settle indirectly via a low-cost participant.

Chapman *et al.* (2008) study the drivers of tiering using a dynamic, general equilibrium model in which both the mode of settlement and the structure of participation are determined endogenously. The authors find that settlement banks perform an important role in monitoring smaller banks' credit history and choosing the optimal settlement mode on their behalf. As such '...a tiered structure can improve efficiency by supporting inter-bank monitoring and cost-saving.'[135]

The literature on tiering in payment systems discussed here provides important insights into the determinants of the structure of payment systems. However, given the wide diversity of factors affecting an individual bank's decision about whether to participate directly or indirectly, it may be that no single model can account completely for the different levels of tiering observed internationally (as in Table 10.1).

10.2 Risks in tiered structures

Settlement banks are proximate infrastructure providers, acting in effect as the payment system through which their customer banks settle their obligations. In respect of both customer-bank payments settled across its own books and those channelled through the payment system, a settlement bank creates systemic externalities similar to those of a dedicated payment system. This is true both in respect of the provision of settlement services for clean payments and the provision of settlement services for the cash leg of a securities transaction. That is, a settlement bank creates links between the participants of its *system* (i.e. customer banks); and any disruption to the provision of the settlement bank's services can have spillover effects. These

---

[135] Chapman *et al.* (2008), p. 36.

are equivalent to the two principal sources of systemic risk described in Chapter 7: interactions between participants within a system; and interactions between a system and the rest of the economy.

The remainder of this section, therefore, discusses the risks posed by tiered payment structures, relative to structures in which all banks are direct settlement members. Issues analogous to those discussed in previous chapters are considered: the credit exposures built up between a settlement bank and its customers (Section 10.2.1); liquidity risk in the provision of wholesale-payments services (Section 10.2.2); the dependence of a customer bank on the operational and financial resilience of its settlement bank (Sections 10.2.3 and 10.2.4); and legal risks around the finality of internalized settlement (Section 10.2.5).

10.2.1 *Credit exposures between a settlement bank and its customer banks*

The main source of credit risk in a tiered structure is the intraday credit typically extended by a settlement bank to its customers to facilitate timely settlement. These overdraft facilities are provided intraday: the expectation is that outstanding balances will be extinguished by the end of day, as incoming payments arrive. Settlement banks may charge a penal rate when credit needs to be extended overnight (unless overnight overdraft limits have been agreed in advance), whereas intraday credit may not attract an explicit fee.

Intraday credit is also provided by the settlement institution in dedicated RTGS-style payment systems. However, a crucial distinction is that these daylight credit extensions are typically secured against high-quality collateral, thereby mitigating the settlement institution's exposure to the default of its members. An overdraft extended by a settlement bank, on the other hand, may be unsecured. Furthermore, limits may also be uncommitted (the settlement bank is not obliged to provide credit and can instead delay outward payments until funds are available) and unadvised (the customer may not be aware of the limit).

These exposures can be sizeable. Harrison *et al.* (2005) estimate that, among CHAPS sterling members, intraday exposures can account for about 3% or more of a settlement bank's total (worldwide consolidated) assets. In this paper, the authors model the effect of tiering on credit risk by comparing a bank's credit-loss distribution under a scenario of 'no tiering' (when it only processes payments on behalf of its non-bank customers) with that under a scenario of 'tiering' (when it also provides wholesale payments services to second-tier banks). The authors view a settlement

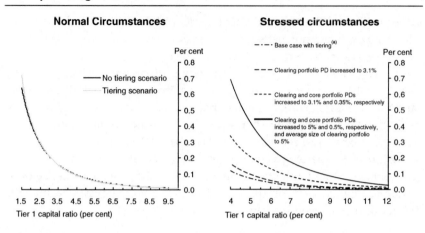

Figure 10.5: Probability of default of first-tier bank against capital

Source: Harrison *et al.* (2005).

(a) Base case: Average size of the clearing portfolio: 3.5% of the settlement bank's assets. Probability of default (PD) for the clearing and the core portfolio: 0.2%.

bank as holding two portfolios of assets: a 'clearing portfolio' that consists of a single, large asset representing the settlement bank's loans to its second-tier banks; and a well-diversified 'core portfolio' that represents the settlement bank's other exposures. Their key results are presented in Figure 10.5. The left panel shows that in normal circumstances, tiering does not have a large impact on a first-tier bank's default probability, since tiering exposures are small relative to the settlement bank's total credit exposure. The right panel (which presents the probability of default for the settlement bank under various scenarios for the size and probability of default of the core and the clearing portfolios) shows that in stressed circumstances, when second-tier banks make greater use of their credit lines and are more likely to default, the credit risk that settlement banks face can increase substantially.

A key concern for policymakers is therefore how settlement banks manage and monitor the usage of intraday credit by their customers. Even with credit limits in place, attention might need to be given to how actively these are monitored in practice. If the settlement bank only monitors limits by identifying *ex-post* breaches, and then makes a decision as to whether it should extend further credit, it may be unaware of the level of its routine intraday exposures to customer banks.

Credit exposures may, of course, also arise in the other direction. When a customer bank holds positive intraday balances with its settlement bank, it has an unsecured credit exposure to that bank.

10.2.2 Liquidity risks in the provision of wholesale-payments services

As mentioned earlier, the magnitude of liquidity demands and the cost of generating intraday liquidity are important driving forces behind a bank's decision as to whether or not to participate directly in an RTGS system. An indirect participant essentially transfers the liquidity management burden associated with meeting its obligations to its settlement bank, potentially leaving the settlement bank more susceptible to liquidity problems. In particular, there is a risk that a settlement bank may use up a high proportion of its liquid resources in making payments on behalf of customers, leaving it constrained in the event that it faces an unexpected liquidity need from its proprietary transactions.

Equally, settlement banks may become dependent on the liquidity provided by customer banks' incoming payments: these can be a cheap source of liquidity for the settlement bank in meeting its own obligations, or those of its other customers.

10.2.3 Operational risk: a customer bank's dependence on the resilience of its settlement bank

A customer bank is dependent on the continued and uninterrupted ability of its settlement bank to send and receive payments on its behalf, just as a direct participant is dependent on the operational resilience of the central payment system. Box 10.2 provides an example. As we have seen, when a dedicated payment infrastructure provider suffers an operational problem, a negative externality is imposed on system participants: the cost of the provider's disruption is borne by those unable to process their payments and others reliant on the smooth flow of liquidity in the system, with potential further spillover effects. This single-point-of-failure risk is a key concern for payment-system overseers.[136]

An operational shock to the service provided by a settlement bank imposes a similar negative externality on its customer banks, again with potential spillover effects beyond the direct customer banks. This dependence on the settlement bank creates what is often termed 'node risk'. As

---

[136] See Section 6.1 for a discussion of operational risk.

Box 10.2: FAILURE OF A DOMESTIC CORRESPONDENT BANKING NETWORK

The potential for correspondent banks to cause contagion in the financial system was acutely evidenced in the US during the Great Depression. Richardson (2006) studies documentation submitted to the Federal Reserve by banks that suspended their operations, either permanently or temporarily, during the crisis. Banks suspensions are attributed to a number of different causes, including failure of a correspondent bank. 15% of temporary suspensions and 4% of terminal suspensions between January 1929 and March 1933 were due to closure of a correspondent.

When Caldwell – a large Tennessee bank with an extensive correspondent network – collapsed in the late 1930s, nearly 100 banks subsequently suspended operations. This was in part, due to runs triggered by known affiliations with the Caldwell organization or geographical proximity to Caldwell-controlled entities. However, it also reflected the severing of correspondent links to institutions controlled by the Caldwell conglomerate. Correspondent networks appear to have propagated the panic particularly during the initial weeks.

---

large settlement banks become increasingly important nodes in the financial system, the question arises as to whether the regulatory authorities should seek to ensure a degree of resilience similar to that required for dedicated infrastructures.

For customer banks, mitigation of the risks of an interruption at a settlement bank will naturally involve having in place workarounds or contingency arrangements. These may involve customer banks holding accounts with more than one settlement bank, such that payments can be rerouted in the event of a disruption at the primary provider. It is important that these arrangements are operationally robust themselves and that payments can be switched at short notice. This may be easier to achieve for outgoing payments than for receipts from counterparties.

In addition to interrupting the ability of customer banks to send and receive payments, a temporary outage at a settlement bank could also create a liquidity sink for the system as a whole. As discussed in Chapter 6, a liquidity sink can arise when a stricken bank is able to receive but unable to send payments, thereby depriving the overall payment system of the recycled liquidity that is crucial to its smooth functioning. To the extent that tiering concentrates payment flows in large settlement banks, there may be a higher chance that a temporary outage results in a liquidity sink.

A final issue is that such arrangements are dependent on the willingness of the settlement bank to send payments on its customer banks' behalf. Since the credit provided by a settlement bank may be uncommitted and unadvised, it may be withdrawn at any time. In the event of a perceived financial problem at a customer bank, the settlement bank may immediately cut the credit line. Indeed, while a customer bank might expect that its settlement bank would continue to provide credit in such circumstances, a settlement bank might be tempted to withdraw the credit line at the first sign of difficulty, trading off the long-term negative effects on its reputation as a reliable correspondent with a desire to limit its credit losses. From a regulatory standpoint, it would seem important that settlement banks' and customers banks' expectations in respect of likely behaviours in stressed circumstances are reasonably well aligned.

10.2.4 *Business Risk*

As with dedicated infrastructures (Section 6.2), a financial problem at a settlement bank can spill over and interrupt its provision of wholesale-payments services. This risk is comparatively greater for a settlement bank, since it will likely have a much broader range of business activities from which a financial problem might arise.

Mitigation of the risk that the failure of a large settlement bank spills over to the financial system as a whole is an important stability issue. Options in a crisis might include stripping out the critical infrastructure functions of a failing institution, such that customer banks can continue to send and receive payments until alternative arrangements can be put in place. But that would typically require careful planning, and a degree of 'separability' of the critical functions from the rest of the business.

10.2.5 *Legal risks and finality of settlement*

The finality of settlement for payments settled via a settlement bank is less well defined than for payments settled directly in a dedicated payment system. For instance, the European Union's Settlement Finality Directive allows for designated systems' rules on payments to be robust to any legal challenge on the question of settlement finality (see also Section 3.2.1). However, this only covers payments between direct participants settled inside the dedicated payment system. The point of finality for the customer bank will not typically be so clearly defined.

Moreover, internalized payments – those between two second-tier banks, settled across the books of the correspondent – do not enter the dedicated payment system at all and so do not enjoy the same level of protection against legal challenge. The finality of such payments would typically be covered by Service Level Agreements between the settlement bank and its customer, and the legal position of such agreements would be a matter of ordinary contract law.

10.3 Other firms providing payment and settlement infrastructure

There are other instances, besides the provision of cash settlement services in high-value payments and securities settlement, in which banks and other financial institutions perform infrastructure-like services. For instance, custodians in many respects perform a role for their customers akin to that of a securities settlement system; and general clearing members (GCMs), or third-party clearers, perform a role for their customers akin to that of a central counterparty. In each case, the service provider's activities again give rise to the two principal sources of systemic risk identified throughout this volume: they create interactions between their customers; and they create interactions between themselves and the rest of the economy.

10.3.1 Custodians

CPSS (2003) defines a custodian as an entity, often a bank, that safekeeps and administers securities for its customers and that may provide various other associated services, including clearing and settlement, cash management, foreign exchange and securities lending. Other banks, money managers, broker/dealers, institutional investors, hedge funds and private equity firms may access securities settlement systems (SSSs) and central securities depositories (CSDs) indirectly via a custodian.

As with correspondent banking, facilitation of cross-border transactions is often at the heart of custody arrangements. Indeed, in recent years some big global custodians have come to dominate the market, providing custody services for all their customers' transactions across the globe (often via a behind-the-scenes network of subcustodians, or local agents in different markets).

The risk issues that arise here with regard to securities settlement are akin to those discussed above in respect of clean payments. The custodian is essentially its customers' access point to dedicated SSSs and CSDs, and where a custodian acts for both counterparties to a securities transaction,

---

Box 10.3: BANK OF NEW YORK CUSTODY DISRUPTION 1985

On the morning of November 21, the Bank of New York (BoNY) experienced an IT systems failure which left its custody function able to receive but unable to transfer securities.[137] As the bank was one of the largest custodian and settlement banks for US government securities, this caused significant disruption to settlement processes.

Figure 10.6 illustrates the flow of funds and securities in Fedwire Securities when BoNY acts as an intermediary in a government securities trade.

Figure 10.6: Schematic overview of the flow of money and securities via BoNY

The systems failure meant that BoNY was unable to instruct Fedwire Securities to transfer securities to buyers' accounts. As a result buyers were not prepared to release funds to BoNY. Sellers, on the other hand, continued to transfer securities to BoNY, in respect of which BoNY continued to settle funds. Since it was unable to transfer these securities to the end-buyer, and receive funds in return, BoNY rapidly ran short of liquidity. Ultimately, the Federal Reserve extended considerable intraday liquidity until the systems problem was resolved.

settlement may be internalized across the custodian's own books. Thus, a customer bank is dependent on the custodian's ability and willingness to process securities transactions on its behalf and to maintain records of the securities transactions settled. A temporary operational outage, or financial failure, of a large custodian could therefore have widespread repercussions (see Box 10.3). Furthermore, through the provision of settlement services, custodians can increase the interconnectedness of financial institutions by, for example, providing intraday credit to facilitate timely settlement.

10.3.2 *General Clearing Members*

As described in Chapter 5, a central counterparty (CCP) interposes itself as a legal counterparty to both sides of transactions executed on a particular exchange – i.e. it becomes the buyer to every seller, and the seller to every buyer.[138] Members of a central counterparty therefore replace their bilat-

---

[137] See Danmarks Nationalbank (2000) for details.
[138] CPSS (2004).

eral counterparty exposures with a single counterparty risk to the CCP (Hills *et al.*, 1999). As set out in more detail in Chapter 5, the CCP manages the credit and liquidity risks associated with the provision of this service by requiring members to post initial margin and by requiring payment of variation margin in response to changes in the value of members' positions.

Membership of exchanges is often split into three broad categories: individual clearing members, who clear their own and their customers' trades; GCMs, who in addition clear the trades of non-clearing members (NCMs); and NCMs, who do not have access to the central counterparty and so must use a GCM to clear their trades.

As such, a GCM in essence offers CCP-like services to its NCM customers, standing between its customer and the central counterparty itself. Any disruption to the GCM's activities will therefore impact its NCM customers and potentially spill over to the wider market.

The financial interlinkages created between a GCM and its customers are also potentially important. A GCM stands behind its NCM customers' trades within the central counterparty and is therefore responsible for the collection of margins from its NCMs and their payment to the central counterparty. How a GCM manages its exposures to its NCM customers is critical. For instance, does the GCM extend daylight credit by paying margin to the central counterparty on their behalf before receiving it from its NCM customers? Or does it have agreements in place that allow it to borrow from its customers by delaying the pass-through of margin payments from the central counterparty?

11

The evolving infrastructure landscape and challenges for central banks

At the time of writing, financial innovation, globalization and regulatory change are transforming the structure of trading and post-trade services (see Jenkinson, 2007). Stresses in the financial system during 2007 and 2008 have also presented challenges for infrastructure providers and their participants, which may shape the evolution. Section 11.1 traces out how the trading landscape has responded to the challenges of financial globalization and regulatory change. We then consider how developments at this level might in turn influence the evolution of payment and settlement systems. Sections 11.2 and 11.3 consider the implications for financial and monetary stability, and how central banks might respond. We conclude in Section 11.4 with some suggestions for future research in the economics of payment and settlement systems.

11.1 Forces for change in the infrastructure landscape

Over the past decade, the forces for change in the provision of trading and post-trading services have in many ways mirrored those in the financial system more broadly.

The rapid decline of the costs of storing, processing and transmitting information,[139] and the development of new software applications that exploit increased processing speed, have fuelled financial innovation and have played a crucial role in facilitating the global integration of financial markets. In response, there has been consolidation amongst incumbent infrastructure providers, and new providers have entered the market.

---

[139] Hancock *et al.* (1999) investigate the evolution of costs in Fedwire, the US large-value RTGS system, and find that real average production costs fell by about 60% between 1979 and 1996.

Regulatory change has provided further impetus to these developments. In this section, we consider these developments and explore some of the risk implications.

11.1.1 *Regulation and public intervention*

In a number of jurisdictions, public intervention has recently lowered significantly the costs of entry for innovative providers of trading, clearing and settlement services and increased the scope of the market in which they operate.

In the US, a series of amendments to the Securities and Exchange Act, collectively referred to as 'Regulation National Market System', or RegNMS, were implemented to increase competition in securities trading. One of these amendments requires that trades be executed on the platform offering 'best execution', thereby significantly reducing barriers to entry for new trading platforms.

The European Commission's Markets in Financial Instruments Directive (MiFID), introduced in 2007, is even more ambitious in scope, aiming to provide a harmonized regulatory regime for investment services across the member states of the European Economic Area. It also contains a best-execution requirement.

Both MiFID and RegNMS are fostering a fresh wave of competition and innovation at the trading platform level, shifting the balance of power away from the exchanges towards the traders, and adding further impetus to incumbent exchanges' cross-border ambitions as they seek to defend their positions. Incumbents have responded by lowering their trading

---

Box 11.1: THE EUROPEAN CLEARING AND SETTLEMENT CODE OF CONDUCT

The European Clearing and Settlement Code of Conduct is an industry initiative in response to concerns voiced by the European Commission on the lack of post-trade competition. It addresses issues around the balance of power between infrastructure providers and market participants. All European exchanges, clearinghouses and securities depositories have been asked to sign the Code on a voluntary basis (although there remains the threat of a clearing and settlement Directive if the Code is not seen to facilitate increased competition).

At the time of writing, the Code applies only to cash equities, but the scope may be widened to securities and derivatives in due course. The Code is being introduced in three stages: applying *price transparency* to post-trade services; tackling *access and interoperability* issues to enable trading venues to be served by more than one provider; and *service unbundling* to discourage cross-subsidization of post-trade services.

---

fees, merging, and absorbing market entrants. For example, in 2007, there were mergers between: the London Stock Exchange and Borsa Italiana; the New York Stock Exchange (NYSE) and Euronext (a pan-European stock exchange that itself originated from a merger of the stock exchanges in Amsterdam, Brussels, and Paris); and NASDAQ and OMX.

Similarly, the recently agreed Code of Conduct in the EU seeks to promote competition in the post-trade space. It requires interoperability and open access between clearing and settlement providers (initially in equities) and thereby seeks to break the stranglehold of 'vertical silos' in some markets, where providers of post-trade services are owned by the trading platforms (see Box 11.1).

11.1.2 Global integration of financial markets: interdependencies

Banks' cross-border activities have been expanding more rapidly than those of the supporting infrastructure, leading to frictions in cross-border settlement. In response, some large multinational banking groups are taking the opportunity to leverage their connections, for example to central securities depositories, to provide cross-border clearing and settlement services (see Chapter 10).

Incumbent infrastructure providers are also adapting to the new demands. With a few exceptions, the provision of infrastructure has traditionally evolved along national lines (or even, at first, regionally within countries). Reflecting the increased importance of electronic and geographically integrated markets, cross-border alliances and mergers between incumbent providers have become increasingly common. Some examples are provided in Box 11.2.

But it is by no means certain that these trends will result in a few large, multinational providers. Technological advance has reduced the barriers to entry for new infrastructure providers, as the fixed cost of building processing capacity has fallen. New entrants may be in a better position to benefit from technological innovations than incumbent providers constrained by legacy systems. To the extent that technology facilitates interoperability (for instance, smart order routing between competing trading platforms, or liquidity bridges between settlement systems), a series of interoperable links may mitigate any loss of network effects associated with a move from concentrated to fragmented provision of infrastructure. Where this is true, it may be that markets are indeed now able to support several providers, and that a competitive equilibrium of this type is sustainable.

Box 11.2: RECENT MERGERS AMONG PROVIDERS OF FINANCIAL INFRASTRUCTURE SERVICES

Over the past decade, a large number of mergers have created multinational providers of infrastructure services. Figure 11.1 demonstrates a number of horizontal and vertical interlinkages that have developed in Belgian, Dutch, French and UK cash equity markets.

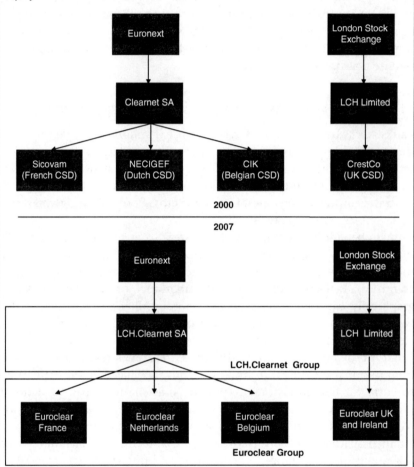

Figure 11.1: The clearing and settlement landscape in a sample of European equity markets in 2000 and 2007

In 2003, the UK-based and French-based central counterparties, the London Clearing House and Clearnet SA, merged (horizontally) to become LCH. Clearnet Group – two central counterparties operating under one corporate structure. LCH.Clearnet Group has a settlement relationship with Euroclear Group that itself formed from the acquisition of a number of settlement systems in other countries, including Sicovam in 2001, NECIGEF in 2002, CRESTCo in 2002 and, more recently, CIK in 2006.[140] The national CSDs are now, respectively, known as Euroclear France, Euroclear Netherlands, Euroclear UK and Ireland and Euroclear Belgium.

For some components of the financial infrastructure, however, one might argue that the underlying scale and network effects are sufficiently strong that a competitive equilibrium with multiple providers is unlikely. In such cases, we may well be witnessing a struggle for supremacy that will result in a new concentrated equilibrium, but with 'the market' redefined on an international scale.

Increased cross-border activities, and competition between providers of infrastructure services that were previously offered by national monopolies, create complex interdependencies between systems – at both the domestic and the international level. Interdependencies take a variety of forms: direct linkages between systems; indirect linkages, arising from the activities of large financial institutions in multiple systems; and broader common dependencies, such as systems' common reliance on a single third-party service provider. As a result, the settlement flows, operational processes, and risk-management procedures of each individual system now depend on other systems, nationally and internationally.[141]

Interdependencies are already strong at the domestic level. For example, banks often participate in several domestic infrastructures: if they are short of liquidity in one system, they might source this from another that settles in the same settlement asset. Some systems, primarily in the United States, have formal cross-margining, cross-guarantee, or cross-netting agreements for their common participants. Direct interdependencies also arise between systems. For instance, domestic large-value RTGS systems often settle net payments from ancillary systems, such as other large-value systems and securities settlement systems that settle on a net basis. A prolonged outage of the RTGS system could thus prevent settlement in these ancillary systems. And some domestic payment and settlement systems rely on common providers of communication and messaging services.

---

[140] Euroclear Group also incorporates an ICSD in Belgium, Euroclear Bank.
[141] CPSS (2008b).

An important milestone in the settlement of foreign exchange was the introduction of Continuous Linked Settlement (CLS), a settlement system that facilitates the simultaneous transfer of the two legs of a foreign-exchange transaction (see Chapter 5). With CLS ultimately settling net in the large-value payment systems of the fifteen participating countries, it naturally reinforces the links between them and therefore creates increased international interdependencies.

As is the case in the domestic context, overlapping system membership in several countries can create system interdependencies. If, for example, credit concerns were to emerge about an international banking group, it might suffer significant outflows simultaneously in multiple systems, triggering strategic responses by other participants and potentially disrupting the flow of liquidity in each system. In practice, about a dozen banks participate directly in a substantial number of large-value payment systems internationally.

And, finally, reliance on a common messaging service, SWIFT, makes payment systems internationally vulnerable to malfunctions of this service (see Chapter 6).

11.1.3 *Innovative business processes: globally centralized liquidity management*

One driver of increased demand for cross-border payment and settlement services is the increasing prevalence of global liquidity management in multinational banks.[142] At a basic level, a bank is liquid if its cash inflows are sufficient to meet its cash outflow obligations as they fall due. The process of liquidity management essentially involves managing the timing mismatches between inflows and outflows, ensuring that the bank has enough cash (or is able to generate it in time) to meet its payment obligations.

Liquidity management can be more complicated for large, international financial groups since the obligations of all entities within the group – in each and every market and currency in which they operate – must be managed. Centralization can be advantageous for a bank that can cover a liquidity deficit in one currency with a liquidity surplus in another currency.

Two main mechanisms are available to transfer this surplus liquidity: the cross-border use of collateral, and the transfer of cash between currencies in the form of a foreign-exchange transaction. Manning and Willison (2006)

---

[142] See CPSS (2006).

focus on the former. In a model with optimizing banks, they show that, even with an aggregate reduction in liquidity holdings, routine cross-border use of collateral can reduce liquidity risk in payment systems. Of course, centralized liquidity management only provides this insurance if liquidity demands are imperfectly correlated across currencies: if the bank faced high liquidity demands in both systems – for example, because its creditors lost faith in its ability to repay their funds and sought to withdraw their deposits – it would be left short of eligible collateral in at least one system.

Schanz (2009) focuses on the cross-border transfer of liquidity via the foreign-exchange market. He argues that the greater informational efficiency of centralized liquidity management, achieved via intragroup cross-currency lending, can be highly advantageous to a bank that is short of funds in one currency but not in others. This is particularly so in stressed circumstances, when there might be heightened asymmetric information in domestic interbank markets. Schanz's starting point is the assumption that only *external* credit relationships suffer from asymmetric information between the borrower and the lender: intragroup transfers are assumed to take place under symmetric information. Hence, Schanz's first key result is an adverse selection one: in a crisis, a subsidiary that is not granted emergency funding by an affiliated entity is inferred by the market to be of low credit quality, and hence will be unable to obtain refinancing from any external lender.

Schanz then shows that the transition from local to global liquidity management has two consequences for financial stability. First, the transmission of solvency shocks from one institution to another becomes less likely because banks with high solvency risks would not be able to refinance themselves at all in response to liquidity outflows (neither in the domestic interbank market, nor via the intragroup transfer of liquidity). This reduces interbank exposures. But, since this implies that such banks would have to delay settlement of obligations beyond their due-date, 'technical default' becomes more likely.

Global liquidity management implies a demand for arrangements that facilitate the cross-border transfer of securities and recycling of cross-currency liquidity surpluses. There have, therefore, been active calls from industry participants (e.g. Payments Risk Committee, 2003) for central banks to accept a wider range of foreign-currency collateral and to work with private providers to enhance infrastructural arrangements for mobilizing such collateral. Partly in response, the central-banking community has been investigating these issues, with the Committee on Payment and

Settlement Systems publishing a first report on cross-border collateral arrangements in 2006 (CPSS, 2006).

In the light of the liquidity dislocation arising from the market turmoil of 2007/2008, public-policy interest in issues around global liquidity management has increased substantially. At the time of writing, follow-up work to the 2006 CPSS report on cross-border use of collateral has been given greater priority. Furthermore, new inter-central-bank currency-swap arrangements have been implemented to facilitate central-bank liquidity provision in foreign currency to an internationally active bank.

11.1.4 Innovative products: post-trade processing of financial derivatives

Innovative financial products are usually initially traded, cleared and settled on a bilateral basis. It is only when a product becomes more widely traded – and perhaps standardized – that market participants will consider more centralized infrastructural arrangements. We focus here on the example of over-the-counter (OTC) derivatives.

For most OTC derivatives products, clearing and settlement of obligations occurs bilaterally between the counterparties to the contract. That is, throughout the life of the contract, the two counterparties retain direct bilateral cash-flow obligations to one another. For instance, under a credit default swap (CDS) contract, the seller of protection is obliged to pay the nominal value of the contract to the buyer of protection in the event of a reference-entity default. In return, the buyer of protection is obliged to pay regular quarterly premia to the seller. Calculation and settlement of such cash flows, and the management of replacement cost risk over the life of the contract has traditionally been the responsibility of the two parties to the contract, with little centralized infrastructure in this market to support these processes. This may be explained, at least in part, by the tailored, bespoke nature of OTC contracts and the lack of a deep and liquid secondary market.[143] At the time of writing, this is beginning to change.

Until the onset of financial market turbulence in 2007 and 2008, the global OTC derivatives market had experienced extremely rapid growth, with outstanding notional values increasing more than three-fold, to $683 trillion, in the four years to June 2008. With post-trade processes largely manual across the range of products, the pace of growth began to put strains on dealers' back-offices. One issue, first highlighted in CPSS (1998),

---

[143] See Ledrut and Upper (2007) for a discussion of some of the challenges to post-trade processing in OTC derivatives markets.

was the failure to confirm trades on a timely basis. Absence of legal confirmation jeopardizes the enforceability of transactions and can generate market and credit risks by allowing errors in trade records and management information systems to go undetected.

As trading volumes continued to grow, and backlogs of trade confirmations began to accumulate, several regulatory authorities and committees internationally began to take a strong interest in post-trade processes in this market (CPSS, 2007). Indeed, in September 2005 the Federal Reserve Bank of New York convened a group of the major international dealers in the credit derivatives market and their regulators, seeking commitments to improve post-trade arrangements. With an initial focus on credit derivatives, this group encouraged a number of important enhancements to the market infrastructure for OTC derivatives, promoting increased automation in the processing of trade confirmations and working with the Depository Trust and Clearing Corporation (DTCC), the US clearing and settlement provider, to establish a Trade Information Warehouse, a central repository of information on all credit derivatives trades executed in the OTC market. As a direct result of these efforts, levels of automation in post-trade processing increased substantially: in 2008, major dealers confirmed more than 90% of credit derivatives trades electronically, as against less than 50% when this initiative was launched three years earlier.

Efforts to enhance the centralized infrastructure in this market have been given even greater priority at the time of writing in response to renewed operational strains during the market turmoil of 2007/08 and concerns over counterparty credit risk and a lack of transparency.[144] A particular focus has been the promotion of central counterparty clearing for the OTC derivatives market, and in the credit default swaps market in particular. A number of providers have developed services in response, with one of these, ICE Trust in the United States, launching in March 2009 and clearing a significant volume of index trades during its first months of operations.

While the demand for certain OTC products has retreated in early 2009, regulators face the challenge of developing policies which can reopen, strengthen and underpin those segments of the market that play an important role in tailored risk and portfolio management, and contribute to efficient price discovery. Improved transparency and disclosure, effective risk management, and resilient operational processes are all sure to play their part in strengthening this market.[145] An important

---

[144] See Financial Stability Forum (2008).
[145] Some interim recommendations in these areas were included in IOSCO (2009).

policy question that clearly arises in this area is how counterparty credit risks might be more explicitly reflected in supervisory assessments of market participants, so as to encourage market participants to continue to innovate and reduce the risks involved in clearing and settling these instruments.

11.2 Implications for financial stability and central bank oversight

The trends and developments described in the previous section imply fundamental changes in the infrastructure landscape. As we have seen, cross-border provision of infrastructural services has increased, interdependencies between systems have intensified, and new infrastructural services have emerged – for instance, to support OTC derivatives markets. Industry and regulatory responses to the financial turbulence of 2007/08 will also shape the evolution. Some of these developments point towards increased concentration in infrastructure provision, and the possible emergence of a small number of large regional or global providers. Others point towards fragmentation, with a number of competing providers, some of which may be banks operating as infrastructure. Whatever the eventual outcome, these developments pose a number of challenges for overseers of payment and settlement systems. Some of these are explored below.

11.2.1 Implications for system resilience

Whether the ultimate end-point is a concentrated or a fragmented infrastructural landscape, changes underway will have important implications for system resilience. The potential implications need to be well understood by overseers, in order that they can prioritize efforts and respond appropriately as the landscape evolves. For instance, a concentrated structure may reduce the probability that settlement risk crystallizes, but increase the potential impact. A fragmented structure may imply the reverse.

Consider first a concentrated structure. To the extent that a system operates as a single point of failure in a given market, with no scope to re-route flow to an alternative provider, crystallization of an operational or business risk may disrupt a higher volume of settlements, imposing higher costs on market participants. The impact may also be more rapidly and more widely dispersed, potentially across markets and across borders.

At the same time, however, a single large provider may have not only greater resources, but also a sharper incentive to invest in system resilience. After all, many of the effects that are external to a small provider will be internalized by a single large provider.[146] A qualification to this is that a systemically important infrastructure provider may count on support by the public sector in a crisis, leading to a corresponding reduction in its investment in system resilience. In such cases, stronger governance or public intervention may be required to secure the appropriate level of 'self-insurance'.

In the case of a fragmented market structure, the loss of positive network externalities may reduce efficiencies and raise both costs and liquidity risks. Furthermore, the incentive to invest in resilience may be reduced, since the external costs of failure are less likely to be internalized. This may increase the probability that a settlement risk crystallizes.

The example of liquidity risk is instructive here. In a settlement system, a bank participating directly in more than one system may find that it has excess liquidity in one system but is short of liquidity in another. Unless technology can be deployed to build an effective liquidity bridge and create a 'virtual pool', there may be processing delays and, perhaps, outright settlement failures in the system in which the bank is short of liquidity. Even with a bridge, there may be costs to mobilizing liquidity across it. Were fragmented systems to fully consolidate, such frictional costs could be avoided. Similarly, in trading, unless orders can be rapidly rerouted between platforms, market depth might be compromised.

The overall impact should settlement risk crystallize is, however, likely to be lower, since any individual provider controls a lower volume of flow. Furthermore, as long as there is some scope for re-routing and alternative systems have sufficient capacity to receive re-directed flow, an operational disruption or failure of a provider can be accommodated more easily.

11.2.2 Implications for the scope and conduct of oversight

Increasing interdependencies between systems, and the blurring of the border between banks and providers of payment and settlement services, create a range of issues for overseers. Oversight in a decentralized system with many links and different channels for contagion is much more complex than in a simple, compartmentalized system. With concentrated

---

[146] See Chapter 7 for a description of these external effects.

and international provision, a difficult question arises as to how leverage can be brought to bear by independent national overseers. This issue is central to the debate underway at the time of writing around regional versus global provision of central counterparty services in the credit derivatives market. In either case, it seems that central banks will need to decide which parts of the changing infrastructure landscape need to be overseen; to what degree; against which standards; and (particularly in the case of firms that take on infrastructure functions) by whom. Concrete actions for overseers might include:

- *Setting the right scope for oversight*: As new systems emerge, it is important that all systemically important payment and settlement systems fall within the scope of oversight. But objective criteria need to be developed and applied consistently, perhaps taking into account the size of flows, interdependencies with other systems/markets, and the degree of substitutability. It is also important that all systemically important providers of infrastructure are subject to equivalent high standards, irrespective of whether the service is being offered by a traditional infrastructure provider or a bank.
- *International cooperation*: With infrastructure providers increasingly operating across borders, and international interdependencies increasing (see Section 11.1), central banks may need to work together ever more closely, sharing risk assessments, cooperating in oversight and co-ordinating their actions.
- *Dialogue with banking supervisors*: Where new infrastructure services are offered by commercial bank providers (see Chapter 10), central banks need to cooperate closely with banking supervisors to ensure that financial stability risk emanating from their roles as providers of infrastructure are reflected within regulatory assessments. Such cooperation would also be valuable in the context of members' intraday liquidity management within systems, their strategic behaviour within systems, and their contingency plans in the event of system disruption. And, to the extent that there is a multicurrency dimension here, an international dialogue may be necessary.
- *Developing an appropriate regulatory and oversight framework to accommodate financial innovation*: As (OTC) markets continue to evolve and financial innovation leads to new product and markets, the post-trade infrastructure needs to keep pace. It will be important for the regulatory regime to reflect risks arising from the use of insufficiently robust clearing and settlement processes and to provide incentives for market par-

ticipants to develop and use infrastructure that is systemically robust. This also points to the need for closer cooperation between central banks as overseers and banking supervisors.

- *Reappraisal of oversight standards*: There may be a need to re-visit international standards for oversight (such as the CPSS Core Principles and CPSS-IOSCO recommendations for securities settlement systems and central counterparties, see Chapter 9) to ensure their continued relevance. For example, at the time of writing, an effort was underway to revise standards for operational risk, and CPSS-IOSCO recommendations for central counterparties were to be revised to encompass clearing services for OTC derivatives products. Furthermore, with cross-border provision of services and emerging competition between infrastructure providers, there may also be a need for 'best-practice guidelines' to aid the interpretation of existing standards and thereby ensure their consistent application across jurisdictions.

11.3 Implications for the implementation of monetary policy

In response to the stresses in the financial system beginning in mid-2007, central banks around the world made changes to their operational frameworks and accommodated an increase in the demand for central-bank money in the banking system. The provision of central-bank liquidity, often against a wider range of eligible collateral assets and over longer maturities, helped to ensure that money markets continued to function even as banks hit liquidity constraints and counterparty credit concerns mounted. In Europe, for instance, the Eurosystem's balance sheet almost doubled in size between June 2007 and April 2009, to €1.51 trillion, equal to 16 per cent of nominal GDP of the euro area (Papademos, 2009).

Prior to the financial turbulence, however, there had been some debate as to the future role of central-bank money and, in particular, whether increased competition from banks offering settlement services in their own (commercial-bank) money might ultimately lead to a decline in the demand for central-bank money. If so, this could affect central banks' ability to implement monetary policy. Longer term, then, as the financial system stabilizes and central banks exit from the extraordinary policy measures taken during the period of financial turbulence, there may be a question as to whether a trend away from central-bank money might reassert itself.

Private banks find themselves structurally short of central-bank money for several reasons. First, central-bank money is the most widely accepted, and hence preferred, medium of exchange between economic agents (Chapter 1). Second, central-bank money is also the preferred settlement asset for high-value payment and settlement systems because the central bank is not normally the source of credit risk. Third, there may be regulations that require banks to hold a certain amount of central-bank liabilities (minimum-reserve requirements), or to use a payment or settlement system that settles in central-bank money.

Central banks typically implement monetary policy by varying the interest rate at which they make their money available to the banking system. Through a variety of transmission channels, a variation in this interest rate ultimately affects real economic activity and prices. Views differ as to whether the central bank would still be able to influence real activity if the private sector's demand for central-bank money were to decline permanently and substantially.[147]

As long as there is a residual structural demand for central-bank money, the central bank's ability to influence real activity should in principle remain unchanged: it can still affect the residual demand via changes in the interest rate. In practice, however, this residual demand may come to be more volatile (especially over short horizons), making it difficult for central banks to forecast the quantity of (some measure of) money demanded by the banking system at a given level of the interest rate, or indeed to target a monetary aggregate directly.

A residual structural demand at any desired level could of course always be ensured simply by imposing minimum reserve requirements on commercial banks. But the case in which the structural demand for central-bank money falls to zero is nevertheless interesting. This might happen if commercial-bank money were to become a perfect substitute, for example when the commercial bank on whose books claims are ultimately settled is regarded as no riskier than the central bank. (It might be, for example, that this bank is perceived to become too systemically important to fail, and so could rely on public-sector support if needed.) In such a situation, it is debated whether the central bank could still affect interest rates. Goodhart (1998a) argues that central banks could still affect interest rates by operating in financial markets at large. A central bank could increase interest rates by selling assets out of its portfolio at a lower price (promising a

---

[147] See, for example, Woodford (2000, 2001, 2003), and Berk (2003).

higher return) than its private-sector competitiors. Interest rates could be lowered by buying assets at a higher price.

Of course, this type of intervention is bound to make losses, and may therefore also reduce the central bank's independence from the finance ministry. And it is not clear that it would be effective. A large literature shows that (similar) central-bank interventions in foreign-exchange markets do not appear to work well.[148]

There is, as yet, no firm evidence of a marked gravitation away from central-bank payment systems. Indeed, in countries with competing large-value payment systems (e.g. the US (Fedwire and CHIPS) and the euro area (TARGET and Euro 1)), the central-bank-operated system has tended to grow faster.[149]

Furthermore, the financial turmoil in 2007/8 is a stark reminder that access to central-bank liquidity can provide an indispensable lifeline for money markets and can support the smooth functioning of payment systems even in times of considerable stress. This points to the continuing value of direct settlement in central-bank money; and also in indirect payment system participants' maintaining close operational links with the central bank via the establishment of reserve accounts and access to standing facilities.

11.4 Directions for future research in large-value payment systems

Throughout the financial market turbulence from mid-2007, the market infrastructure around the world continued to function smoothly. This may in part reflect advances in system design, which have insulated the main payment and settlement systems from an increase in counterparty credit risks. It may also reflect the considerable liquidity injected into overnight and longer-term money markets by central banks around the world. While this provision of liquidity was aimed primarily at relieving strains in these markets, it might also have reduced the scope for liquidity risks to crystallize in payment and settlement systems. Empirical research

---

[148] Costa and De Grauwe (2001) argue that if, for example, commercial banks sold some of their assets to the central bank, they might be unwilling to hold the central bank's liabilities in their portfolio, and redeem them at the central bank against the asset they just sold. This redemption would eliminate the increase in the central bank's liabilities, and increase the supply of the asset, thereby reducing its price and return to the initial level.

[149] Some evidence on this is available in Bech *et al.* (2008), alongside some other useful background on trends in large-value payment systems.

can use data that is now becoming available to study, in more detail, the link between central bank provision of liquidity and the performance of payment and settlement systems.

As noted in this chapter, growing interdependencies can serve as channels for contagion from operational or financial disruptions. It is crucial, then, that central banks, system operators and market participants improve their understanding of the various interdependencies between payment and settlement systems, ensuring that effective risk controls are established to contain the potential transmission of risk. This is also an area, therefore, in which further research will be valuable.

Building on seminal contributions – surveyed in Chapter 6 – that have pioneered the econometric analysis of the impact of operational shocks on behaviour in payment systems, as well as the potential for 'spillovers' into interbank markets, further research could employ techniques used in financial econometrics to build a much more complete picture of the interdependencies between different systems. These techniques might also be used to quantify interactions between systems and the markets that are being served, or indeed markets that might be affected indirectly. Careful consideration might be given here to the distinction between behaviour in normal times and under conditions when financial markets are already stressed and subject to heightened uncertainties.

A third area where further research is needed is to understand better the underlying determinants of the evolution of the landcape, as well as behaviour within sytems as the landcape evolves. Game-theoretic approaches may provide intuition, but they are not able to capture fully the complexity of interaction in payment systems. Particular challenges also arise in modelling the evolution of the infrastructural architecture and its transition to a new equilibrium. Research in this field may therefore usefully build on agent-based modelling techniques – described in Chapter 4 – that are now being applied to understand complex interactions within systems. They might also be used to study the transition from one set of infrastructural arrangements to another.

The final key area of research that is motivated by the developments described in this chapter goes right back to the central theme of Part I of this book. Central banks have leverage over monetary and financial stability not least because of their role in providing the final settlement asset in payment systems. In a world where settlement in commercial-bank money can offer tailor-made solutions that, for political economy reasons, are not in the gift of central banks – such as settlement across multiple currencies – settlement might over time move away from central banks' books. A key question faced by central banks is therefore whether their role in ensuring financial and monetary stability may then become more difficult. This question is difficult to answer with modelling techniques that are used in traditional monetary economics – where neither money, nor payments, play an essential role. However, progress could be made when analysis is built on recent and important theoretical advances – surveyed in Chapters 2 and 4 – that introduce explicitly the tightly linked concepts of money and payments into the mainstream of modern monetary economics.

Further research in these areas will help to ensure that central banks are well placed to face challenges to their pursuit of monetary and financial stability that will emerge from the ongoing rapid pace of change in payment and settlement systems.

Glossary

CCP: Central Counterparty. See Section 5.3.

CNS: Continuous Net Settlement. See Section 4.6.3.

CPSS: The Bank for International Settlement's Committee on Payment
           and Settlement Systems.

CSD: Central Securities Depository. See Box 2.3.

DNS: Deferred Net Settlement. See Section 3.1.

DvP: Delivery versus Payment. See Section 5.2.

ICSD: International Central Securities Depository. See Box 2.3.

IOSCO: International Organization of Securities Commissions.

IOU: I-Owe-You, an acknowledgement of debt.

LVPS: Large-Value Payment System.

PvP: Payment versus Payment. See Section 5.1.

QART: Queue-Augmented RTGS. See Section 4.6.2.

RRGS: Receipt-Reactive Gross Settlement. See Box 4.4.

RTGS: Real-Time Gross Settlement. See Section 3.3.

SSS: Securities Settlement System. See Section 5.2.

References

Adams, M., Galbiati, M., and Giansante, S. (2009). Emergence of Tiering in Large Value Payment Systems, *Bank of England Working Paper*, forthcoming.

Alesina, A. and Summers, L. (1993). Central Bank Independence and Macroeconomic Performance: Some Comparative Evidence. *Journal of Money, Credit & Banking*, 25 (2), 151–162.

Allen, H., Christodoulou, G., and Millard, S. P. (2007). Financial Infrastructure and Corporate Governance, *Bank of England Working Paper*, No. 316.

Angelini, P. (1998). An Analysis of Competitive Externalities in Gross Settlement Systems, *Journal of Banking & Finance*, Elsevier, 22 (1), 1–18, January.

——Maresca, G. and Russo, D. (1996). Systemic Risk in the Netting System, *Journal of Banking and Finance*, 20, 853–868.

Arjani, N. (2006). Examining the Trade-Off Between Settlement Delay and Intraday Liquidity in Canada's LVTS: A Simulation Approach. *Bank of Canada Working Paper*, No. 2006–20.

——and McVanel, D. (2006). A primer on Canada's Large Value Transfer System, Bank of Canada.

Armentier, O., Arnold, J. B., and McAndrews, J. J. (2008). Changes in the Timing Distribution of Fedwire Funds Transfers, *Economic Policy Review*, 14 (2), 83–112, Federal Reserve Bank of New York.

Arrow, K. J. and Debreu, G. (1954). Existence of an Equilibrium for a Competitive Economy, *Econometrica*, 22 (3), 265–290.

Ashtor, E. (1973). Banking Instruments Between the Muslim East and the Christian West, *Journal of European Economic History*, 1, 553–573.

Baer, H. L., France, V. G., and Moser, J. T. (2004). Opportunity Cost and Prudentiality: An Analysis of Collateral Decisions in Bilateral and Multilateral Settings, *Research in Finance*, 21, 201–27.

Baltensperger, E. (1974). The Demand for Reserves, *American Economic Review*, 64 (1), 205–210.

Bank of England (1994). *Quarterly Bulletin*, 34 (2), London.

——(2005). Strengthening Financial Infrastructure, *Financial Stability Review*, June, 79–89.

——HM Treasury, and FSA (2006). *UK Financial Sector: Market Wide Exercise 2006 Report*, London.

References

Barbera, S. and Jackson, M. O. (2004). Choosing How to Choose: Self-Stable Majority Rules and Constitutions, *Quarterly Journal of Economics*, 119 (3), 1011–1048.

Barro R. J. and Gordon R. (1983). A Positive Theory of Monetary Policy in a Natural Rate Model, *Journal of Political Economy*, 91, 589–610.

Bartolini, L., McAndrews, J.J., and Hilton, S. (2008). Settlement Delays in the Money Market, *Federal Reserve Bank of New York Staff Reports*, No. 319.

Basel Committee on Banking Supervision (BCBS) and The Joint Forum (2006). The Management of Liquidity Risk in Financial Groups.

Bech, M. L. (2008). Intraday Liquidity Management: A Tale of Games that Banks Play, *Economic Policy Review*, 14 (2), 7–23, Federal Reserve Bank of New York.

——**and Garratt, R. (2003).** The Intraday Liquidity Management Game, *Journal of Economic Theory*, 109 (2), 198–219.

——**and Soramäki, K. (2005a).** Gridlock Resolution and Bank Failures in Interbank Payment Systems, in Liquidity, Risk and Speed in Payment and Settlement Systems – a Simulation Approach, *Bank of Finland Studies E: 31–2005*.

————**(2005b).** Systemic Risk in Netting Systems Revisited, in Leinonen, H. (ed.), Liquidity, Risk and Speed in Payment and Settlement Systems – a Simulation Approach, *Bank of Finland Studies E: 31–2005*.

——**Madsen, B., and Natorp, L. (2002).** Systemic Risk in the Danish Interbank Netting System. *Danmarks Nationalbank Working Paper*, No. 8–2002.

——**Preisig, C., and Soramäki, K. (2008).** Global Trends in Large-Value Payments, *Economic Policy Review*, 14 (2), 59–81, Federal Reserve Bank of New York.

Becher C., Galbiati M., and Tudela M. (2008a). The Timing and Funding of CHAPS Sterling Payments, *Economic Policy Review*, 14 (2), 113–133, Federal Reserve Bank of New York.

——**Millard, S., and Soramäki, K. (2008b).** The Network Topology of CHAPS Sterling, Bank of England Working Paper No. 335.

Becht, M., Bolton, P., and Röell, A. (2002). Corporate Governance and Control, *European Corporate Governance Institute Finance Working Paper* No. 02/2002.

Bedford, P., Millard, S., and Yang, J. (2004). Assessing Operational Risk in CHAPS Sterling: A Simulation Approach, *Bank of England Financial Stability Review*, June.

Berentsen, A. and Monnet, C. (2007). Monetary Policy in a Channel System, *CESIFO Working Paper*, No. 1929.

Berger, A. N., Hancock D., and Marquardt J. C. (1996). A Framework for Analyzing Efficiency, Risks, Costs, and Innovations in the Payments System, *Journal of Money, Credit and Banking*, 28 (4), 696–732.

Berk, J. M. (2003). New Economy, Old Central Banks?, *Economic Notes*, 32 (1), 1–35, Banca Monte dei Paschi di Siena SpA.

Bernanke, B. S. (1990). Clearing and Settlement During the Crash, *Review of Financial Studies*, 3 (1), 133–151.

Beyeler, W. Glass, R., Bech, M., and Soramäki, K. (2007). Congestion and Cascades in Payment Systems, Physica A: Statistical Mechanics and its Applications, 384, (2), 613–718.

Bleiberg, E. (2001). Prices and Payment, in D. B. Redford (ed.), *The Oxford Encyclopaedia of Ancient Egypt* (Vol.3), Oxford University Press, New York, USA.

Board of Governors of the Federal Reserve System (2006). Consultation Paper on Intraday Liquidity Management and Payment System Risk Policy, *Federal Register*, 71 (119), 35679–35687.

—— **(2008)**. Policy on Payments System Risk, *Federal Register*, 73 (46), 12417–12443.

Bollerslev, T., Engle, R.F., and Wooldridge, J.M. (1988). A Capital Asset Pricing Model with Time-Varying Covariances, *Journal of Political Economy*, 96, 116–131.

Buckle, S. and Campbell, E. (2003), Settlement Bank Behavior and Throughput Rules in an RTGS Payment System with Collateralized Intraday Credit, *Bank of England Working Paper*, No. 209.

Central Bank of Ireland (1971). Survey of Economic Effects of Bank Dispute 1970, Dublin.

Chakravorti, S. (2000). Analysis of Systemic Risk in Multilateral Net Settlement Systems, *Journal of International Financial Markets, Institutions and Money*, 10, 9–30.

Chapman, J., Chiu, J. and Molico M. (2008). A Model of Tiered Settlement Networks, *Bank of Canada Working Paper* 2008–12.

—— **and Martin, A. (2007)**. Rediscounting under Aggregate Risk with Moral Hazard, *Federal Reserve Bank of New York Staff Reports*, No. 296.

CHIPS (2007). Clearing House Interbank Payment System Self Assessment of Compliance with Core Principles for Systemically Important Payment Systems.

Coase, R. A. (1960). The Problem of Social Cost, *Journal of Law and Economics*, 3, 1–44.

Coleman, S. P. (2002). The Evolution of the Federal Reserve's Intraday Credit Policies. *Federal Reserve Bulletin*, 88, 67–84.

Committee on Payment and Settlement Systems (CPSS) (1992). Delivery versus Payment in Securities Settlement Systems, Bank for International Settlements, Basel.

—— **(1996)**. Settlement Risk in Foreign Exchange Transactions, CPSS Publications No 17, Bank for International Settlements, Basel.

—— **(1997)**. Statistics on Payment and Settlement Systems in Selected Countries (Red Book), Bank for International Settlements, Basel.

—— **(1998)**. OTC Derivatives: Settlement Procedures and Counterparty Risk Management, Report by the Committee on Payment and Settlement Systems and the Euro-currency Standing Committee of the Central Banks of the Group of Ten Countries, Bank for International Settlements, Basel.

—— **(2001a)**. Core Principles for Systemically Important Payment Systems, CPSS Publications No. 43, Bank for International Settlements, Basel.

References

Committee on Payment and Settlement Systems (CPSS) (2001b). Recommendations for Securities Settlement Systems, *Report by the Committee on Payment and Settlement Systems and IOSCO*, CPSS Publications No. 42, Bank for International Settlements, Basel.

—— **(2003a).** The Role of Central Bank Money in Payment Systems. CPSS Publications No. 55, Bank for International Settlements, Basel.

—— **(2003b).** Payment and Settlement Systems in Selected Countries, CPSS Publications No. 53, Bank for International Settlements, Basel.

—— **(2003c).** Glossary of Terms used in Payments and Settlement Systems. Bank for International Settlements, Basel.

—— **(2003d).** Policy Issues for Central Banks in Retail Payments-Consultative Report, CPSS Publications No. 50, Bank for International Settlements, Basel.

—— **(2004).** Recommendations for Central Counterparties. *Report by the Committee on Payment and Settlement Systems and IOSCO*, CPSS Publications No. 64, Bank for International Settlements, Basel.

—— **(2005a).** New Developments in Large Value Payment Systems, CPSS Publications No. 67, Bank for International Settlements, Basel.

—— **(2005b).** Central Bank Oversight of Payment and Settlement Systems, CPSS Publications No. 68, Bank for International Settlements, Basel.

—— **(2006).** Cross-Border Collateral Arrangements, CPSS Publications No. 71, Bank for International Settlements, Basel.

—— **(2007a).** Progress in Reducing Foreign Exchange Settlement Risk, CPSS Publications No. 81, Bank for International Settlements, Basel.

—— **(2007b).** Statistics on Payment and Settlement Systems in Selected Countries (Red Book), Bank for International Settlements, Basel.

—— **(2007c).** New Developments in Clearing and Settlement Arrangements for OTC Derivatives, CPSS Publications No. 77, Bank for International Settlements, Basel.

—— **(2008a).** Statistics on Payment and Settlement Systems in Selected Countries (Red Book), Bank for International Settlements, Basel.

—— **(2008b).** The Interdependencies of Payment and Settlement Systems, CPSS Publications No. 84, Bank for International Settlements, Basel.

Costa, C. and De Grauwe, P. (2001). Monetary Policy in a Cashless Society, mimeo, Banco de Portugal and University of Leuven.

Dale, S. and Rossi, M. (1996). A Market for Intra-day Funds: Does it Have Implications for Monetary Policy?, *Bank of England Working Paper*, No. 46.

Danmarks Nationalbank (2000). *Payment Systems in Denmark*, Kopenhagen.

Davies, G. (2002). *A History of Money from Ancient Times to the Present Day*, University of Wales Press, Cardiff.

Day, T. and Lewis, C. (2004). Margin Adequacy and Standards: An Analysis of the Crude Oil Futures Market, *Journal of Business*, 77 (1), 101–135.

Devriese, J. and Mitchell, J. (2006). Liquidity Risk in Securities Settlement, *Journal of Banking and Finance*, 30 (6), 1807–1834.

Eichenwald, K. (1988). The Day the Nation's Cash Pipeline Almost Ran Dry, *New York Times*, 2 October 1988.

Emmons, W. R. (1997). Recent Developments in Wholesale Payment Systems, *US Federal Reserve Bank of St Louis Review*, November/December, 23–43.

Engle, R. F. and Russell, J. R. (1998). Autoregressive Conditional Duration: A New Model for Irregularly Spaced Transaction Data, *Econometrica*, 66 (5), 1127–1162.

Ercevik, K. and Jackson, J. (2007). Simulating the Impact of Hybrid Functionality on CHAPS Banks, Paper presented at the 5th simulator workshop in Helsinki, 28–29 August 2007, Bank of Finland.

European Central Bank (2000). Role of the Eurosystem in the Field of Payment System Oversight, Frankfurt.

—— (2006). Business Continuity Oversight Expectations for Systemically Important Payment Systems (SIPS), Frankfurt.

—— (2007). User Information Guide to the TARGET2 Pricing, October.

Federal Reserve Board (2007). Assessment of the Compliance of the Fedwire Securities Service with the Recommendations for Securities Settlement Systems, Washington, USA.

Fenn, G.W. and Kupiec, P. (1993). Prudential Margin Policy in a Futures-Style Settlement System, *Journal of Futures Markets*, 13 (4), 389–408.

Ferguson, N. (2008). *The Ascent of Money - A Financial History of the World*, Allen Lane, London, UK.

Figlewski, S. (1984). Margins and Market Integrity: Margin Setting for Stock Index Futures and Options, *Journal of Futures Markets*, 4 (3), 385–416.

Financial Stability Forum (2008). Report of the Financial Stability Forum on Enhancing Market and institutional Resilience, Bank for International Settlements, April.

Fish, S. and Willison, M. (2008). The Impact of Market Structure and Competition on Risk in Payment Systems, mimeo, Bank of England.

Fisher, I. (1933). *Stamp Scrip*, Adelphi Company, New York.

Fleming, M. J. and Garbade, K. (2005). Explaining Settlement Fails. *Current Issues in Economics and Finance*, 11 (9).

Freeman, S. (1996a). Clearinghouse Banks and Banknote Over-issue, *Journal of Monetary Economics*, 38 (1), 101–15.

—— (1996b). The Payments System, Liquidity, and Rediscounting, *American Economic Review* 86 (5), 1126–38.

—— (1999). Rediscounting under Aggregate Risk, *Journal of Monetary Economics*, 43, 197–216.

Friedman, M. (1969). *The Optimum Quantity of Money: And Other Essays*, London: MacMillan.

—— and Schwartz A. (1963). *A Monetary History of the United States, 1867–1960*, Princeton University Press, New York, USA.

References

Furfine, C. H. and Stehm, J. (1998). Analyzing Alternative Intraday Credit Policies in Real Time Gross Settlement Systems, *Journal of Money, Credit, and Banking*, 1998, 30 (4), 832–848.

Galbiati, M. and Soramäki, K. (2008). An Agent-Based Model of Payment Systems, Bank of England Working Paper 352.

Gemmill, G. (1994). Margins and the Safety of Clearing Houses, *Journal of Banking and Finance*, 18 (5), 979–996.

Gerali, A. and Passacantando, F. (2007). The Loss of Confidence on Bank Money in the Great Depression, paper presented at *Payments and Monetary and Financial Stability, ECB-Bank of England Conference 12–13 November 2007*, European Central Bank and Bank of England.

Gibbons, R. (1992). *Game Theory for Applied Economists*, Princeton University Press, New Jersey, USA.

Glaser, M. and Haene, P. (2008). Operational Disruptions in the Swiss Payment System, SPEED, 2 (3), 27–31.

Gönenç, R., Maher, M., and Nicoletti, G. (2003). The Implementation and the Effects of Regulatory Reform: Past Experience and Current Issues, *OECD Economic Studies*, 2001 (1), 5–107.

Goodhart, C. A. E. (1988a). *The Evolution of Central Banks*, MIT Press, Cambridge, Mass., USA.

——**(1998b).** The Two Concepts of Money: Implications for the Analysis of Optimal Currency Areas, *European Journal of Political Economy*, 14 (3), 407–432.

Gouriéroux C., Josiak J., and Le Fol, G. (1999). Intra-Day Market Activity, *Journal of Financial Markets*, 2, 193–226.

Green, E. J. (1997). Money and Debt in the Structure of Payments, *Bank of Japan Monetary and Economic Studies*, 15, 63–87.

——**(2007).** *The Role of Central Banks in Payment Systems*, in Haldane *et al.* (2007), 45–56.

Greenspan, A. (2007). *The Age of Turbulence*, The penguin Press.

Grierson, P. (1977). *The Origins of Money* (Athlone Press, London).

Haldane, A. and Latter E. (2005). The Role of Central Banks in Payment Systems Oversight, *Bank of England Quarterly Bulletin* 45 (1), 66–71.

——**Millard, S., and Saporta, V. (eds) (2007).** The Future of Payment Systems, *Routledge International Studies in Money and Banking*, 43, Routledge, Abingden, UK.

Hancock, D. and Wilcox, J. (1996). Intraday Management of Bank Reserves: The Effects of Caps and Fees on Daylight Overdrafts, *Journal of Money, Credit and Banking*, 28, 850–908.

——, **Humphrey, D.B. and Wilcox, J. A. (1999).** Cost Reductions in Electronic Payments: The Roles of Consolidation, Economies of Scale, and Technical Change, *Journal of Banking and Finance*, 23, 391–421.

Hardouvelis, G. and Kim, D. (1995). Margin Requirements, Price Fluctuation and Market Participation in Metal Futures, *Journal of Money, Credit and Banking,* 27 (3), 659–671.

Harrison, S., Lasaosa, A., and Tudela, M. (2005). Tiering in UK Payment Systems: Credit Risk Implications, *Bank of England Financial Stability Review,* December, 63–70.

Hart, O. and Moore, J. (1996). The Governance of Exchanges: Members' Cooperatives versus Outside Ownership, *Oxford Review of Economic Policy,* 12 (4), 53–69.

Hausman, J. A., Leonard, G. K. and Tirole, J. (2003). On Nonexclusive Membership in Competing Joint Ventures, *Rand Journal of Economics,* 34 (1), 43–62.

He, P., Huang, L. and Wright, R. 2005. Money and Banking in Search Equilibrium. *International Economic Review,* 46 (2), 637–70.

Heller, D. and Lengwiler, Y. (2000). What Drives the Turnover Ratio?, mimeo, Swiss National Bank and University of Basel. Available at http://ssrn.com/abstract=250880.

——**Nellen, T. and Sturm, A. (2000).** The Swiss Interbank Clearing System, mimeo, Swiss National Bank.

Hills, B., Rule, D., Parkinson, S. and Young, C. (1999). Central Counterparty Clearing Houses and Financial Stability, *Bank of England Financial Stability Review,* 6, June, 122–34.

Holthausen, C. and Rochet, J.-C. (2005). Incorporating a Public Good Factor into the Pricing for Large-Value Payment Systems, *ECB Working Paper,* No. 507.

————**(2006).** Efficient Pricing of Large Value Interbank Payment Systems, *Journal of Money, Credit, and Banking,* 38 (7), 1797–1818.

Humphrey, D. B. (1986). Payments Finality and Risk of Settlement Failure, in: Anthony Saunders and Lawrence White (ed., 1986), *Technology and the Regulation of Financial Markets,* Lexington Books/Salomon Brothers Center Series on Financial Institutions and Markets, New York, 97–120.

Humphrey, D. B. and VanHoose, D. D. (2001). Sweep Accounts, Reserve Management, and Interest Rate Volatility, *Journal of Economics and Business,* 53, 387–404.

Inaoka, H., Ninomiya, T., Taniguchi, K., Shimiza, T., and Takayasu, H. (2004). Fractal Network Derived from Banking Transaction – An Analysis of Network Structures Formed by Financial Institutions, *Bank of Japan Working papers* No. 04-E-04.

Innes, A. M. (1913). *What is Money?,* reprinted in Wray (2004).

Jackson, J. and Manning, M. (2007a). Central Bank Intra-Day Collateral Policy and Implications for Tiering in RTGS Payment Systems, in Haldane *et al.* (2007), 138–159.

————**(2007b).** Comparing the Pre-Settlement Risk Implications of Alternative Clearing Arrangements, *Bank of England Working Paper* No. 321.

James, K. (2003). A Statistical Overview of CHAPS Sterling, *Bank of England Financial Stability Review,* June, 115–121.

References

Jenkinson, N. (2007). *New markets and new demands: challenges for central banks in the wholesale market infrastructure*, Speech held at the Bank of England/European Central Bank Conference on Payments and Monetary and Financial Stability, Frankfurt, 12 November 2007.

——and Manning, M. (2007). Promoting Financial System Resilience in Modern Global Capital Markets: Some Issues, *Bank of England Quarterly Bulletin*, Autumn, 453–461.

Jevons, W. S. (1875), *Money and the Mechanisms of Exchange*, D. Appleton & Company, New York.

Johnson, K., McAndrews, J. J., and Soramäki, K., (2004). Economizing on Liquidity with Deferred Settlement Mechanisms, *Federal Reserve Bank of New York Economic Policy Review* 10 (3), 51–72.

Joskow, P. J. (2007). Incentive Regulation in Theory and Practice – Electricity Distribution and Transmission Networks (revised), mimeo, MIT.

Kahn C. M. and Roberds, W. (1998). Payment System Settlement and Bank Incentives, *Review of Financial Studies*, 11 (4), 845–70.

——(2001a). Real-Time Gross Settlement and the Costs of Immediacy, *Journal of Monetary Economics*, Elsevier, 47 (2), 299–319.

——(2001b). The CLS Bank: A Solution to the Risks of International Payments Settlement?, *Carnegie-Rochester Conference Series on Public Policy*, 54 (1), 191–226.

——(2005). Payments Settlement: Tiering in Private and Public Systems, University of Illinois and Federal Reserve Bank of Atlanta, mimeo.

——(2009). Why Pay? An Introduction to Payment Economics, *Journal of Financial Intermediation* 18 (1), 1–23.

Keynes, J. M. (1914). What is Money? *Economic Journal*, 24, 419–21.

Kindleberger, C. P. (1993). *A Financial History of Western Europe*, Oxford University Press, New York, USA.

Kiyotaki, N. and Wright, R. (1989). On Money as a Medium of Exchange, *Journal of Political Economy*, 97 (4), 927–54.

————(1991). A Contribution to the Pure Theory of Money, *Journal of Economic Theory*, 53 (2), 215–235.

————(1993). A Search-Theoretic Approach to Monetary Economics, *American Economic Review*, 83 (3), 63–77.

Klee, E. (2007). Operational Problems and Aggregate Uncertainty in the Federal Funds Market, *FEDS Paper No. 2007–49*, Board of Governors of the Federal Reserve System, Washington.

Kleidon, A. W. and Whaley, R. E. (1992). One Market? Stocks, Futures, and Options During October 1987, *The Journal of Finance*, 47 (3), Papers and Proceedings of the Fifty-Second Annual Meeting of the American Finance Association, New Orleans, Louisiana January 3–5, 851–877.

Knott, R. and Mills, A. (2002). Modelling Risk in Central Counterparty Clearing Houses: A Review, *Bank of England Financial Stability Review*, December, 162–74.

Kocherlakota, N. (1998). Money is Memory, *Journal of Economic Theory,* 81 (2), 232–251.

—— **(2005).** Optimal Monetary Policy: What We Know and What We Don't Know, *International Economic Review,* 46 (2), 715–729, May 2005.

Koeppl, T., Monnet, C., and Temzelides, T. (2006). A Dynamic Model of Settlement. *European Central Bank Working Paper,* No. 604, forthcoming in the *Journal of Economic Theory.*

Kohn, M. (1999). Early Deposit Banking, *Dartmouth University Working Paper,* No. 99–03.

Kroszner, R. S. (1999). Can the Financial Markets Privately Regulate Risk?: The Development of Derivatives Clearinghouses and Recent Over-the-Counter Innovations, *Journal of Money, Credit and Banking,* 31, 596–618.

Kupiec, P. H. (1998). Margin Requirements, Volatility, and Market Integrity: What Have We Learned Since the Crash?, *Journal of Financial Services Research,* 13 (3), 231–255.

Kuussaari, H. (1996). Systemic Risk in the Finnish Payment System: An Empirical Investigation, *Bank of Finland Discussion Paper,* No. 3.

Kydland F. E. and Prescott E. C. (1977). Rules Rather Than Discretion: The Inconsistency of Optimal Plans, *Journal of Political Economy,* 85, 473–92.

Lacker, J. M. (1997). Clearing, Settlement and Monetary Policy, *Journal of Monetary Economics,* 40 (2), 347–381.

—— **(2004).** Payment System Disruptions and the Federal Reserve following September 11, 2001, *Journal of Monetary Economics,* 51 (5), 935–65.

Lai, A., Chande, N., and O'Connor, S. (2006). Credit in a Tiered Payments System. *Bank of Canada Working Paper* 2006–36.

Lasaosa, A. and Tudela, M. (2008). Risks and Efficiency Gains of a Tiered Structure in Large Value Payment Systems: A Simulation Approach, *Bank of England Working Paper* No. 337.

Ledrut, E. (2007). Simulating Retaliation in Payment Systems: Can Banks Control Their Exposure to a Failing Participant?, *DNB Working Paper,* 133 (March).

—— **and Upper, C. (2007).** Changing Post-Trading Arrangements for OTC Derivatives, *BIS Quarterly Review,* December, 83–95.

Lester, B. (2006). A Model of Interbank Settlement, *Society for Economic Dynamics 2006 Meeting Papers,* No 282.

——, **Millard, S., and Willison, M. (2007).** *Optimal Settlement Rules for Payment Systems,* in Haldane *et al.,* (2007), 87–99.

Lockwood, B. and Thomas, J. P. (2002). Gradualism and Irreversibility, *Review of Economic Studies,* 69 (2), 339–356.

Lublóy, Á. (2006). Topology of the Hungarian Large-Value Transfer System, *Magyar Nemzeti Bank Occasional Papers,* 57.

—— **and Tanay, E. (2007).** Operational Disruption and the Hungarian Real-Time Gross Settlement System (VIBER), *Hungarian Review of Financial Institutions* (Hitelintézeti Szemle) 6 (4), 324–357.

References

Lucas, R. Jr. and Stokey, N. (1987). Money and Interest in a Cash-in-Advance Economy, *Econometrica*, 53, 491–514.

Magyar Nemzeti Bank (2005). *Report on Financial Stability*, Budapest.

Mailath, G. J. and Samuelson, L. (2006). *Repeated Games and Reputations: Long-run relationships*, Oxford University Press.

Manning, M. and Willison, M. (2006). Modelling the Cross-Border Use of Collateral in Payment Systems, *Bank of England Working Paper*, No 286.

——and Russo, D. (2008). Central banks, Stability and the Financial Infrastructure, *Payments and Monetary and Financial Stability, ECB-Bank of England Conference 12–13 November 2007*, European Central Bank and Bank of England.

Martin, A. (2004). Optimal Pricing of Intraday Liquidity, *Journal of Monetary Economics* 51 (2), 401–24.

——and McAndrews, J. (2008a). Why are There No Intraday Money Markets?, *Federal Reserve Bank of New York Staff Report*, No. 337.

————(2008b). Liquidity-Saving Mechanisms, *Federal Reserve Bank of New York Staff Report*, No. 282, revised.

Marx, L. M. and Matthews, S. A. (2000). Dynamic Voluntary Contribution to a Public Project, *Review of Economic Studies*, 67 (2), 327–358.

Matutes, C. and Padilla, A. J. (1994). Shared ATM Networks and Banking Competition, *European Economic Review*, 38, 1057–1069.

Mazars, E. and Woelfel, G. (2005). Analysis, by Simulation, of the Impact of a Technical Default of a Payment System Participant. An Illustration with the PNS System. *Banque de France Financial Stability Review*, 6, June.

McAndrews, J. and Potter, S. M. (2002). The Liquidity Effects of the Events of September 11, 2001, *Federal Reserve Bank of New York Economic Policy Review*, 8 (2), 59–79.

——and Rajan, S. (2000). The Timing and Funding of Fedwire Funds Transfers, *Federal Reserve Bank of New York Economic Policy Review*, 6 (2), 17–32.

——and Trundle, J. (2001). New Payment System Designs: Causes and Consequences, *Financial Stability Review*, December, 127–136.

——and Wasilyew, G. (1995). Simulations of Failure in a Payment System, *Working Paper*, No. 95–19, Federal Reserve Bank of Philadelphia.

McPhail, K. (2003). Managing Operational Risk in Payment, Clearing, and Settlement Systems, *Bank of Canada Working Papers* 2003–2.

Menger, C. (1892). On the Origins of Money, *Economic Journal*, 2, 239–55.

Merrouche, O. and Nier, E. (2009). Payment Systems, Inside Money and Financial Intermediation, Working Paper No. 371, Bank of England.

Millard, S. P. (2006). Foundations of Money, Payments and Central Banking: A review essay Paper presented at the 2006 Money Macro and Financial Reserved Group Conference, No. 106.

——and Saporta, V. (2007). *Central Banks and Payment Systems: Past, Present and future*, in: Haldane *et al.* (2007), 15–44.

——and Willison, M. (2006). The Welfare Benefits of Stable and Efficient Payment Systems *Bank of England Working Paper,* No 301.

——, Speight, G., and Willison, M. (2007). Why Do Central Banks Observe a Distinction between Intraday and Overnight Interest Rates?, mimeo, Bank of England.

Mills, D. C. (2006). Alternative Central Bank Credit Policies for Liquidity Provision in a Model of Payments, *Journal of Monetary Economics,* 53 (7), 1593–1611.

——and Nesmith, T. D. (2008). Risk and Concentration in Payment and Securities Settlement Systems, *Journal of Monetary Economics,* 55 (3), 542–553.

Moen, J. R. and Tallman, E. W. (2000). Clearinghouse Membership and Deposit Contraction during the Panic of 1907, *The Journal of Economic History* 60 (1), 145–163.

Morgan, D. (1987). The Mongols, Blackwell, Oxford, UK and New York, USA.

Moser, J. T. (1998). Contracting Innovations and the Evolution of Clearing and Settlement Methods at Futures Exchanges, *Federal Reserve Bank of Chicago Working Paper Series,* No. 1998–26.

——and Reiffen, D. (2008). *Clearing and Settlement of Trades Made at Exchanges, Companion to Financial Derivatives,* Robert W Kolb and James A. Overdahl (eds.) Blackwell Publishing, Oxford.

Mueller, R. C. (1997). *The Venetian Money Market – Banks, Panics, and the Public Debt 1200–1500,* Johns Hopkins University Press, Baltimore, MD, USA.

Murphy, A. E. (1978). Money in an Economy without Banks: the Case of Ireland. *The Manchester School of Economic & Social Studies,* 46 (1), 41–50.

Nield, I. (2006). Changes to the Liquidity Management Regime, *Reserve Bank of New Zealand: Bulletin,* 69 (4).

Norman, B. P., Shaw, R. E. and Speight, G. E. (2007). The History of Interbank Settlement Arrangements: Exploring Central Banks' Role in the Payment System, mimeo, Bank of England.

Norman, P. (2007). *Plumbers and Visionaries. Securities Settlement and Europe's Financial Market,* John Wiley & Sons, Chichester, UK.

Northcott, C. A. (2002). Estimating Settlement Risk and the Potential for Contagion in Canada's ACSS. *Bank of Canada Working Paper,* No. 2002–41.

Office of Fair Trading (2003). *UK payment systems,* London.

——(2007). Final Report of the Payment Systems Task Force, London.

Papademos, L. (2009). Europe in the economic and financial crisis: How to bring back prosperity to everyone?, speech held at a policy debate organised by the European people's party, Brussels, 4 May 2009.

Quinn, S. (1997). Goldsmith-Banking: Mutual Acceptance and Interbanker Clearing in Restoration London, *Explorations in Economic History,* 34 (4), 411–432.

Radford, R. A. (1945). The Economic Organisation of a P.O.W. Camp, *Economica New Series,* 12, (48) (November), 189–201.

Renault, F., Bech, M. L., Beyeler, W., Glass, R., and Soramäki, K. (2007). Congestion and Cascades in Coupled Payment Systems, paper presented at 'Payments and Monetary and Financial Stability', ECB-Bank of England Conference 12-13 November 2007, European Central Bank and Bank of England.

Richardson, G. (2006). Bank Distress During the Great Contraction, 1929 to 1933, New Data from the Archives of the Board of Governors, *NBER Working Paper*, No. 12590.

Ripatti, K. (2004). Central Counterparty Clearing: Constructing a Framework for Evaluation of Risks and Benefits, *Bank of Finland Research Discussion Paper*, No. 30/2004.

Rochet J.-C. (2007). *How Should We Regulate Banks' Liquidity?*, in Haldane *et al.* (2007), 175–186.

———and Tirole, J. (2004). *Two-Sided Markets: An Overview*, mimeo, IDEI and GRE-MAQ, Toulouse.

Sargent T. J. and Velde, F. R. (2002). *The Big Problem of Small Change*, Princeton University Press, New Jersey, USA.

Schanz, J. (2009). Models of Foreign Exchange Settlement and Informational Efficiency in Liquidity Risk Management, *Bank of England Working Paper*, forthcoming.

Schmitz, S. W., Puhr, C., Moshammer, H., and Elsenhuber, U. (2006). Operational Risk and Contagion in the Austrian Large-Value Payment System ARTIS, in: Oesterreichische Nationalbank (Austrian Central Bank) (ed.), *Financial Stability Report*, 11, 96–113.

Schoenmaker, D. (1995). A Comparison of Alternative Interbank Settlement Systems, *London School of Economics Financial Markets Group Discussion Paper*, No. 204.

Selgin, G. (2004). Wholesale Payments: Questioning the Market-Failure Hypothesis, *International Review of Law and Economics*, 24 (3), 333–350.

———and White, L. H. (1987). The Evolution of a Free Banking System, *Economic Inquiry*, 25 (3), 439–57.

——— ——— (2002). Mengerian Perspectives on the Future of Money, in: Michael Latzer and Stefan Schmitz, (eds.) *Carl Menger and the Evolution of Payments Systems: From Barter to Electronic Money*, Edward Elgar, Cheltenham, UK, 133–58.

Soramäki, K., Bech, M. L., Arnold, J., Beyeler, W. E., and Glass, R. J. (2006). The Topology of interbank payment flows, Federal Reserve Bank of New York Staff No. 243, March.

Soramäki, K., Bech, M. L., Arnold, J., Beyeler, W. E., and Glass R. J. (2007). The Topology of Interbank Payment Flows, *Physica* A, 379, 317–333.

Stella, P. (2008). Central Bank Financial Strength, Policy Constraints and Inflation, *IMF Working Paper*. 08/49.

———and Klueh, U. H. (2008). Central Bank Financial Strength and Policy Performance: An Econometric Evaluation, *IMF Working Paper*, No 08/176.

Svensson, L. E. O. (1985). Money and Asset Prices in a Cash-in-Advance Economy, *Journal of Political Economy*, 93 (5), 919–944.

Telser, L. G. (1981). Margins and Futures Contracts, *Journal of Futures Markets*, 1 (2), 225–253.

Temzelides, T. and Williamson, S. (2001). Payments Systems Design in Deterministic and Private Information Environments, *Journal of Economic Theory*, 99, 297–326.

Tirole, J. (2001). Corporate Governance, *Econometrica*, 69 (1), 1–35.

Tucker, P. (2004). Managing the Central Bank's Balance Sheet: Where Monetary Policy Meets Financial Stability, *Bank of England Quarterly Bulletin*, Autumn, 359–382.

Tymoigne, É. (2006). An inquiry into the nature of money: An alternative to the functional approach, *The Levy Economics Institute, Economics Working Paper*, No. 481.

Williamson, S. D. (2003). Payments Systems and Monetary Policy, *Journal of Monetary Economics*, 50 (2), 475–495.

Willison, M. (2005). Real-Time Gross Settlement and Hybrid Payment Systems: A Comparison, *Bank of England Working Paper*, No 252.

Woodford, M. (2000). Monetary Policy in a World Without Money, *International Finance* 3, 229–260.

—— **(2001).** Monetary Policy in the Information Economy, *Proceedings, Federal Reserve* Bank of Kansas City, 297–370.

—— **(2003).** *Interest and Prices: Foundations of a Theory of Monetary Policy*, Princeton University Press, New Jersey, USA.

Wray, L. R. (2004). *Credit and State Theories of Money*, Edward Elgar, Cheltenham, UK.

Index